A Moving Child Is a Learning Child

How the Body Teaches the Brain to Think
(Birth to Age 7)

Gill Connell and
Cheryl McCarthy

free spirit
PUBLISHING®

Library of Congress Cataloging-in-Publication Data
Connell, Gill.
      A moving child is a learning child : how the body teaches the brain to think
(birth to age 7) / Gill Connell, Cheryl McCarthy.
                  pages cm.
      Summary: "This book explains the learning link between the body and the brain and what early childhood educators and caregivers can do to guide it. The authors discuss children's movement and introduce the Kinetic Scale: a visual map of the active learning needs of infants, toddlers, preschoolers, and primary graders. Includes tips, activities, and PowerPoint presentation"—Provided by publisher.
      ISBN 978-1-57542-435-4 (pbk.) —ISBN 1-57542-435-5 1. Movement education. 2. Learning—Physiological aspects. 3. Thought and thinking—Physiological aspects. I. McCarthy, Cheryl. II. Title.
      GV452.C66 2014
      372.86—dc23
                                                2013036127

Photo credits: Cover © Inti St Clair/Blend Images/Corbis; back cover © Ilka-erika Szasz-fabian | Dreamstime.com. Interior credits on corresponding pages and on page 324.

Editors: Meg Bratsch, Christine Zuchora-Walske, and Marjorie Lisovskis
Cover and interior design: Michelle Lee Lagerroos
Illustrations: Heidi Panelli

10 9 8 7 6 5 4 3 2
Printed in the United States of America

Free Spirit Publishing Inc.
Minneapolis, MN
(612) 338-2068
help4kids@freespirit.com
www.freespirit.com

To my mum Leah, for the twinkle in my eye, the love in my heart, and the hug that holds me safe and close each day. To my dad Jack, for a lifetime of love, understanding, guidance, and clarity of purpose.

G.C.

To Mom, for my smile. To Pop, for my strength. And to you both, for the love that defines me. Thank you. (And Mom, you were right. I can do anything I set my mind to.)

C.M.

Contents

List of Digital Reproducible Forms

You may download these printable forms at **www.freespirit.com/moving-forms**. Use the password **2grow**.

Charts

What Real Learning Looks Like

The Evolution of Independent Movement

The Kinetic Scale

The Evolution of Communication

The Journey of Can-Do

The Kinetic Scale: Snugglers

The Kinetic Scale: Squigglers

The Kinetic Scale: Scampers

The Kinetic Scale: Stompers

The Kinetic Scale: Scooters

Foreword

by Darell Hammond, founder and CEO, KaBOOM!

Active play is joyful, fun, and creative. Play is the essence of childhood. And it is also essential to child development.

The benefits of active play are often linked to physical health—which of course, in an era concerned with childhood obesity rates, is critically important. Yet this book tells the lesser-known and surprising story of the myriad ways in which play and movement are vital to our children's learning.

Gill and Cheryl's groundbreaking book introduces a developmentally complex (yet easy to implement) tool that supports the full, natural development of movement and learning in young children. The Kinetic Scale shows us what constitutes a "balanced diet" of movement, enabling teachers, parents, and caregivers to facilitate learning through active play while respecting each child's individual needs.

It's a story that needs to be heard. At home, at school, and in communities, our children are being denied vital opportunities to move their bodies, exercise their imaginations, and interact with other kids. Children spend an average of eight hours a day in front of a screen. Almost half of all low-income students do not get any recess. Only one in five children lives within walking distance of a park or playground. This directly affects these children's physical development and, more importantly, their social, emotional, and cognitive development.

As a society, we are failing to give children the balance of active play they need to become healthy and successful adults. This is why I champion the importance of play, because our children's futures depend on it—and it is why Gill and Cheryl are working to share the message of moving to learn in a way that offers us all new insights and practical, engaging ways to support it.

That kids' brains require play should be a no-brainer. In this important book, the authors demonstrate what a grave injustice we're doing to our kids by denying them opportunities to move and play. More than that, through illuminating brain research, they show us why our children need to be on the move, and how we can make this happen for the young children in our care.

It is all of our responsibility to give kids the childhood they deserve by ensuring they get the play they need to learn and grow.

Darell Hammond is the founder and CEO of the nonprofit KaBOOM!, which has built more than 2,300 playgrounds in areas of need throughout the United States.

INTRODUCTION
Let's Get Moving!

Put a table and chairs in a room and bring in some adults. What do they do? They come in and sit down.

Now take the adults out of the room and bring in a group of kids. Same table and chairs. What do they do? One little girl rushes to the window and spins around aimlessly with a great big smile on her face. Under the table, a boy builds a fort. Three little ones decide now's a good time for a race. One girl needs to go to the bathroom. Two toddlers bump into each other and spill to the floor. A little boy can't figure out how to take his coat off. A baby crawls by only stopping to examine the lint on the floor . . . with his mouth. And, one little girl insists on showing you how she growls like a lion. If you have young children in your life, you know these kids. In fact, at one point in your life, you *were* these kids.

Kids move—often in unexpected ways, and often for no apparent reason. But if you know how to "read" the moves, you'll find there's a reason for *every* move they make, and much of it has little to do with the movement itself. You see, movement is the essential and often overlooked starting point for children's learning. Our intent with *A Moving Child Is a Learning Child* is to help you understand how all those wiggles and giggles facilitate learning and what you can do to guide this process.

About This Book

As you already know, in working with young children, theory without practice only gets you so far. But so does practice without theory. Our goal with *A Moving Child Is a Learning Child* is *both*. We call this the "Here's Why, Here's How" approach. So here's how our journey will unfold.

1

In the first part of the book, **Part 1: Movement Matters,** we explain the importance of movement and introduce you to a new tool we call the Kinetic Scale.

Part 2: A Moving Child endeavors to give you a simple-yet-comprehensive understanding of movement and its relationship to learning.

Part 3: Language: The Bridge to Formal Learning explores the role that all types of language play in helping young children "translate" their physical exploration of the world into higher-level thinking, reasoning, and abstract learning.

In **Part 4: A Learning Child,** we'll lay out methods and practices for kinetic learning in the classroom, on the playground, at home, or anywhere little ones are moving and learning.

While on the move, children instinctively use different play patterns to explore their world. **Part 5: Put It in Play** walks you through classic play patterns and their role in stimulating a child's movement and learning.

Finally, **Part 6: Smart Steps** wraps up with 36 thoughtfully selected activities that keep the fun and learning moving.

Many of the diagrams and activities in *A Moving Child Is a Learning Child* are provided as printable PDFs at the Free Spirit Publishing website (see page ix for information about how to access the PDFs).

For ease of reading, we alternate the use of male and female pronouns chapter by chapter when writing about children. Unless a specific note is made, all the information applies to girls and boys alike.

Throughout the book, you will find three recurring elements: "Gill's Notebook," "Family Moves," and "Motorvators."

Gill's Notebook

Based on journals Gill has kept in over 30 years of working with early childhood teachers and caregivers, these first-person entries relate personal stories and practical suggestions about guiding movement in early childhood.

Family Moves

Families can get in on the action with these ideas for sharing information and activities that encourage movement at home. Handouts to share with families are included in the digital file at the Free Spirit website. (See page ix.)

Motorvators

Because we don't want you to wait until the final chapters to get your little ones up and moving, we've included "motorvators" throughout the book—quick, easy, anytime, anywhere ideas for adding high-energy, purposeful activities to your day.

In fact, here's one you can try right now . . .

Snail the Whale

Here's Why
Fidgeting doesn't always mean a child isn't concentrating. In fact, quite often it means he's *trying* to concentrate. First, make sure a squirmy child doesn't need to go to the bathroom, and then try a little balancing activity.

Here's How
Tell the child the tale of poor old "Snail the Whale":

> There once was snail named Whale
> Who couldn't find the end of his tail.
> Three spins to the left . . .
> Three spins to the right . . .
> Never failed to help Whale find his tail.

Where's Your Tail?
Now make a game of it! Get up and look for your own "tail." Then ask the child if he can find his. Spin slowly three times to the left, then slowly three times to the right. (*Slow* is the key here—about one revolution per eight seconds.)

Once he's found his tail, what's the best way to keep from losing it again? Sit down!

"Finding his tail" may help the child settle down and sit still . . . at least until that tail goes missing again!

So, if you've found *your* tail and you're ready to start, so are we. Let's get moving!

PART 1

Movement Matters

CHAPTER 1

Introduction to Movement: How the Body Teaches the Brain

All learning begins with the body. It has to. It's our point of reference—our own personal, portable true north, so to speak. And for children, it's even more so because the body is the brain's first teacher. And the lesson plan is movement.

A Moving Child Is a Learning Child

From grasping your finger to grasping her rattle to grasping the mechanics of crawling, standing, walking, jumping, and those hurtling-headlong hugs, every move a young child makes—intentional or accidental—leads to learning. Every move develops her physical capabilities, of course. But at the same time, movement is building sensory perceptions and critical pathways in the brain necessary to reach her full potential.

It's been well reported that within the first years of childhood, approximately 90 percent of the neural pathways in the brain will be set for life.[1] Those pathways determine how a child thinks and learns, but more importantly, they will shape who she becomes . . . her passions and pursuits, triumphs and challenges, inner reflections, outer reactions, and outlook on life . . . all flowing through the neural network built by her earliest physical and sensory experiences.

With breathtaking simplicity, nature has created this move-to-learn process to be both dynamic and self-perpetuating, building the body and brain simultaneously. As such, the more a child moves, the more she stimulates her brain. The more the brain is stimulated, the more movement is required to go get more stimulation. In this way, nature gently coaxes the child to explore beyond her current boundaries toward her own curiosity to acquire new capabilities. (This dynamic process is illustrated in the chart on pages 10–11, "What Real Learning Looks Like.")

> The body is the brain's first teacher.

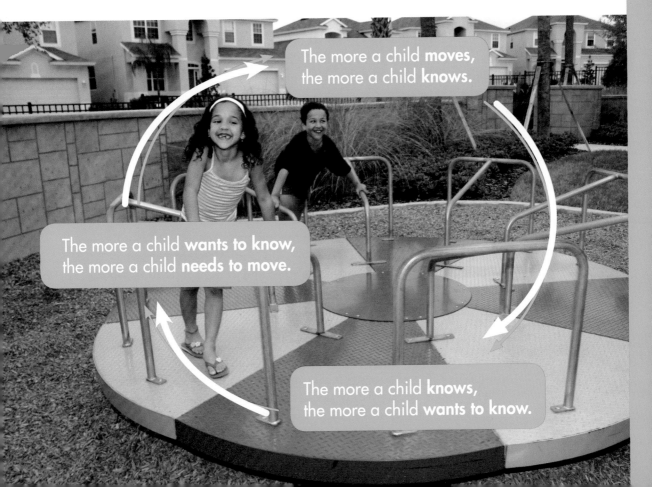

The more a child **moves,** the more a child **knows.**

The more a child **wants to know,** the more a child **needs to move.**

The more a child **knows,** the more a child **wants to know.**

The Brain Has Priorities

We'll talk in more detail about early brain development in Chapter 2. But there are a couple of things we want to draw your attention to here.

During these early years, the brain sets the priorities on a child's developmental calendar, and movement is one of its top priorities (after survival functions such as breathing, heartbeat, and digestion). Now, that doesn't mean other areas of development aren't happening at the same time, but it does mean movement is where the brain is focusing a good deal of its attention.

> **Without automated movement a child will not be able to think.**

Indeed, movement is so important to the brain's master plan, it eventually becomes fully automated, so that the child is able to move without having to think about it.[2] And this may well be the most critical, yet overlooked, aspect of early childhood development. Stated plainly, without automated movement a child will not be able to think.

The human brain is only capable of doing one thinking task at a time. One *conscious* task, that is. But the brain *is* capable of layering that one thinking task on top of one or more automated processes. This is the illusion we call "multitasking," and it explains why as an adult you can walk and talk at the same time. You don't have to think about walking, which leaves your brain free for talking.

Family Moves

Print the "Snail the Whale" Motorvator from the digital file and share it with parents so that little ones can find their tails anywhere they go!

By contrast, a young child has her hands full just controlling muscle movements. Only when she has settled into her own body will her mind be free to think about other things like the ABCs and 123s, remembering "please" and "thank you," pondering the stars, and wondering why cats drink out of puddles.

Interfering with Nature

But here's the problem. Compared with past generations, children today are living far more sedentary lives. We'll examine this in more detail in Chapter 3. But the key point is this: We are tampering with thousands of years of predetermined, movement-based biology, and the unintended consequences are just beginning to show up in research studies and news reports.

And the reasons are obvious. A young child can learn only what her brain is primed and ready for. And in the early years, that's everything the body has to teach—the tangible, physical, and sensory qualities of the world around her. It's no wonder preschool learning rarely happens sitting down. And for that matter, it barely happens right side up.

A young child is a literal, physical creature who needs to experience life in her own way, in her own time, on her own terms, and with her own body. And when she does, she's learning all she needs to know, and then some.

And it hardly ever looks like learning.

Chapter Summary

- **All learning begins with the body and is linked to movement.** Every move develops physical capabilities while building sensory perceptions and critical pathways in the brain.

- **The brain prioritizes movement on a child's developmental calendar.** Movement is so important, it's one of the functions the brain automates in the early years of life. And that's critical to children's learning.

- **The human brain is capable of doing only one thinking task at a time.** But it can layer that thinking task on top of one or more automated processes. When movement becomes automated, the child's mind will be free to think.

What *Real* Learning Looks Like

Love

Perseverance

Mathematics

Reasoning

Language

Visualization

Spelling

Reading

Judgment

Control

Movement is the foundation of all the skills and attributes shown here. *A Moving Child Is a Learning Child* explains how this dynamic move-to-learn process works.

Trust

Handwriting

Responsibility

Concentration

Adaptability

Power

Courage

Science

Creativity

Individuality

Compassion

CHAPTER 2

Containerized Kids

//

By nature's design, kids are born to move. This plays out in every aspect of children's early development. It also explains why wiggles and giggles come so naturally to them. We'll spend the rest of this book getting to know all those wiggles and giggles. But before we do, let's put nature's design in context to today's kids' lifestyle.

Kids and Containers

Stop and consider all the modern products that, by intent or default, contain or constrain children's movements:

- Car seats
- Strollers
- Front packs
- Backpacks
- Slings
- Cribs
- Bassinets
- Baby carriers

- Portable baby chairs
- Bouncy seats
- High chairs
- Baby swings
- Play yards
- Exercise saucers
- Baby jumpers
- Baby walkers

If a family owns more than two or three of these products, or if the child-care setting routinely relies on this kind of equipment, chances are the child for whom they are intended is spending many of his waking hours in confinement, unable to move at will, separated from the vibrant sensations of life by plastic walls with well-intended padding.

Now, that is *not* to say that all baby equipment should be abolished. Quite the contrary. Car seats, strollers, cribs, play yards, and the like keep children safe in dangerous or uncontrollable environments like moving cars, crowded malls, and darkened nighttime rooms.

But often, caregivers *do* control the environment at home and elsewhere. In these circumstances, children deserve the right and the room to move. And for kids, that means the floor. The floor is a child's first, best playground— an experimental laboratory for learning, even from the youngest age.

Although they can't get around on their own, even infants need to understand that space comes in different sizes, shapes, and textures. Floor time gives them different perspectives and helps them see how they fit into their world. So get out the vacuum, remove sharp or breakable objects, and do whatever else is necessary to make the space safe. Then lay out a blanket and let baby explore.

Then one day, out of the blue, a child figures out how to get himself from here to there. At last—independent mobility! But of course, that's usually when the portable play yard pops up. And after the play yard comes a series of other well-intended containers to keep kids safe—and sedentary. Consider these modern "container" trends:

- Many kids are indoors most of the day more than ever before.

- Modern playgrounds and play areas often provide a high level of safety but a low level of challenge.

- Electronic screens beckon kids with mesmerizing but two-dimensional, tactile-free effects.

- Today's high-tech toys, games, and other play experiences offer great fun. But if they don't leave enough room for a child's own discoveries, they could intensify children's natural penchant for instant gratification while setting up false expectations of immediacy in other pursuits (including learning).

- Kids tend to be driven or accompanied everywhere instead of walking or biking on their own or with playmates.

- Enrichment classes offer fun, learning, and stimulation, but by their very nature can't provide the self-directed exploration that free play does.

> Car seats, strollers, cribs, play yards, and the like keep children safe in dangerous or uncontrollable environments. But often, caregivers *do* control the environment. In these circumstances, children deserve the right and the room to move.

- "Academic creep" is narrowing the early learning experience through more and more focus on school readiness and standards.

- "Recess recession" is happening around the globe. Schools are shortening or skipping recess in favor of more classroom work and test readiness.

> **Family Moves**
>
> Print the "Kids Need Room to Move" handout from the digital file and share it with parents to help family adults understand the importance of container-free movement for young children.

Just like the products meant to keep kids safe, these "containerizing" trends distract, block, or limit a child's ability to follow his natural interests. For instance, a toddler in his stroller might be fascinated by a dozen different things he sees. But because he's being pushed from behind, he has no power to do anything but watch those fascinations whiz by. Curiosity is nature's great motivator. When a child is free to follow what interests him, he's not only learning, he's learning *how* to learn by developing a confident, self-motivated, and dynamic approach to new ideas.

Born Risk-Takers

In the field of early childhood development, the word *risk* often refers to physical challenges that may cause injury. Now, no caregiver wants to see a child get hurt. But avoiding physical risk altogether is risky in its own way. The consequences are not always as obvious as a skinned knee or sprained ankle, but can be equally—or even more—harmful down the road.

Children are born to take risks. In fact, a child's growth and development depends on it. A young child lives life on the edge of discovery, constantly stretching his current abilities to conquer new things. And when he does, he's wiring his brain with three essential values he will carry with him for the rest of his life:

> No caregiver wants to see a child get hurt. But avoiding physical risk altogether is risky in its own way. Children are born to take risks.

1. Courage to try

2. Perseverance to try again

3. Independent decision making to make and modify his choices and bring him closer to his goal

Embedded in his mind from early childhood, these values will become part of the child's identity and approach to learning—whether the subject is riding a two-wheeler or learning two times two. And that's the "readiness" we're all searching for. Containers *aren't* always physical. They can equally—and more powerfully—be a self-limiting state of mind.

So, whenever you confront a choice to "contain" a child, ask yourself, "Is this container necessary? Is it for his safety and well-being, or is it for my peace of mind? What will this container stop him from doing, learning, or understanding? What will this container stop him from trying, failing, or conquering?"

Because in life, experience is the root of all learning.

Inexperience is the root of all fear. And fear is the greatest container of all.

Chapter Summary

- **Children deserve the right and the room to move.** While safety seats, cribs, strollers, and other "containers" are needed at times to keep children safe, they also limit children's movements. Choose to give the child freedom to move as much as possible.

- **Children are born to take risks.** They need to take risks so they learn courage, perseverance, and independent decision making. When you confront a choice to "contain" a child, ask yourself if it's necessary. Is the container for the child's safety and well-being? What will the container stop him from learning, trying, failing, or conquering?

CHAPTER 3

How Movement Helps Unlock the Brain for Learning

//

Freeing the body for movement unlocks the brain for learning. We'll talk about that how that works in a bit. But first, we'll take a look at some brain basics, because as the brain goes, so goes learning.

Neuroscience is a fascinating, complicated subject and one where the experts will tell you we still have much to learn. Still, let's review some fundamental science relevant to our understanding of how children grow and learn.

Some Brain Basics

Different centers in the brain handle different major functions. In the early years of life, those centers learn to work together in harmony to create what we experience as human thought, feeling, movement, and expression. And broadly, that brain development happens from the bottom up. So let's take it from the bottom.

The Brain Stem: Survival

The brain stem is on constant alert to matters of our survival, managing functions such as breathing, heart rate, digestion, and so on. It works behind the scenes without conscious thought most of the time. But whenever the brain senses danger or stress, real or imagined, it directs energy into the brain stem for immediate action. It's that snap-to-attention moment when we sense something is amiss, such as a strange sound or an unexpected event. When that happens, the lower parts of the brain take over, and in extreme cases, can all but shut down other parts of the brain until the situation is resolved.

This is one of the reasons why when a child is upset, it's nearly impossible to reason with her.[4] And while understanding this may not solve the crisis any sooner, it should make it easier for you to see it for what it really is (and keep you calm in the process).

The Senses: Perception

The senses gather information the brain needs to understand and navigate the world. In fact, sensory perceptions are so important to our everyday functioning that all parts of the brain and some parts of the nervous system are involved in processing the information.

> Repetition helps the brain learn to move the muscles automatically—one of the brain's biggest priorities in the early years.

In early childhood, the brain is so hungry for information, you can see the senses in action all day, every day—and especially in the things that encourage children to move.

So for our purposes, even though sensory processing doesn't reside in any one place in the brain, we consider the senses a part of brain structure in the "Brain Basics" diagram.[5] We'll discuss this more in Chapter 5.

The Cerebellum: Moving

The cerebellum is command central for most physical movement and muscle control, while playing a supporting role in some cognitive functions. Think of it as the part of the brain that learns how to move every muscle, then stores that information—muscle memory—for future use.

The learning that happens in the cerebellum is often why children love to do the same game over and over. Repetition helps the brain learn to move the muscles automatically—one of the brain's biggest priorities in the early years.

The Limbic System: Feeling

The limbic system manages our emotional lives. It houses emotional memories, builds impressions of our experiences, and influences our day-to-day reactions. In other words, the limbic system determines behavior.

This region of the brain is immature in young children, so their emotional reactions tend to be black-and-white. That's why broccoli may send a child screaming from the room or why he attaches to a favorite toy and won't let go! Emotional memory is powerful stuff—in both children and adults.

The Cortex: Thinking

The most complex part of the brain, the cortex directs what we consider higher-level human thought, including:

- Imagination and creation—the ability to develop a new idea

- Projection and prediction—the ability to forecast the consequences of different choices, such as stepping off a curb before the light turns green or mixing blue and yellow paint

- Interpretation of symbols—the ability to understand and use symbols, such as letters and numbers, for formal learning pursuits like reading, writing, mathematics, and science

Apple Is for A

Quite often, our modern idea of *early learning* gets whittled down to that last point: learning letters and numbers. But a young child's brain is concerned with developing the whole child—not just the future student. Early childhood learning is a process of compiling tangible, physical, real-life, in-the-moment experiences one on top of the next. And the reason is simple. All learning, at any age, stands on the shoulders of prior knowledge—from the known to the unknown. That's how the brain is designed.

For instance, consider the old saying "A is for Apple." It's shorthand for describing how children learn their letters. But in fact, it's not correct. You see, for little ones, the sentence is backward and meaningless. It starts with the unknown instead of the known.

For kids, "Apple is for A" is what makes sense. It starts with the known (Apple) and relates it to the unknown (A). It moves from the tangible to the intangible, from the concrete to the symbolic. And that's how children learn.

Brain Basics

Cortex
Formal learning
Abstract thinking
Symbolic understanding
Consequential thinking

Limbic System
Emotional engagement
Understanding and interpreting emotional messages
(including body language)

Cerebellum
Muscle control
Muscle memory
Motor skills
Fundamental movement patterns

Senses
Seeing
Hearing
Smelling
Tasting
Touching
Balance (Vestibular)
Intuition (Proprioception)

Brain Stem
Survival
Breathing, digestion, blood pressure
Primitive reflexes[3]

Perry, B. "Introduction to the Neurosequential Model of Therapeutics (NMT)." Houston, TX: Child Trauma Academy, 2010.
Adapted with permission.

But of course, "Apple is for A" only makes sense if a child has had experience with apples first. And by experience, we mean personal, sensory experiences with real apples—seeing them, smelling them, holding them, tasting them, hearing them crunch, rolling them around the plate, enjoying them in applesauce, apple juice, apple pie, and so on.

Multiple experiences that engage multiple senses plant information deeply in the brain. And more, they engage the emotions that form opinions and judgments. Judgment poses the important question, "How do I feel about apples?" Whether the answer is love 'em or leave 'em, it's the combination of tangible experiences and the formation of judgment that creates the child's personal reality of apples. And once something is real, the child can then transfer it to related but unknown ideas, such as the letter A.

Motorvator

What Do Apples Sound Like?

Here's Why

To help children build their range of sensory experiences, their sense of adventure, and excitement for learning, challenge them to explore their physical world in different ways. For instance, when children explore apples, the first sense they engage is likely sight, then touch, then smell, and finally taste. But what about hearing? What do apples *sound* like?

Here's How

For any subject a child shows interest in, consider the senses typically *left out*. Challenge the child to discover the subject using those untapped senses.

For example: "What does it sound like when you bite into an apple? *Crunch*. What else goes *crunch*? What does an apple sound like when you roll it on a plate? Can you make that sound for me?" Explore the sounds fully and introduce new language and ideas to this safari of the senses!

And make sure to leave room for imagination. If apples talk, so be it. Have an apple chat!

Next, let's take a closer look at the mechanics of acquiring knowledge, forming opinion, and developing thought.

Wiring the Brain

By some estimates, there are approximately 200 billion neurons (nerve cells) in the brain. But only a small number of those neurons are connected at birth[6]—just enough to enter the world and survive in our atmosphere. Those "factory-installed" functions include breath-ing, blood pressure, reflexes, digestion, and so on. The rest of the brain's connections must be "wired." And that happens at an intense rate, from the first breath to the first day of school. In fact, experts believe about 90 percent of the brain's neural connections are in place by age five.[7] In other words, a child's preschool years are the pivotal period for growing critical, lifelong neu-rological capabilities.

Family Moves

Print the "Apple Is for A" handout and the "What Do Apples Sound Like?" Motorvator from the digital file and share it with parents to help them understand how physical experiences help young children get ready for learning.

A Bit About Neurons

Ongoing research in the area of human thought and memory has yet to form a consensus opinion on how the brain actually stores information. Broadly,

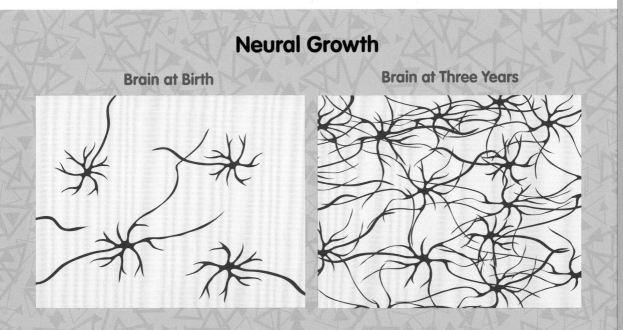

Neural Growth

Brain at Birth　　　　　**Brain at Three Years**

researchers believe that neurons hold specific pieces of information—part genetic, part experiential or environmental—that when connected with other neurons, form thought or memory.[8] That means neurons perform two essential functions: storing information and passing information along. Picture the neural network as a complex interactive puzzle in which the pieces seek each other's company and form their own ideas about things.

In order to create that puzzle, the neurons need to communicate. Now, neurons don't physically touch one another. Instead, they use tiny electrical impulses to share information across the synaptic gaps (the spaces between neurons). This allows the neurons to broadcast information to lots of other neurons all at the same time.

> About 90 percent of the brain's neural connections are in place by age five. A child's preschool years are the pivotal period for growing critical, lifelong neurological capabilities.

Think of it like posting on Facebook. You say something once, and instantly all your friends can see it. ("I like apples.") When they respond, all your friends see what everyone else said. Information spreads quickly and efficiently. And the process is more than just an information exchange. It also forms judgments" ("I like apples, too"), opinions ("I prefer green apples"), actions ("Let's go apple picking"), and reactions ("Then I can make an apple pie").

Neural communication happens at lightning speed all across the brain. A single bit of information may travel through thousands or even millions of neurons in a fraction of a second. And as it travels, each of those neurons is contributing to the brain's understanding, judgment, and cataloging (memory) of the information. That's why two people can experience the exact same event and walk away with completely different understandings and memories. In short, neurological processing explains the complex, dynamic, sometimes-fascinating, sometimes-confounding world of human individuality. [9]

Myelination

Even though neural impulses travel at lightning speed, the human mind requires even faster transmission to achieve mature thinking, reasoning, and creativity. So in the early years of life, a process called myelination occurs in the brain.

Now, each brain cell is made up of a neuron (the central core) and transmitters. The dendrites receive information and the axon passes it along.

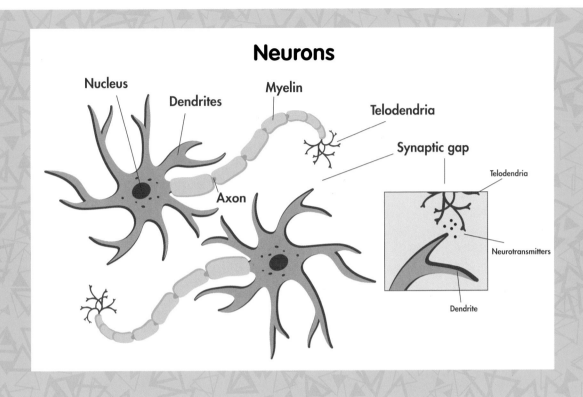

Myelination specifically involves the axon. It's a fatty substance (the myelin sheath) that acts like insulation protecting the axon from damage or disruption from all the other neural activity going on in the brain.

Remarkably, myelination both speeds up processing power and helps cement experiences into permanent conscious or subconscious memories. In short, myelination makes the brain faster and "stickier."[10]

Myelination begins at the moment of birth and continues for many years. But the first five years—and especially the first three—are the most important. Even though the brain records every experience, those involving multiple inputs—physical, sensory, and emotional—will trigger the myelination process. The stronger the experience, the more myelin will grow. And if the experience is repeated over and over, still more myelin will form.

In part, this explains the essential trial-and-error nature of early childhood. Think about when a baby is first learning to pull herself up. She tries a lot. She plops a lot. Over and over, as she's striving to get vertical, her brain is recording every movement and every sensation. Only when the muscles have enough strength and the brain has enough experience can she accomplish her goal. (So *that's* what the top of the coffee table looks like!)

Automaticity

Chapter 1 discussed automated movement. Automation—or what we call *automaticity*—is one of the most critical aspects of early childhood development. Yet it happens so gradually, it almost escapes notice.

What Is Automaticity?

> Movement is at the forefront of all early childhood development. Automaticity—movement without having to think about it—creates efficiencies in the brain and frees up processing power for more complex thinking, reasoning, imagining, and inventing, and yes, learning to spell your own name.

This is so important it bears repeating. Automaticity is the process of automating repetitive functions so that they no longer require conscious thought. That's because the human brain is *incapable* of doing more than one *thinking* task at a time. But it *can* layer one thinking task on top of one or more automated tasks.

A great example is handwriting. When children are first learning to write letters, they're not thinking about *what* they're writing, they're thinking about *how* they're writing. If you want to know what that feels like, try writing your name with your nondominant hand. Forming the letters will feel awkward and strange. You may even find yourself reversing some letters or having to stop and think about which letter comes next (even in your own name!). Your brain is prioritizing between the movement (your hand) and the cognitive process (what you want to write), and in this case, the movement is winning. In short, when the brain is confronted with having to choose, it always prioritizes from the bottom up.[11]

That's why we say movement is at the forefront of all early childhood development. Automaticity—movement without having to think about it—creates efficiencies in the brain and frees up processing power for more complex thinking, reasoning, imagining, and inventing, and yes, learning to spell your own name.

Split Attention Versus Switched Attention

Now, you may be thinking, "I'm a great multitasker. I can talk on the phone and write an email (two thinking tasks) at the same time." But in fact, you're not doing them simultaneously. While it may feel as though you are, you're actually switching your attention rapidly back and forth.

Switched attention develops over years of practice through millions of experiences. Children lack that experience, of course, and, on top of that, have immature short-term memory. That's why many struggle to switch attention between tasks.

For example, a young child may be learning how to pour her own milk. Left undisturbed, she'll succeed to the best of her physical ability. But interrupt her with a question and one of three things will happen:

1. She'll stop pouring and answer you.

2. She'll keep pouring and not answer you.

3. Where's the mop?

So what's the key to developing automaticity?

Again, Daddy! Again!

Repetition aligns the brain and body. It creates muscle memory and automates movement. But repetition *doesn't* mean drills. In fact, it's just the opposite.

When a child does something over and over, that means her brain is working through the steps of memorizing the activity. (Myelination is happening, too.) Her brain rewards her with positive feelings (a sense of fun) so she *wants* to continue. And when the brain has had enough, she's had enough, and she moves on to something else.

The best thing you can do to facilitate this is to cooperate with her brain. Let nature take its course again and again . . . and yes, again!

Gill's Notebook

Growing Memory: Forgetting to Remember

One day my two-year-old granddaughter and I were planning to take our monthly trip to the library. We've been going to the library together since she was an infant. To see, smell, and touch that many books in one place, and then take home whichever ones she wants, never gets old for her (or me).

When it was time to go, I asked Caitlin, "Please put on your coat and shoes and bring your library book."

A few minutes later, Caitlin came to the door with her unbuttoned coat on, but no shoes and no book. And all I could think was, "Oh, how silly of me. I forgot to remember she's still working on remembering things."

The Mechanics of Memory

Memory is an essential part of learning, and there's more to it than simply retaining information. It must be stored so it's accessible when needed. And for that, the brain needs to create its own system for cataloging information.

In a young mind with few points of reference, that's a tall order. In these early years, the brain is constantly arranging and rearranging information. And because *all* the brain's neurons store information—there's no "memory central"—where and how information gets stored colors the memory and interpretation. In other words, the human brain remembers information in context. And little ones don't have a lot of context yet.

> Preschoolers typically can hear and follow two *fewer* instructions than their age.

This system is so complex that science has many different theories about the storage and retrieval of memories. For our purposes, let's discuss the three basic types of memory.

Three Types of Memory
Short-Term Memory

The reason Caitlin couldn't follow three simple instructions is that her young brain hadn't yet mastered the use of her short-term memory. That, and the fact that she was two years old and easily distracted, made it appear as though she lacked attention span. But in fact, little ones come equipped with the same amount of short-term memory capacity as we adults have. They just don't use it very well.

Short-term memory is part of the reason the brain is as fast as it is. By managing immediate information in a temporary manner, the brain can be responsive and reactive to what's happening at the moment, while it takes time to sort and place that information into long-term memory. In fact, here's a rule of thumb you might find useful:

Age Minus 2 (or Thereabouts)

Preschoolers typically can hear and follow two *fewer* instructions than their age. Two-year-old Caitlin could probably remember and follow one simple instruction—and sometimes would still get it wrong. By age four, she might be able to remember two verbal instructions at once (age $4 - 2 = 2$ instructions); at age five, three instructions (age $5 - 2 = 3$ instructions), and so forth.[12]

Working Memory
Working memory is the brain's ability to take action on information in short-term memory while it builds bridges to long-term memory.

Long-Term Memory
Long-term memory is the brain's vast, complete catalog of experiences—the home of "the known." As such, it is the key to processing all new learning. With each new encounter, the brain searches the long-term memory banks to contrast, compare, define, and eventually organize and store the new information for future use.

SARAH ALICE LEE

Learning Modalities

Memory is enhanced when we take into account a child's natural learning style or what's called her *learning modality*. Now, it's generally agreed there are three major types of learners: visual, auditory, and kinesthetic.

Visual Learners

Visual learners seek out visual cues to help them understand tasks. For instance, if you tell a visual learner, "Please go get your library book," she'll start scanning the room for visual information while you're still talking. It may seem as though she's not listening, but chances are she's hearing everything and using her eyes to aid her understanding.

Insisting that a visual learner look at you while you're talking to her will defeat her. Instead, let visual learners use their eyes to help them understand, remember, and carry out tasks. Even better, offer visual cues with pictures or body language.

Auditory Learners

Auditory learners seek audible cues to assist their understanding. If you tell an auditory learner, "Please go get your library book," chances are she will look straight at you and listen to every word before reacting.

Be sure you have an auditory learner's full attention before you speak, make eye contact with her, and have her repeat instructions back to you. Additional auditory stimulation, such as rhyming or singing the instructions, will help her understand what you're asking.

Kinesthetic Learners

One school of thought suggests that all children start out as kinesthetic learners, [13] which is defined as those who learn by doing. Kinesthetic learners often appear impulsive. When you ask a kinesthetic learner, "Please go get your library—," she's off before you can even finish your sentence.

To help a kinesthetic learner listen, understand, and remember, be sure to get her attention, make eye contact, use body language, and provide positive physical cues like holding her hand or patting her shoulder. Have her repeat instructions back to you, making the experience even more interactive.

And note: No matter which learning modality a child exhibits, try not to repeat yourself too often. This will only teach her *not* to pay attention the first time! And that's not the sort of thing you want her to remember.

Chapter Summary

- **The brain has priorities.** The brain develops from the bottom up. In early childhood, survival functions and movement are prioritized for development before emotional and cognitive development.

- **Apple is for A.** Children must learn concretely (apple) before they can advance to abstract and symbolic learning (letters and numbers).

- **Neural connections are built in early childhood.** Movement facilitates this process of "wiring" the brain.

- **Young children are wiring their brains.** The process of myelination occurs for many years, but most intensely in the first two. Myelination speeds up the brain's processing and cements experiences into permanent memories.

- **The brain can do only one conscious thinking task at a time.** It is essential to automate movement in the early years so that the brain can move on to develop higher thinking and reasoning tasks. Automaticity is achieved through many varied physical experiences and repeated muscle movements.

- **Experience develops memory.** Young children need context to store and retrieve memories properly. Context comes from physical, tangible experiences.

- **Young children have limited memory skills.** By and large, preschoolers remember two fewer instructions than their age.

- **Children have different learning styles.** There are three major learning modalities: visual, auditory, and kinesthetic.

PART 2

A Moving Child

CHAPTER 4

How a Moving Child Develops

//

It's hard to imagine, but when babies are born, they don't fully understand they have a body. This knowledge is called body awareness—an innate sense of the complete self—and it emerges over time as the body and brain get to "know" each other through everyday life experiences.

This is important for one simple, obvious reason. You can't control what you don't know you have. Body awareness is a precursor to deliberate muscle control.

The Snowflake Effect

Much the way a snowflake grows in an orderly fashion from the center outward, children's awareness and control of their bodies builds from the top down and from the inside out.[14] By nature's design, this logical progression ensures the larger muscles are ready to support and transport the smaller muscles for more refined, detailed activity.

In the early months of life, the body and brain "introduce" themselves. First, babies master their head and neck muscles when they can lift their heads at will. Next, they begin developing control from their shoulders out to their arms, while forming the beginnings of muscle tone in the fingers for later grasping, pinching, and holding. Of note, much of early hand movement is actually the primitive reflexes at work, not deliberate fine motor control. We'll discuss reflexes in more detail in Chapter 5.

Next, the upper torso comes into focus, building the strength and control necessary to hold the body upright. And from there, control begins to emerge over the lower torso, large muscles in the legs, and finally the feet for crawling, sitting up, standing, and walking.

Straightforward as this may seem, body awareness isn't a simple "on" switch. It's an ongoing process that creates a complete and reliable "relationship" between the brain and each part in the body over the early years of life.

The Evolution of Independent Movement

Every step along the path to independent movement builds on the one before. It all happens naturally when the child's body and brain are ready.

As a rule, nature is very organized and has a generalized master plan for children's development. The diagram on pages 34–35 shows you the typical way children's movement evolves from before birth to fully coordinated movement.

But please note! *This progression is a guideline, not a mandate.* Each child develops uniquely. No chart—including this one—can tell you precisely what to expect or when to expect it. That's because the child's brain is a wise steward of his individual needs. It is running the show, so to speak, and setting its own priorities. If he skips a step or follows a different order from what we're showing you here, it's not necessarily cause for concern. As long as he is progressing, getting to each step in his own time and way, he's on the road to making the most of what his body and brain were designed to do.

Snowflake Effect

Children learn to understand their bodies from the top down and from the inside out.

The Evolution of Independent Movement: A Guideline, Not a Mandate

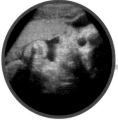

Prenatal primitive reflexes: involuntary movement

Primitive reflexes in place at birth

Head control: first attempts

Awakening of senses with touch, massage, and skin-to-skin contact

Hand and foot recognition

Crawling Matters

Crawling has enormous developmental benefits for young children. Both arms and both legs move in opposition to one another, which not only develops physical coordination, but also accelerates the growth of critical connections between the right and left sides of the brain.

Some children skip the crawling stage in favor of bottom shuffling, or they shoot straight up to walking. If that happens, encourage the child to crawl with push-along toys, such as toy cars and trucks.

Pincer grip

Crawling

Changing hands

Releasing grasp voluntarily

Sitting independently

Navigating small spaces

Pulling up to stand

Marching

Balancing on one foot

Handedness: early signs

Temporal awareness

Manipulative skills emerging

Hopping

Climbing in opposition: opposite arm, opposite leg

Galloping

Midlines developing: isolated or complex whole-body movements

Hand and foot dominance developing

Hip tips:
attempting to roll over

Sensory discoveries:
especially mouth

Rolling over onto
tummy

Pushing up from
tummy

Postural reflexes
emerging

Studying facial
expressions

Rocking

Up on all fours

Commando crawling

Mouthing things

Grasping

Cruising

Bobbing up and
down, aided

Standing, unaided

Climbing up
furniture or stairs

Eye-hand
coordination:
self-feeding

Walking
unaided:
toddling or
waddling

Jumping forward
on two feet

Upper body
strength
developing

Jumping on
two feet

Bobbing up and
down, unaided

Running

Leaping from standing

Crossing the midline

Leaping from running

Skipping

Automated coordinated
movement

Building a Moving Child

As you can see, the early years are jam-packed with increasing physical ability. And it's a self-rewarding system—each accomplishment building on the last and unlocking the possibility of still more.

Parents and teachers call these milestones. Professionals in physical education and health and wellness call this the process of developing fundamental movement patterns (FMPs)—the outward exhibition of advanced, coordinated skills.[15]

Fundamental Movement Patterns

Movement is a three-dimensional, dynamic puzzle that children are working to figure out all the time. To help us understand these complexities, experts have broken down all human movement—the different ways the human body moves—into three fundamental movement patterns (FMPs) that include:

Locomotion: The ability to move your body from here to there
Stability: The ability to maintain balance while still or in motion
Manipulation: The ability to effect objects with part of your body or with an instrument (such as a bat or racquet)

All whole-body movements are made up of a combination of these patterns, and mastering them in both their simple and complex forms will eventually add up to a well-coordinated, proficient, and reliable set of physical skills.

However, what's *not* seen is the underlying complex weave of "developmental engineering" that makes it all possible.

And for that, we need a new way of looking at movement...

Introducing the Kinetic Scale

In order to understand not only the moving child but the learning child, we need a deeper understanding of movement itself. So let's start by breaking down the basic elements of movement—the raw ingredients, if you will. And to do that, we've devised a tool to help you visualize the dynamic relationship among all of those ingredients. We call it the Kinetic Scale.

We'll get into more detail in the following chapters, but here's a quick snapshot to give you a sense of how it all comes together.

The Kinetic Scale

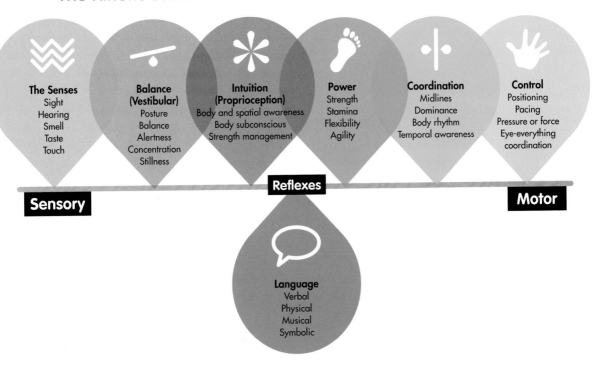

The Senses	Balance (Vestibular)	Intuition (Proprioception)	Power	Coordination	Control
Sight	Posture	Body and spatial awareness	Strength	Midlines	Positioning
Hearing	Balance	Body subconscious	Stamina	Dominance	Pacing
Smell	Alertness	Strength management	Flexibility	Body rhythm	Pressure or force
Taste	Concentration		Agility	Temporal awareness	Eye-everything coordination
Touch	Stillness				

Sensory   **Reflexes**   **Motor**

Language
Verbal
Physical
Musical
Symbolic

The **reflexes** underpin and enable all early childhood movement, triggering critical developmental stages. Since all early movement depends on the reflexes, they serve as the platform for what we call the six physicalities.

Three sensory tools and three motor tools make up the six **physicalities**. Together, they ensure a rich movement "diet," which builds the body *and*

> Early childhood development is comprised of thousands, if not millions, of tiny interrelated and interdependent advancements occurring in the body and brain simultaneously.

fosters the deep and intricate neural wiring in the brain that occurs in the early years.

Language in all its forms enriches the learning power of movement by providing the brain with the stimulation it needs to translate physical, tangible experience into conceptual, abstract thinking. In other words, exposure to rich and plentiful language stimulation optimizes a child's early movement development for learning.

Nature's Developmental Engineering

Early childhood development is comprised of thousands, if not millions, of tiny interrelated and interdependent advancements occurring in the body and brain simultaneously. But books are built one chapter at a time. So as we move forward to explore each of these ingredients, please keep in mind that each is playing its own unique part in concert with the others to fulfill nature's plan for building the *whole* child.

So, in Chapter 5 we'll begin our journey where movement itself begins—the reflexes.

Chapter Summary

- **The snowflake effect:** Children gain awareness and control of their bodies in sequence, from the top down and from the inside out.

- **The evolution of movement:** Movement development in the early years happens step by step, building one competency upon another in a long journey toward fully coordinated, automated movement.

- **Each child is unique:** Growth charts can provide only broad guidelines. Each child develops uniquely, according to the needs of his brain. Following a different order or skipping a step is not cause for concern as long as the child continues to show signs of progress.

- **The Kinetic Scale:** Early childhood movement involves an intricate weave of developmental engineering that encompasses the raw ingredients of movement including the reflexes, sensory tools, and motor tools. When combined with language, they form the foundations for children's learning and understanding about themselves and their world.

CHAPTER 5

The Origins of Movement: Primitive and Postural Reflexes

///

Thousands of years ago, according to Margot Sunderland, author of *The Science of Parenting,*[16] when the human body began to evolve from walking on four feet to walking on two, necessary changes were made to our basic physiology for this new, upright posture. In particular, the pelvic region needed to be narrowed to provide for efficient bi-pedal movement. From there, changes needed to be made to the female reproductive system resulting in a narrower birth canal. As a result, nature made some logical "design trade-offs," shortening the gestation period to allow for smaller babies, which in turn required far more development of the body and brain *after* birth than any other creature on earth.

With a smaller brain at birth, nature needed to provide ways for human infants to survive before, during, and after arrival. The solution was a system of reflexes.

Reflexes are defined as automatic, involuntary responses to stimulation. In other words, they are nature's "starter kit" for our moving life.

Human babies have two types of reflexes: primitive and postural. Most primitive reflexes form in utero and are designed principally for navigating the birth canal, surviving the first months of life, and initiating movement. Postural reflexes develop soon after birth. They remain with us until movement in an upright position is automated, and in some cases much longer than that.

Primitive Reflexes

Primitive reflexes govern many aspects of a newborn's life, from navigating the birth canal to finding the breast. Because these reflexes aid in the transition from the womb to the world, they are meant to be temporary. Once they have served their purpose, the natural process of early movement releases the reflexes, rendering them dormant. As this happens, the postural reflexes begin to emerge which unlock the more complex movement patterns children need as they grow.

Delayed Release of Primitive Reflexes

Generally, releasing the primitive reflexes happens in an orderly fashion, but of course, it differs slightly for each child. That said, there are occasions when primitive reflexes do not release within a normal window of time. And that may—and let us underscore *may*—affect or even delay other aspects of development.

There can be many reasons for delayed release, including genetic predisposition, premature birth, and assisted delivery among others. Add to that today's "containerization" trend (see Chapter 2), and these factors could be compounded by a lack of natural, physical play and movement which is nature's way of releasing these reflexes.

Now, the effects of lingering primitive reflexes vary greatly and may be hard to pinpoint. After all, there are thousands of other developmental events going on at the same time these reflexes are in effect. But a delay could result in developmental "gaps" most typically in physical development, but also in the areas of cognitive, social, and emotional growth. The longer a primitive reflex remains after its intended life cycle, the longer it may take a child to unravel its effects. But that does *not* mean a child will never be able to recoup what's been missed. It may simply mean more time and attention needs to be paid to those "gaps" later on.

Dozens of primitive reflexes govern all aspects of a child's early movements. Some of the more prominent ones are:

- Startle reflex (Moro reflex)
- Grasp reflex (Palmar reflex)
- Food-finder reflex (rooting reflex)
- Push-away reflex (plantar reflex and Babinski response)
- Squirming reflex (spinal galant reflex)
- Aligning reflex (tonic labyrinthine reflex or TLR)
- Fencing reflex (asymmetrical tonic neck reflex or ATNR)
- Rocking reflex (symmetrical tonic neck reflex or STNR)

Startle or Moro Reflex

What Does It Do? The startle or Moro reflex develops in utero to stimulate the first breath after birth and to help baby adjust to the sensations of her new surroundings. Throughout the first months of life, this reflex serves as baby's natural alarm bell. When a baby is startled, her body goes stiff. Her arms, legs, and fingers spread-eagle, and her eyes open wide. This reaction usually lasts only a few seconds, then baby relaxes again.

> The startle or Moro reflex develops in utero to stimulate the first breath after birth and to help baby adjust to the sensations of her new surroundings.

Releasing the Reflex. To release this reflex, baby needs a low-stress environment and, when possible, simulated sensations of the womb. For instance, the ancient practices of swaddling or skin-to-skin care makes newborns feel warm, snug, and safe, much like the walls of the uterus.

And the startle reflex is also aligned with baby's vestibular system—her sense of balance—which can be stimulated through very gentle, slow rocking and spinning movements.

Related Development. The startle reflex generally releases between three and four months. If there is a challenge in releasing this reflex it may affect a child's balance and motor development, contribute to motion sickness, or even make her timid about trying more complex movement activities.

Grasp and Food-Finder Reflexes

Grasp or Palmar Reflex

What Does It Do? The grasp or palmar reflex is responsible for three seemingly unrelated—yet essential—early movements. First, it explains a baby's disproportionately strong hand grip to her tiny frame. It's thought to be a residual survival mechanism from long ago, when babies needed to hold onto their mothers' hair while crossing rugged terrain. Similarly, the toes of the feet will also curl up when stimulated. And third, this reflex triggers sucking movements in the mouth to assist in feeding. If you watch carefully, you might see a newborn's hands pulsing ever so slightly. When that happens, the mouth muscles also suck involuntarily.

Releasing the Reflex. By gently touching the palm of a newborn's hand or the center of her foot, you will see her fingers or toes immediately curl into a "grasp." Many adults naturally play with baby's hands and feet during feeding and playtime, providing the perfect stimulation for release of this reflex over time, usually within five to six months. Feeling a wide variety of textures with the hands and feet is also great stimulation for this reflex.

Of note, sometimes primitive reflexes may leave an echo effect after they've been released. In this case, thumb sucking, fiddling with fingers (such as stroking a favorite soft toy), or playing with her hair can become a very natural, self-soothing habit after the grasp reflex has released.

Related Development. The palmar reflex provides baby's first tactile interactions with the world. It is stimulated by the everyday acts of touching, holding, and playing with objects. When it begins to release, voluntary hand movements, such as the pincer grip (the ability to hold objects between the thumb and index finger), emerge for more deliberate manipulative skills.

The grasp reflex also ensures that baby will take nourishment by stimulating the sucking instinct, working in coordination with the food-finder reflex.

Food-Finder or Rooting Reflex

The food-finder reflex centers on finding the source of food. You can see it by gently stroking an infant's cheek. This simulates the feeling of the breast and she will turn her head toward that sensation. Both the grasp and food-finder reflexes work to develop the muscles around the mouth so that when they release around the age of six months, she'll be ready for the deliberate use of those muscles for taking nourishment independently and forming sounds and words someday soon.

Push-Away Reflex (Plantar Reflex and Babinski Response)

What Does It Do? The push-away reflex accomplishes two important survival tasks by helping baby move her body by pushing with her feet. During the birth process, she uses this reflex to push against the uterine wall to help Mom with delivery. After birth, that same instinct helps baby move closer to the breast for feeding.

Releasing the Reflex. When you hold a baby upright with her feet on your lap, her legs reflexively push away from you. That's the push-away or plantar reflex. (Parents sometimes mistake this as an early attempt to stand, but it's simply her reflexes in full gear.) Likewise, if you place a baby on the floor and press gently on the soles of her feet, she'll push away. Many babies can do this for minutes at a time, squiggling across an entire blanket. At the same time, you may also see another reflex—the Babinski response—in which the big toe stands up and the other toes fan out.

> The push-away reflex is baby's first inkling of independent locomotion.

Related Development. The push-away reflex is baby's first inkling of independent locomotion. It builds muscle strength in the toes, feet, and legs, which she will use to begin crawling in a few months.

Squirming or Spinal Galant Reflex

What Does It Do? As a baby's back rubs against the uterine and vaginal walls during birth, the squirming reflex helps baby wriggle through the birth canal.

Releasing the Reflex. The squirming reflex is essential for the birth process but appears to have little use after that. To see it in action, hold and support baby on her tummy and gently stroke her back on either side of the spine. You'll see the muscles on that side contract.

Firm baby massage, gentle rolling and stretching movements, and baby's own natural wiggles work to release this reflex, usually between the ages of three and nine months.

Motorvator

Egg Rolls

Here's Why
A squirmy child may need some stimulation to help release the squirming reflex. You can do this activity very gently with newborns and infants. Older children can do egg rolls on their own. For safety's sake, use the floor only—never a bed or other furniture.

Here's How
For infants: Lie face-up with baby lying face-up on your chest. Fold your knees into the "cannonball" position. Continually support baby while you slowly and gently rock to the left and right several times and forward and back like a rocking chair. As you do this, talk to baby or sing "The Egg Roll Song" (to the tune of "Row, Row, Row Your Boat.")

The Egg Roll Song
Roll, roll, roll along.
Sing a silly song.
Scramble.
Scramble.
Scramble.
Scramble.
Good thing our shells are strong!

With toddlers and preschoolers, you can do this same activity or show them how to do it on their own. Start by rolling side to side then curl up and rock forward and backward—a precursor to somersaulting.

Related Development. If release is delayed, potty training may take longer. And in older children, it may be related to fidgeting, or "ants in the pants." Simple back rubs and natural play such as rolling activities will work to release this reflex.

Aligning or Tonic Labyrinthine Reflex (TLR)

What Does It Do? Because the baby was curled up in a ball for months in the womb, nature has provided the TLR or aligning reflex to assist in stretching out the body for proper posture and movement. It develops in utero but manifests at birth.

You'll see this reflex in two very different body positions. The first is the familiar fetal position. The other is the exact opposite—an overextended backward arch.

Releasing the Reflex. Releasing the aligning reflex is an ongoing process through the first three years. For infants, different holds can stimulate the curling and arching movements. For instance, hold the child in the crook of your arm, and her body will naturally curl up. Support her at the small of her back, and she will arch backward. And baby massage is also great stimulation for this and other primitive reflexes.

Related Development. The aligning reflex affects many aspects of development, including posture, balance, muscle tone, and more. Releasing this reflex fosters a smooth transition from the prone to upright position and ensures proper posture. Children who haven't fully released the aligning reflex may have trouble maintaining balance or show clumsiness, poor muscle tone, or for lack of a better description, floppiness.

Fencing or Asymmetrical Tonic Neck Reflex (ATNR)

What Does It Do? During birth, the fencing reflex helps position baby's body so her shoulders can squeeze through the birth canal. After birth, the reflex helps keep baby's head turned to one side, which is designed to prevent the accidental obstruction of the airways while she is lying on her tummy.

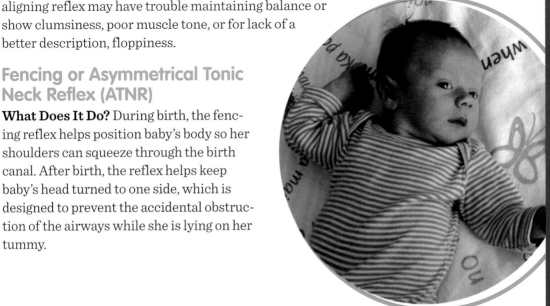

The fencing reflex is the reflexive connection between the arms and head, so that they move automatically as a single unit. When baby turns her head, the corresponding arm stretches out, the eyes look toward the hand, and the other arm folds in.

Family Moves

Print the "Egg Rolls" Motorvator and the "Skin-to-Skin" handout from the digital file and share them with parents of infants. Also share "Gill's Notebook: No Propping, Please" to help parents understand the importance of allowing young children to develop naturally and on their own timeline.

Releasing the Reflex. While baby lies on her back, lift one arm out to the side. Watch as her head follows her arm. Then try it with the other arm. Next, gently touch her left arm to her right foot. Repeat with the other arm and foot. This gives baby a sense of more advanced movements while challenging the fencing reflex to release.

Related Development. While the fencing reflex is essential in the early months of life, releasing this reflex is important to advancing motor development. At five to six months, babies may now have the strength to get up on all fours. When this occurs, you'll see baby begin to rock in preparation for crawling. This is the rocking reflex kicking in. This period (usually three to six weeks or so) releases the fencing reflex so that arms can begin to move independent of the head.

Rocking or Symmetrical Tonic Neck Reflex (STNR)

At this unique turning point in infant development, the rocking reflex acts as a bridge to the body's final, postural reflex stage. As this "exchange" is made, the brain and body are learning a whole new pattern of coordinated movement—opposite arm and leg movement, as well as the ability to move one side of the body independent of the other. If this critical period is delayed, children will struggle with their coordination to begin crawling.

Imagine the brain as a master reflex control board. The brain ramps up the posturals as it fades out the primitives in a precise order tailored and timed to each child's developmental needs.

Postural Reflexes

Sitting, standing, walking, running, and all the other sophisticated move-ments children need to master rely on a straight and steady upright posture. The postural reflexes focus on helping children get and stay upright and on their two-footed way.

Imagine the brain as a master reflex control board. The brain ramps up the posturals as it fades out the primitives in a precise order tailored and timed to each child's developmental needs.

Many postural reflexes are at work during and after this period. Let's look at some of the more prominent ones:

- Straightening reflex (Landau reflex)
- Head-righting reflex
- Crawling and swimming reflex (amphibian reflex)
- Falling reflex (parachute reflex)

Straightening or Landau Reflex

The straightening reflex helps babies achieve and maintain a straight pos-ture by centering the head on the neck and shoulders. It appears shortly after birth, sometime between three and 10 weeks of age, and works to develop overall muscle tone. This is an essential bridge from prone to upright. But like all the reflexes, it does not act in isolation.

Head-Righting Reflex

Within weeks of birth, infants can lift their heads a bit when lying on their tummies or while being held. These are the very first signs of the head-righting reflex, which will culminate by about the age of five to six months when baby can lie on her back and lift her head toward her chest. This is a big turning point that often goes unheralded. Nature is signaling it's time to work on getting vertical.

Like everything in child development, going from prone to upright is a multistep process involving all parts of the brain and body. And in the case of getting vertical, the key is strong, deliberate control of the head. When nature switches on the head-righting reflex, the muscles in the neck, shoulders, back, and torso are prompted to try to lift and hold the head at the top of baby's body while she is in any position, moving or still. You see, the head is the heaviest part of her little body. Without control of the head, she'll likely tip over, whether she's attempting crawling, sitting independently, standing, or walking.

Meanwhile, the rocking reflex is prompting the release of the fencing reflex (ATNR) so that as baby gets up on all fours, the head and arms can move independently. But the head-righting reflex must also activate during this period to make crawling possible. This chain of events ensures that once baby gets moving, she's got a better chance of maintaining her balance, and of course, with her head up, she can see where she's going.

Crawling and Swimming or Amphibian Reflex

Almost like a dress rehearsal for crawling, this reflex stimulates an involuntary opposite-arm, opposite-leg movement. You'll see the signs of it when you lift one arm and the opposite knee bends at the same time, usually between four and six months. When that happens, watch out! Here comes crawling.

And during this period, another remarkable milestone is right around the corner: the ability for baby to sit up on her own.

Falling or Parachute Reflex

Nature knows baby will do a lot of plopping and flopping while she's working to get vertical. The falling or parachute reflex emerges as baby begins to crawl and sit up on her own to protect her body (and especially her head). For instance, when learning to sit up, she splays her legs to form a wide base. This helps her stay upright, but her balance isn't yet refined, so she'll likely tilt from time to time. When that happens, her arms reflexively reach out like a parachute to break her fall.

A Word About Sitting Up

Sitting up independently takes both physical and vestibular maturity according to each baby's own timetable. Often, parents or caregivers prop baby up in containers or with lots of soft pillows thinking they are helping that process. But in fact, propping baby up is unnecessary and might even interfere with the process. The falling reflex needs to do its job so that baby is equipped with all she needs to protect herself without containers or pillows.

Gill's Notebook

No Propping, Please

We all want the best for the children in our care. We'll do whatever we can to help them grow up happy and healthy. But if we do everything *we* can, we may prevent them from doing everything *they* can.

A common example is propping up a child before she's ready to sit on her own. Cute and well-meaning as this may be, when a child is propped up by pillows or containers, she doesn't have to do the work necessary to get to that position on her own. And if this happens often enough, it can actually interrupt or leave gaps in her natural development process.

So what does it take to sit up on your own for the first time?

- **Strength:** Core muscle strength provides a stable base for the rest of the body. At the same time, upper body strength is needed to hold the head centered over the shoulders.

- **Primitive reflex release and postural reflex emergence:** During the period babies are learning to get themselves up on all fours and eventually turn and sit for themselves, the brain is dialing back primitive reflexes while triggering the postural reflexes in order to encourage the body to move in new ways.

- **Balance:** As with everything, balance underpins the ability to sit and stay upright, but to do this on her own, baby must learn to find her own sense of balance.

Children who get lots of floor time on their backs and tummies naturally build the strength and balance necessary to crawl and sit up when the reflexes are ready. Children who don't may struggle with one or more of these essential components.

But more, when a child doesn't have the freedom to move and explore, her senses are not engaged. This creates what I call a "lazy brain." That is, when the world "comes to you," there is little motivation to go and discover things on your own. After all, the word "motivation" is derived from the Latin, *moveo*, or *to move*. When children move, they stimulate the brain, motivating curiosity, which in turn stimulates more movement, and the cycle begins again.

So if you want to *motivate* a child, be sure to *motorvate* her, by giving her the time and space she needs to move to and through the learning all by herself.

Chapter Summary

- **Movement starter kit:** Reflexes initiate movement before birth, then foster controlled, deliberate movement development through the early years.

- **Nature's movement control panel:** The brain uses reflexes to trigger tiny advancements that add up to major milestones.

- **Reflex individuality:** Each child's reflex schedule depends upon her brain's unique needs.

- **Stimulating the reflexes:** A child's daily routine of eating, sleeping, and playing is usually all she needs to release her primitive reflexes and trigger her posturals.

CHAPTER 6

The Origins of Learning: The Senses

The senses are the filters through which we internalize the world around us and come to know our own bodies. Now, contrary to what we all learned in school, there are actually *seven* senses. They include the familiar ones (sight, hearing, smell, taste, and touch) plus two more: our internal sense of balance (known as the vestibular system) and intuition (our sense of spatial orientation and movement, technically referred to as proprioception). For our purposes, we call these the sensory tools. Here's why . . .

The Origins of Learning

Put simply, the senses are the very beginnings of learning. They deliver the raw information the brain needs to make sense of the world.

Physical experiences (movement) stimulate the senses, which collect information and deliver it to the brain for analysis, interpretation, reaction, and storage as memory. Think of the senses as scouts. They bring news of the world to the brain so it can decide what to do next. They act as the fuel that keeps a child's move-to-learn cycle moving.

For instance, a young infant stares at a shiny object for weeks and weeks, then one day reaches out to touch it. As simple as that sounds, it's actually a signal that his brain has decided it needs more information, so it sends the hand (the sense of touch) to go get it.

As such, movement and the senses share a special and reciprocal relationship in the learning process:

1. **The senses motivate movement.** We all know that when a child wants something, he works out a way to get it, by hook or by crook. The senses begin that process and movement gets the job done The infant *saw* the shiny object first, then *reached* for it. (Chances are you do the same thing every time you go shopping.)

2. **The senses are stimulated by movement.** When the baby raised his arm, that sensory-triggered movement fired up additional sensory stimulation. Prompted by what he saw, he engaged his sense of intuition to get his hand to the shiny object. This, in turn, enabled his fingers to touch the object.

> Movement and the senses share a reciprocal relationship in the learning process: the senses both *motivate* and *are stimulated by* movement.

This infant not only learned something about the shiny object, he also sharpened his senses a little bit more. And his brain now has vital early clues to help him eventually master deliberate movement. And once he's discovered he can do that—well, what else can he do?

This is experience—the essence of learning by doing. And the senses are the pathway to all experiences.

Sensory Learning

As the senses develop, so does a child's ability to recognize what he's sensing, which is the first step in any learning process. But they help us do a lot more than that.

The senses help us figure out how we *feel* about things. This in turn determines what we think, learn, and do in different situations. In fact, there are four steps in the process of digesting sensory information and turning it into workable knowledge: recognition, association, judgment, and response.

As a child gathers experience and begins to *recognize* and remember more and more, his brain needs to develop strategies for managing new information. It starts by *associating* the new with what he already knows, which enables him to make initial assumptions. For example, if a toddler's favorite food is strawberries, he might assume that raspberries would be good, too. They're small and red, and you told him they were like strawberries.

But to really know raspberries, he has to taste them. Only then can he form his own *judgment*.

Judgment leads to *response*. And with little ones, that's easy to spot. If he likes raspberries, he'll grab some more. If he doesn't, he'll spit them out. Anything new can spark a highly charged response. Whatever his reaction, he'll be a little wiser for the experience and a little more prepared for the next new thing.

Sensory Integration

Any sense—or combination of senses—can be the jumping off point for learning something new. In fact, the more senses brought to bear, the better! For instance, the baby used touch to find out more about the shiny object, while the toddler used touch, taste, and smell to find out if he liked raspberries.

Because the brain is so hungry for knowledge, it sends out as many sensory scouts as necessary to gather data and report back to the brain. However, to make sense of all of this information, the brain must learn to integrate it—to put it all together and form a complete picture.

Think of it like a jigsaw puzzle. Until the brain integrates all the pieces, the child may not fully understand the picture. Sensory integration, therefore, greatly affects not only what a child perceives, but also how he interprets, understands, and responds to sensory information—in other words, how he learns.

Now, all of that seems logical enough until you put it inside the complex human mind, and especially a young mind that is growing and changing each day, in part because of the very sensory information it's trying to learn how to process. This is tricky to say the least, but it's one of the reasons why some children come to love raspberries while others prefer bananas, or why some love the color red, others blue, and so forth. In other words, sensory integration is one of the most important foundations in the formation of individuality.

Sensory Profile

Because each of us has a unique set of experiences and a unique body and brain, we all perceive and interpret things a little bit differently. That is, we each have our own sensory profile.

Because a child is growing, his sensory profile is constantly adapting in response to his environment and experiences. Indeed, individual senses sharpen according to the type and amount of stimulation they are exposed to.

For example, a child who gets lots of visual stimulation will build a strong sense of sight and reliance on his eyes to feed information to his brain. And that's great. However, if that same child does not also get lots of tactile stimulation, his brain will eventually recalibrate its processing. It will give more weight to what he sees than to what he touches. Over time, this may skew the pool of information his brain considers and could lead to an incomplete or even incorrect interpretation. After all, from a distance, a hedgehog sure *looks* soft.

The Sensory Balancing Act

Sensory processing and integration are a Goldilocks-style balancing act. That is, a child's brain tries to find the sweet spot between too much and too little input to arrive at just right.

Parents often remark on their children's preferences. They say, "My baby likes shiny objects," or, "My toddler likes raspberries." Personal judgment is part of a child's sensory learning process. But it's actually more than just liking or not liking something. A child's brain searches for particular bits of information to complete his understanding. That search often drives his preferences and behavior patterns.

For instance, some children crave new sensations all the time. These kids want to explore many new things all at once (the All-Over-the-Place Kids). At the other end of the spectrum are children who stick to familiar ground (Picky Eater, anyone?). Enthusiasm or reluctance toward stimulation may vary from experience to experience depending on the child's sensory profile. For example,

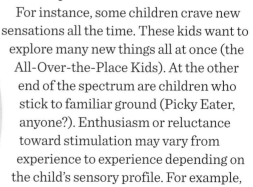

a child may not be able to take his eyes off the fireworks, but covers his ears the whole time to muffle the scary booms.

Striking the right sensory balance, like everything else in early childhood, is a matter of trial and error. When a child gets too little stimulation, he may become distracted and walk away. Too much stimulation and he might be overwhelmed or walk away. When he's actively, physically engaged and having fun, you know he's found "just right"—at least until he's done (for now) . . . and walks away.

Make It Multisensory

Sensory integration supports children's growth intellectually, emotionally, physically, and socially. So providing children with a rich, multisensory environment is crucial. And variety and balance are the keys.

Sensory Integration Supports All Learning

Intellectual learning	Understanding what things are
Physical learning	Understanding how things work
Emotional learning	Understanding what I like and don't like
Social learning	Understanding my relationship to people, places, and things

Some activities stimulate just one sense, while others are a sensory free-for-all. For instance, eye-tracking games are great for sharpening vision, while a game of Simon Says focuses on listening. On the other hand, a trip to the park invites all the senses to come out and play, giving the body and the brain a chance to experience and manage multiple sensory inputs simultaneously. It all works. It's all additive. It's simply a matter of providing a variety of experiences to be sure all the senses "get their turn" and, importantly, are being stimulated in many different ways.

This may seem like a lot to take on. But it's probably already happening naturally through everyday play—as long as the child is spending a good part of his day in *active* play, that is. So, here are a few things to keep in mind that you can do to enrich sensory learning.

Follow the Child's Lead

Sensory play helps a child figure out what *he* likes, not what you want him to like. If he doesn't like the feel of sand between his toes, or if the very mention of green beans makes his lower lip quiver, avoid those experiences for now. You can always try again later.

Be Open to Different Ways of Exploring

One day, a little boy couldn't take his eyes off an open bottle of orange soda on the kitchen table. He picked up the bottle and turned it around and around in his hands, transfixed by the orange bubbles dancing in the light. He lifted it to the window to study it some more, turning it upside down, pouring it all over his face. Oops.

Now, this is not to suggest pouring things on your head is necessary for discovery, but everybody does explore differently. And for little ones, that means examining everyday objects in not-so-everyday ways. When children reach deep into exploration—so deep they don't realize they're about to pour soda all over themselves—you are witnessing inspiration awakening deep in the mind.

Your job is to go with it. Sometimes it will get messy, but the learning payoff is worth it. And by the way, that boy with the soda bottle grew up to be a prominent glass artist, successful entertainment executive, and father to two great kids.

> When children reach deep into exploration—so deep they don't realize they're about to pour soda all over themselves—you are witnessing inspiration awakening deep in the mind.

Be a Sensory Role Model

No matter the sensation—slimy goo, creepy spiders, the smell of a cow pasture—if you don't like something, keep it to yourself. Instead, be an *enthusiastic* tour guide on the child's sensory journey (even if you want to scream "Eeeeek!").

Be a Sensory Adventurer

Watch for opportunities to introduce new and different sensory experiences. Introduce them slowly and gently and let the child's brain, senses, and motor tools do the rest. In other words, give the child freedom to move to the learning instead of bringing the learning to him. That's because movement plus sensory experiences deepens brain stimulation. (Although we do recommend avoiding hedgehog quills if you can.)

In the diagram on pages 58–59, note the variety of sensory opportunities you can create with common materials, experiences, and environments.

Gill's Notebook

"Asensory" Play

The other day, my grandchildren came for a visit and I had a big surprise for them—an empty refrigerator box. Hours of fun later, I found myself thinking about why cardboard boxes are such magnets for kids.

Now, I subscribe to the school of thought that rich sensory experiences are critical for early development. Yet, the very "asensory" nature of a cardboard box offers its own unique exploration of the senses. The brown color suggests nothing in particular. The smooth sides imply little. The cube structure defines empty space. The subtle smell lacks distraction. The sound of the cardboard folding is muted and music-less.

In other words, the very things cardboard boxes *lack* can be valuable contrasts to the more powerful and deliberate stimulation we traditionally think of as "sensory play." In fact, this relief from the sensory world may explain, in part, why kids find the confines of a cardboard box so appealing. And, of course, its very neutrality is the blank slate upon which children so easily imprint their imaginations. Now that's *not* something you want to put in a box.

Sensational Sensations

At first, you may want to introduce these different sensations one at a time. But later, combine different sensations to create a well-balanced diet of multisensory experiences.

Seeing

Visual stimuli:

- Color identification and differentiation (color names, light/dark, bright/muted)
- Object identification and differentiation (treasure hunts, picture puzzles)
- Texture observation (bumpy/smooth, sharp/soft)
- Bold and subtle contrasts (black/white, pink/red)
- Lighting variations (bright/dim)
- Depth perception (climbing up or down steps)
- Assumptions and preferences (raspberries vs. strawberries)

Visual interaction:

- Facial gestures (smiles, surprises)
- Animated movements (finger plays, puppets)
- Comparisons (big/small)
- Different shapes (square, round, triangular)
- Indoor and outdoor environments
- Daytime and nighttime experiences

Smell and Taste

- Recognition and identification
- Differentiation (strong and subtle differences)
- Visual support (with or without)
- Assumptions and preferences (apples vs. oranges)

Hearing

Auditory stimuli:

- Dynamics (loud to soft)
- Pitch recognition (high to low)
- Tempo and rhythm (music, speech)
- Auditory environment (animals, street noises)
- Visualization (hearing without seeing, such as blindfold games or reading stories without pictures)
- Assumptions and preferences (fireworks, lullabies)

Auditory interaction:

- Talking
- Singing and humming
- Reading aloud
- Making silly sounds
- Finger plays
- Dancing to music

Intuition

- Body awareness (parts of the body)
- Spatial awareness (seeing and feeling space)
- Weight (light to heavy)
- Force and leverage (pushing, pulling, lifting)

Touch

- Recognition and identification
- Differentiation (strong and subtle differences)
- Temperature evaluation (warm to cold)
- Visual support (with or without)
- Assumptions and preferences (sandpaper vs. cotton balls)

Balance

- In balance, out of balance, maintaining balance
- Orientation and positioning
- Adjustment (rocking horses, seesaws)

Motorvator

The More the Merrier

Here's Why
Multisensory experiences help deepen learning and memory, especially when paired with movement.

Here's How
Try enriching the sensory stimulation of ordinary children's activities. And remember, the idea is the more senses, the merrier!

- Art time: *Brightly colored* papers are smooth to the *touch* and make a funny *sound* when you crinkle them, which creates a new texture to *feel*.

- Music time: Even the simplest children's song offers a variety of *sounds*. *Move* your body by acting out the words or dancing to the music!

- Outdoor time: Flowers have many different *colors* and *aromas*. *Touch* the soil to feel its granular texture, then add water and feel a completely new sensation—mud!

- Mealtime: Offer a variety of foods that provide different *aromas*, *tastes*, *temperatures*, *sounds*, *colors*, and *textures*. Let the child explore his food with his fingers—even if both of you wind up wearing some of it!

Setting Up Learning for Life

As the sensory puzzle comes together through recognition, association, judgment, and response, the brain is beginning to figure out how to use sensory information to its advantage.

Recognition: Creating Common Ground

The senses are a common language we all share and, as such, provide common ground for understanding and communicating with others. At the most rudimentary level, all societies and cultures are built on the tacit agreement of what things are and what they are called. Likely that's why much of early learning and all of early language acquisition centers around the recognition of people, places, and things—the tangibles in our world that children can understand through their physical and sensory selves.

Association: Searching for the Known

As we discussed in Chapter 3, learning is a journey from the known to the unknown. Anytime we encounter something new, our brains search for ways to understand it using the only available information it has—prior knowledge.

The first association we make is usually finding similarity: "This is like that." Other associations follow, and eventually those associations graduate to the status of prior knowledge, which gives the brain even more to work with.

> **Family Moves**
>
> Print "Gill's Notebook: 'Asensory' Play" and the Motorvator "The More the Merrier" from the digital file and share them with parents to encourage a wide range of sensory experiences at home.

As this cumulative process continues, we not only sharpen our associative skills, we can align incoming data with more than one piece of prior knowledge. This gives the brain associative options, which are the basis for analysis, reasoning, and choice.

Judgment: Developing Analysis and Reasoning

While there are many theories about how the brain processes information, we've identified three sets of analysis and reasoning tools that start developing in early childhood through the senses:

- Categorization (classification and discrimination)
- Context (constancy and relationship)
- Seriation (order and disorder)

Categorization

One of the earliest forms of analysis and reasoning is categorization—sorting things according to their similarities (classification) and differences (discrimination).

Classification is the ability to see two red apples and understand that they are alike. The ability to spot similarities is one of the first

> For a young child, conceptual thinking can only be born out of what he sees, hears, feels, smells, tastes, and bumps into.

tangible experiences children have with abstract thinking—that two different things can be the same. Classification is a key building block for advanced thinking and abstraction. And it readies the mind for the next leap, discrimination.

Discrimination is the ability to see an apple and an orange and understand that they are *not* alike. Now a new definition of "this" and "that" has emerged, and with it, the first inkling that relationships between things can vary. And note the word *things* here. For a young child, conceptual thinking can only be born out of what he sees, hears, feels, smells, tastes, and bumps into.

Context

Next comes the idea that there may be different degrees of similarity and dissimilarity. Here, the question isn't whether two things are or are not alike, but instead, *how* they relate to each other. This introduces the element of context—that how you look at something changes what you see.

One aspect of context is constancy—the ability to understand variations of the same thing. For example, a red apple and a green apple are both apples; a tall woman and a short woman are both women. This is necessary to understand even basic instructions, such as "Please put your toys away." If a child doesn't understand that his truck and his teddy bear are both toys, he cannot follow the instruction.

Relationship is another aspect of context. It's the ability to understand the connection between two apparently different things. For example, apples and oranges are both fruits, or puppies and kitties are both pets—or are both fluffy, or both have four legs. In this way, children are creating their

own personal catalog of relationships that helps them organize the flood of information they gather each day. Like a well-organized library, developing a broad understanding of relationships facilitates future learning by making prior knowledge (the known) easier to retrieve and associate with new learning (the unknown).

Seriation

Once children understand that they can group things, the next step is to understand how things relate within a group. This ability is called seriation. It consists of order and disorder.

Finding or defining order means understanding patterns and sequences. Let's start with patterns.

Patterning is when things in a group recur—stripes on a zebra, steps on a staircase, squares on a checkerboard, or flowers on a Hawaiian shirt. Patterns help us organize complex information, which makes it easier to understand. Some patterns, such as zebra stripes, are easy to see. Others are barely discernible. For instance, a pattern on a Hawaiian shirt appears random, but upon close inspection you can see where the pattern repeats.

Sequencing is ordering things in a linear fashion. Common sequences include the alphabet and numbers, spatial sequences (large to small, front to back, top to bottom), time sequences (morning to night, Monday to Sunday, past-present-future), harmonic sequences (do-re-mi), and more. These common sequences provide the comforting benchmark of correctness. When a child can recite the alphabet from A to Z, he feels reassured, proud, and in sync with the world.

But what happens when there isn't a predetermined order to things? For instance, who goes first in the hopscotch game? Here, there is no right or wrong answer, just an agreed-upon solution devised by the players. But how do they decide?

Mastering the concept of order—patterns and sequences—prepares children for those times when they need to bring order to disorder without a referee of "correct" to guide them.

In our hopscotch example, choosing the order of the players' turns necessitates creating a new sequence. They could decide that the youngest goes first, or the tallest, or they could flip a coin. Regardless of the choice, the *process* of understanding, recognizing, and managing disorder is the essential learning happening here. It's the difference between *knowing* what's correct (established orthodoxy) and *deciding* what's correct (independent decision making). And children need both.

Gill's Notebook

See What You Can See

Doctors were examining a seven-year-old boy for signs of gifted intellect. The clinician handed him a set of blocks, asked him to put them in order, and gave no further instructions. The boy puzzled for a while, then arranged the blocks.

None of the doctors could work out the boy's logic. The blocks were not arranged by color, size, shape, design, or any other discernible attribute. They'd never seen this sequence before. So they asked the boy to explain. He said each block sounded different when shaken so he arranged them from highest to lowest pitch.

The doctors learned a lot that day.

Perception is a funny thing and is uniquely personal. So whenever I can, I give kids the opportunity to show me how *they* see things without imposing conventional wisdom on the activity. More than once I've been surprised by the outcomes, and over the years, I've learned a thing or two, too!

Chapter Summary

- **Sensory tools:** The sensory tools include the familiar senses (sight, sound, smell, taste, and touch), balance (the vestibular system), and intuition (proprioception—our sense of spatial orientation and movement).

- **The origins of learning:** The sensory tools provide the raw information the brain needs to learn about and interact with the world.

- **Movement and the senses:** Movement stimulates the senses to collect information for the brain to analyze. The more a child moves, the more sensory stimulation occurs, which encourages learning.

- **Experience as teacher:** Experience is the best teacher, and the senses are the pathway to all experiences.

- **Four steps of sensory learning:**

  1. Recognition (What is that?)

  2. Association (This is like that.)

  3. Judgment (I [don't] like that.)

  4. Response (What if I do this with that?)

- **Sensory integration and sensory profile:** In order for the brain to get a complete picture, it must learn to integrate multiple sensory perceptions. A wide variety of physical experiences helps the brain learn to manage and interpret sensory information. This process ultimately builds a unique sensory profile.

- **Multisensory play:** Engaging as many senses as possible in a wide variety of experiences is essential for early brain development.

- **Stimulating the senses includes:**

  1. Following the child's interests

  2. Respecting the child's reactions

  3. Letting the child explore in his own way

  4. Being a sensory role model

  5. Staying alert to new sensory experiences to introduce

- **The senses jump-start critical reasoning:**

  1. Categorization (classification and discrimination)

  2. Context (constancy and relationship)

  3. Seriation (order and disorder)

For examples of some sensory activities you can try, please see Part 6, pages 274–295.

CHAPTER 7

The Senses: Sight, Hearing, Smell, Taste, and Touch

///

Now that we understand how the senses foster movement and learning, let's dig a little deeper into the familiar senses: sight, hearing, smell, taste, and touch.

Sight: Seeing, Vision, and Perception

The visual world is often our first impression of things. But sight is more than just clear focus. Indeed, seeing, vision, and perception are three different aspects of sight which all develop simultaneously as a child grows.

Seeing

> Sight is more than just clear focus. Indeed, seeing, vision, and perception are three different aspects of sight which all develop simultaneously as a child grows.

Every eye-opening minute of the day, a child's eyes must transmit massive amounts of visual information to the brain. Research has shown that newborn eyes have all the optical equipment they need. Yet it's equally well documented that newborn vision is very limited. That's because the brain's ability to process and interpret visual stimulus is still immature.[17] In other words, the eyes and brain are learning to understand each other.

In the meantime, the brain also needs to learn how to steer and control the eyes while the eye muscles

build up strength and stamina to do what the
brain requires. As such, seeing is the physical
process of sight, or *how* we see. It's made
up of four elements: focus, teaming, fixation, and eye tracking. Together, this is
what we call "eye fitness."

Focus

Focus is the ability to see clearly
and automatically whenever the
eyes move from one focal point to
another. It develops gradually over
the first year of life.

At first, newborns just see
vague shapes. They can see only
about 8 to 10 inches away. But
that's all they need in the first weeks.
Measure the distance between your
breast and your smile, and you'll see why.

Over the first year of life, details sharpen,
the full spectrum of color emerges, depth perception develops, and focus extends farther. That is, by the
time baby is ready to move on her own, she can see where she's going.

Teaming

Teaming is binocular vision, or the ability of both eyes to see as one. Some
babies are born with their eyes already working as a team, while others may
take a little while to sync up. And with the eyes teamed up, depth perception
kicks in.

Depth perception is our ability to see the world in 3-D, which is critical
to understanding that space has dimension: near/far, shallow/deep, and so
forth. Without depth perception, even the simplest things—like catching a
ball, going down stairs, or steering a bike—would be impossible.

Fixation

Fixation is the ability to keep the eyes deliberately set on a single object or
location without wandering. This is important because focus and comprehension require looking at a subject long enough for the brain to recognize
and interpret it. Fixation is also an essential precursor to eye tracking.

Eye Tracking

Eye tracking is the ability to follow a moving object with your eyes while keeping your head still.

Mature eye tracking has the appearance of smooth eye movement, but in fact, it is actually a series of instantaneous eye fixations, much like a motion picture camera. Look closely and you'll see a young baby's eye movements are short and jerky. But as the eye muscles get stronger they move with greater speed and accuracy without loss of focus, which creates the appearance of smooth eye movement.

It's well known that eye tracking is foundational for reading which, of course, requires very precise eye control. But keep in mind that even though a child may have mastered eye tracking, it does not necessarily mean she's ready for reading just yet.

Motorvator

Runaway Balloon!

Here's Why
Eye tracking activities strengthen the eye muscles for the highly precise movement of reading and observational learning.

Here's How
Keeping the head still is important when working the eye muscles. That might seem tricky with a group of wiggly preschoolers, but it's actually easy.

Have the children sit in a line, one behind the other, facing you. Have each child hold the head of the child in front of her. Tell the children to freeze, keeping their heads perfectly still. Once the children are situated, explain that a balloon is trying to run away, and we have to keep our eyes on it.

Blow up a balloon, but don't tie it into a knot. Point the balloon to the right and let it go, challenging the children to follow it with their eyes only. Repeat the activity to the left. Note: the balloon will scoot away fast, so if that's too difficult, walk the balloon to the left and right of the children's field of vision, being sure to walk it out of sight so that the eye muscles get a good stretch. Have them call out, "Runaway balloon!" when they can't see it any more.

Gill's Notebook

When Is a Child Ready for Reading?

I often find that grown-ups are so excited to start a child on the road to independent reading, they don't stop to consider if she's ready or not. And not just cognitively, but physically. Reading requires a high level of eye fitness which depends on the type and amount of activity the eyes get in the early years.

And by activity, I don't mean time spent in front of a screen. Screen play occurs on a flat, 2-D plane, which has limited value for developing 3-D eye fitness. Focusing near and far is impossible on a screen. Furthermore, small screens (especially smartphones and tablets) do not let the eyes sweep widely to strengthen the muscles and fine-tune eye tracking. In fact, these mesmerizing, confined images create conditions for ocular lock, a frozen stare with no awareness or cognition of what's being seen.[18]

So what happens if you start teaching a child to read, but her eyes just aren't ready? While reading, she may:

- Get red, irritated eyes
- Rub her eyes a lot
- Get watery eyes
- Blink excessively
- Turn away to rest her eyes
- Jerk her eyes across the page
- Display a flicker or jump in her eye movement when the eyes reach the middle of the page

> Exposure to language from television screens and audio tracks does *not* enhance a young child's ability to learn language during the critical period of development from six to eight months.

But far worse than a temporary case of eye strain, if the experience is difficult, frustrating, or even painful, it may leave a lasting negative impression, which could become an even bigger hurdle to reading later on.

In my view, if you want a child to love reading, there are two simple, powerful things you can do:

- Develop her eye fitness through lots of fun, playful, 3-D visual stimulation each and every day.
- Spend time reading with her one-on-one. Children love the individual attention, and sharing a book up close lets you point out important images, ideas, and words along the way.

Vision

Vision is directing the eyes to specific fields of interest. It's made up of three elements: visual figure ground, convergent/divergent focus, and peripheral vision.

Family Moves

Print the Gill's Notebook entries "When Is a Child Ready for Reading?," "A Screen Is No Substitute for You," and "Respect the Mess" from the digital file and share them with parents.

Visual Figure Ground

Okay, the term *visual figure ground* is a mouthful, we agree. But whether you know it or not, you're practicing it right now as you're reading.

Visual figure ground allows us to focus only on important visual information.[19] For example, when you shop for laundry detergent, you probably know the color of the package you want. As you scan the aisle, your visual figure ground lets you ignore all the unwanted colors so you can quickly find the one you want. In other words, visual figure ground is the ability to know what *not* to focus on, which is, in fact, the very definition of focus and concentration.

For young kids, this isn't so easy. With little frame of reference to tell them what's important, they take it *all* in. This is one of the reasons children seem so easily distracted. But through many, varied visual experiences, their eyes and brains will mature and harmonize for the lightning-fast dance known as visual figure ground.

Peripheral Vision

While visual figure ground keeps us focused, peripheral vision keeps us aware of our surroundings. It's defined as the field of vision outside the immediate area of focus, and between the two, we are able to interpret the "full picture" in context.

Peripheral vision plays an important role in pretty much everything we do. For example, in sports, players use it to assess and respond to the changing dynamics of the game. In learning, peripheral vision is critical to reading. As you're scanning these words, your peripheral vision is acting as a forward scout, pointing the way toward the next bit of text on this page. As such, peripheral vision is often used by the brain to prepare us for what's next.

Convergent and Divergent Focus

For optimal and efficient vision, the eyes must be able to automatically switch from short to far distance focus, while training that focus in exactly the intended spot. Convergence brings the eyes together to see something up close. Divergence keeps the eyes parallel to each other to see things far away.

Perception

Visual perception is how the brain interprets, understands, and analyzes what the eyes see. As we discussed in Chapter 6, all sensory perception is unique to the individual, which means we all "see" things a little differently. But because the eyes often lead off our sensory exploration, visual perception plays a particularly important role in early learning, and of course, in the classroom.

Gill's Notebook

Struggling with Reading

Several years ago, I met a cab driver named Henry. He was about 60 years old. Henry and I were exchanging life stories when we stumbled upon the subject of books. I asked him about his favorite book, and he paused. Henry humbly admitted he couldn't read. He recounted painful memories of children taunting him in school and of the day he realized his teachers had given up on him.

I asked him what he sees when he looks at text. He explained as best he could. From what I could piece together, it seemed to me Henry might have visual perception problems that had gone undiagnosed. I suggested that a behavioral optometrist might be able to help him.

Several months later, I got a note from Henry. It turned out Henry does see things differently.

Visual Perception Problems

Visual perception relates to how the brain and eyes "talk" to each other. When something interrupts this communication, the brain may interpret visual information incorrectly. But here's the tricky thing: Visual perception problems are "normal" to those who have them—they are not likely aware of the problems—so it's very easy to overlook or mislabel the symptoms. Indeed, they are commonly mistaken for low IQ, learning disorders, inattentiveness, or misbehavior—the kinds of things Henry has been dealing with his whole life.

Typically, visual perception problems may include one or more of the following:

- Words or letters jumping off the page
- Flaring or shadows around words or letters

- Difficulties with eye tracking
- Difficulty differentiating between black and white on a page
- Reversing letters within a word (for example, *on* becomes *no*) when reading or writing
- Reversing the order of words in a sentence
- Reversing numbers in a sequence or math problem

Signs of Visual Perception Problems

If you are concerned about a child who's struggling with reading, consider the possibility of visual perception problems. Here are some signs to watch out for:

- Difficulty with or dislike of reading
- Difficulty with spelling
- Difficulty understanding concepts of print (where the line starts or which direction the words run)
- Eyestrain
- Staring
- Short attention span
- Off-task behavior
- Avoidance tactics
- Midline issues or laterality problems (see Chapter 11 for details)

If you see one or more of these symptoms recurring, I recommend a behavioral optometry screening as a first step for children over the age of six or seven. This branch of optometry studies what the eye actually sees, which is different from a standard vision acuity test.

But please remember: a child's eyes are developing and learning just like the rest of her. Any issues you suspect may resolve with maturity. Also, anyone can have a bad day or week. These signals are worrisome only if a child shows signs of reading stress over an extended period without making progress in learning.

Hearing

Studies have shown that hearing starts as early as 18 weeks after conception, making hearing a child's introduction to the outside world.[20] But *why* does hearing develop so early?

Experts believe hearing is part of the newborn's survival toolkit. While her other senses develop, hearing helps baby acclimate to her surroundings, becoming familiar with what is and isn't normal. This may explain why soft music soothes babies, while loud or startling sounds frighten them. And that seems logical because hearing is always "on," whether you're awake or asleep. In fact, research shows that a young baby naturally turns her head to sleep with her dominant ear facing upward.[21] (See Chapter 11 for more information on left-right dominance.)

Building Good Listeners

The ability to hear and the ability to listen are two different things. And no one needs to convince you of the importance of good listening skills. After all, following instructions, behaving appropriately with others, and even, at times, staying safe, can depend on being a "good" listener.

There are simple things we can do to help a child fine-tune her "early ears." Spending time talking, reading, and listening to her naturally develops her understanding of the world of sound. Active play, singing or music in any form, and simple word and sound games all work toward building a better listener. In other words, be a purposeful noisemaker.

Turning hearing into listening means developing a relationship between the ears and brain for gathering and interpreting auditory information. That

includes auditory discrimination, auditory figure ground, and what we call "ear tracking."

Auditory Discrimination

Auditory discrimination is the ability to hear and differentiate sound. It develops in the early years through hearing, associating, and interpreting our auditory world. For example, when a baby hears the difference between her parents' voices or the sound her toys make, she's already using auditory information to better understand her world.

Simple as that sounds, auditory discrimination is foundational to academic success. For instance the ability to distinguish individual sounds within a word (phonics) is one of the first steps toward sound to letter correspondence. This, of course, is an essential gateway to vocabulary acquisition, reading, and spelling.

> Children don't have the experience to know what to tune in to and what to tune out. Ironically, this can make it seem as though they're not listening at all—when in fact, they're hearing you . . . and everything else, too!

Auditory Figure Ground

Stop for a moment and actively listen to the sounds all around you. You might hear kids playing happily, birds chirping, or cars passing by. But chances are, until you stopped to listen, you didn't hear any of that "auditory pollution." That's because you have developed auditory figure ground, the ability to tune in and tune out different sounds according to their importance to you. [22] In other words, you know from experience what belongs in your auditory landscape and what doesn't, enabling you to stay focused on this book. But, if those happy kid sounds turned into cries, chances are your ears would switch back on.

Children don't have the experience to know what to tune in to and what to tune out. Ironically, this can make it seem as though they're not listening at all—when in fact, they're hearing you . . . and everything else, too!

Ear Tracking

Because sound is all around us, hearing is an important tool for understanding the dimensions of our world. We call this ear tracking. It's the ability to distinguish the location, proximity, and context of sounds, an ability which is foundational for many life and learning skills. The major components of ear tracking are auditory locating, auditory context, and auditory sequencing.

Auditory Locating

Auditory locating is the ability to track sounds from different locations and distances—and to recognize whether the sound is fixed or in motion. It also calculates whether you're moving closer to or farther away from a sound, to the left or right of it, above or below it, and so on. Auditory locating helps children better understand the scope and dimension of their environment.

Auditory Context

Where a sound is coming from or going toward can affect its meaning. For example, a car engine in the distance is nothing to worry about. But nearby, it could be cause for immediate action. Auditory context helps a child anticipate, predict, and react to changing circumstances.

Auditory Sequencing

We rarely hear a single sound in isolation. In fact, most sound occurs in sequences, rhythms, and patterns—including speech, music, the sounds of

Motorvator

Get Noisy!

Here's Why

Ear tracking helps children understand their world in three dimensions while honing listening skills.

Here's How

Give three children (the Noisies) noisemakers and have them scatter to three different corners of the playground. Gather all the other children and have them close their eyes. Explain that someone is being very noisy on the playground, and we have to go find out what all that noise is about!

Signal one of the Noisies to make a lot of noise, then stop. Have the other children open their eyes and run toward the source of the noise.

Repeat the activity at different distances and locations. Once the children get the idea, have the Noisies make sounds at different volumes to challenge the listeners.

nature, mechanical noises, and so on. As the ear tracks a series of sounds, the brain interprets the sequence to determine its meaning. This is auditory sequencing. It is especially important in learning to speak and understand the spoken word. For instance, the sound of the letters N ("en") and O ("oh") put together in that order means "no." Reverse them and "oh" and "en" means "own."

Gill's Notebook

A Screen Is No Substitute for You

Since my area of expertise is children and movement, I'm sure you can guess where I stand on the subject of television, video, computer screens, smartphones, tablets, and so on for young children. Instinctively, anything that takes children away from active play doesn't sit right with me. But in fact, research has shown that screen time negatively affects natural development processes in many ways. One in particular is language and communication development.

Is All Language Stimulation Good Stimulation?

Common sense tells us that any type of language stimulation must be good for learning. But in fact, research shows that exposure to language from television screens and audio tracks does *not* enhance a young child's ability to learn language during the critical period of development from six to eight months.[23]

> Children learn language mainly through personal, *human* interaction.

The research goes on to say that children learn language mainly through personal, *human* interaction. Chances are, you're doing exactly what children need every day when you talk, laugh, sing, whisper, and giggle together—dialogue in real time vs. the monologue of digital/virtual experiences. Put simply, when it comes to language, there is no substitute for you!

Distractions Interrupt Concentration

Once again, common sense might argue that while screen time isn't an effective teacher of language skills, it doesn't really do any harm, so it's no big deal. Right? Actually, wrong. Other researchers have found that lights and sounds coming from television and video programs can *distract*

children, preventing them from delving deeply into play, which in turn may inhibit their ability to concentrate.[24]

Concentration means shutting out distractions. Many adults can do this even with noise all around them. But we can't expect the same of young children. They simply don't have the experience to filter out unimportant visual or auditory "pollution" in their environment.

Further, when you're distracted, it's hard to stay on task, no matter how old you are. Frustration can set in and may even make you want to quit altogether. When that dynamic is set up in a child's young mind, not only is her ability to concentrate at stake, but her perseverance may be at risk as well.

Atmosphere Matters

Life is busy and noisy. I'm not suggesting we shut children in a soundproof booth. But do pay attention to the atmosphere in which children play. I like to tell parents to think of a young child's playtime as homework. When older children do homework, the TV is usually off. The same rules should apply for little ones, whether at home or in a childcare or school setting.

Joint Attention

And please understand that there's a world of difference between your participation in playtime and the disembodied intrusion of a screen. That's because you provide the child with the exact social interaction she needs to learn language (and a whole lot more!). Experts call this *joint attention*.[25]

For instance, when a parent or caregiver is looking at something, young babies' attention is drawn to the same thing. As you play with a child, you naturally talk about what you both are seeing and doing. Each time you do this, you help her understand her world while providing the words to describe it. And one day soon, she'll be the one telling you all about it!

And Don't Forget Smell, Taste, and Touch

By now you're likely seeing a pattern to how the senses work. In coordination with the brain, the senses recognize and discriminate between different sensations. Over time, the brain learns to tune in and tune out sensations (figure ground) based on what's important and relevant. And, through it all, the brain is learning to track and understand the scope and conditions of the world, which in turn develops personal preferences, reactions, and behavioral responses. This is true of sight and sound, and so it goes for smell, taste, and touch.

In another example of Nature Knows Best, early stimulation of the senses of smell, taste, and touch begins instinctively and simultaneously through the mouthing stage.[26] You see, a young child has more sensory receptors in her mouth than in any other part of the body. Mouthing helps her judge the size, shape, and texture of things while building her senses of taste, smell, and touch. And she's also using sight and sound in the process, which means mouthing is one of the first ways the brain experiences multisensory inputs.

As we've said, multisensory stimulation is critical for developing a well-balanced sensory profile. And the mouthing stage is only the beginning. As a child begins to move on her own, she takes her senses with her, gathering information as she goes. And because it's all new to her, she employs every sensory tool in her toolkit. What does the coffee table taste like? What does Grandma's necklace smell like? What do mashed peas feel like?

Our role as parents, teachers, and caregivers is to make these explorations safe and accessible whenever possible. And while it's easy for us to focus on the things children see and hear, be sure not to leave the other senses less involved and, consequently, the brain less informed. After all, there was a time we didn't know what mashed peas felt like, either.

In another example of Nature Knows Best, early stimulation of the senses of smell, taste, and touch begins instinctively and simultaneously through the mouthing stage. A young child has more sensory receptors in her mouth than in any other part of the body.

Gill's Notebook

Respect the Mess

The traditional definition of *messy play* refers to different kinds of sensory materials children can use with their hands. For instance:

Wet or Viscous
Mud
Slime
Play dough
Clay
Paste
Finger paint
Snow
Soap, bubble bath, bath foam
Water

Dry or Textured
Sand
Dirt
Glitter
Markers
Crayons

Messy play materials are pretty much anything that can and will travel to places unrelated to the designated play space, and often show up weeks later despite the most vigorous cleanup. However, my definition of messy play is a little different. And a lot messier.

More Mess Is Better Mess

It's well accepted that sensory play is important for children's development, yet it often seems to be narrowly defined as hands-only, tactile experiences. I say, why stop at the wrist?

The brain learns best from experiences provided by the entire body, so I recommend whole-body messy play whenever possible. For instance, painting with your toes instead of your fingers gives you a whole new way to express yourself. Or try making mud prints with your elbows! When a child's body is fully immersed in play, sensory receptors in the skin complement all her other senses to develop a full picture of the world and the self. And while messy play molds the brain, it's doing a whole lot more, too.

> How can a child understand "clean" if she doesn't understand "messy"?

Fine Motor Messiness

Think about the last time you held a blob of play dough in your hands. Chances are, you couldn't put it down—you squeezed it, shaped it, poked holes in it, pressed it through your fingers, and so on.

Messy play is a call to action for the fingers, working those tiny muscles to build strength, endurance, and coordination. This development, together with core and upper body development, helps young hands learn to manipulate a crayon, pencil, pen, or keyboard, as well as piano keys, guitar strings, and more.

Cleanliness Is Next to Messiness

What does "clean" feel like? As an adult, you might say, "Clean is when my hands don't feel sticky, gooey, gravelly, or chalky; when there is no dirt on my skin or under my fingernails; when my hands smell of nothing; when I feel comfortable touching something precious or white or shaking someone's hand." In other words, "clean" is "not messy."

Consider this. How can a child understand "clean" if she doesn't understand "messy"?

Messy Mania

Messiness is one thing. But put "messy" in the same sentence with "mania" and that's where most adults draw the line. I say, "In for a penny, in for a pound." Getting messy is a license to get even messier. And when "messier" happens, messy mania kicks in—an exuberant freedom from everyday expectations of conformity and neatness.

In and of itself, this is a great emotional release for kids, but it's also a boundary buster where children learn what it feels like to go beyond where they've been before—and even across the border to "too far." After all, it's one thing to be *told* you'll get cold from snow. It's another to feel snow down your shirt.

And as for the cleanup, let's be honest. There's not a lot of difference between cleaning up "messy" and "messier."

The Power of Mess

Creating change is an important learning experience for a young child. When she discovers she can make a difference in her world—large or small, accidental or deliberate, neat or messy—she awakens to the idea that she has the power to do things herself.

Messy play is a dramatic expression of that power, because the child sees big changes of her own making as she physically transforms herself and the space around her. And yes, the mess at the end of your mop is no fun for you. But the learning for her is worth it.

The After Mess

When a child observes or participates in the cleanup, she's learning to respect her environment. By seeing the transformation from neat to messy and then back to neat, she learns that she is part of something bigger than herself.

And that's a very neat feeling.

Chapter Summary

Sight

- **Eye fitness:** Four mechanical aspects of sight work to create optimal eye fitness: focus, teaming (the ability of both eyes to see as one), fixation (the ability to keep the eyes still to look at a single object), and eye tracking (the ability to follow a moving object with the eyes while keeping the head still).

- **Vision:** Directing the eyes to specific fields of interest involves visual figure ground (which allows focus only on important visual information), peripheral vision (field of vision outside the area of focus), and focus switching.

- **Perception:** To make sense of visual data, the brain and eyes must be in constant, instantaneous communication.

- **Early reading:** Encouraging children to read is wonderful, but it's important to remember that their eyes are still developing. They may not yet have the eye fitness needed for the sustained, controlled eye movements of reading.

- **Reading struggles:** Children may struggle with reading for many reasons, including visual perception problems.

Hearing

- **Auditory discrimination** is the ability to distinguish between sounds. It underpins language development and spelling.

- **Auditory figure ground** is the ability to tune in and tune out different sounds according to importance.

- **Ear tracking** is the ability to understand sound location, context, and sequence.

- **Human interaction and language development:** Language development thrives when babies have personal interactions with others. Screen time is no substitute.

Smell, Taste, and Touch

- **Mouthing:** Nature provides babies with the instinct to mouth, which stimulates smell, taste, and touch simultaneously.

- **Messy play** holds many sensory and life lessons for children.

For examples of some sensory activities you can try, please see Part 6, pages 274–279.

CHAPTER 8

The Sense of Balance: The Vestibular System

Any kindergarten teacher will tell you that three of the most important elements of school readiness are the abilities to sit still, pay attention, and stay focused. The vestibular system governs all three.

The Vestibular System

The vestibular system detects motion and gravity to create our internal sense of balance. It coordinates with all the other senses—especially the eyes—to help us get and stay upright whether we're still or on the move. And more, it helps us listen and learn.

That's because balance underpins pretty much everything we do. Think of trying to do everyday things like eating breakfast, riding a bike, or reading a book while standing on a tightrope. If you were always worried about falling over, how could your brain concentrate on anything else? That's what the vestibular system takes care of for you.

> Developing—and automating—a strong sense of balance, orientation, motion, and gravity is a mandatory prerequisite for children's overall development and readiness for school.

As such, developing—and automating—a strong sense of balance, orientation, motion, and gravity is a mandatory prerequisite for children's overall development and readiness for school.

The vestibular system controls five major aspects of everyday living: posture, balance, alertness, concentration, and stillness. Let's look at each one.

Posture

From the moment of birth, a baby's biological drive is to stand up—to get vertical. Indeed, the vertical drive is so strong it involves nearly every muscle in the body.

Within the first year or so, as a child's muscles develop strength and stamina, the brain is figuring out how to harmonize the reflexes and muscle movements into coordinated action. Meanwhile, the vestibular system is familiarizing the brain with the sensations of movement to develop orientation, stability, and balance. Only when all three come together can the journey to vertical begin.

Balance

Whether we're on the run (dynamic equilibrium) or sitting still in a cozy chair (static equilibrium), the vestibular system is constantly at work behind the scenes to keep us in balance—secure in that inner sense of "rightness" with our spatial orientation.

But children aren't born with a sense of balance. It must be learned. And the only way to learn balance is through movement—all different kinds of movement experienced many times in many varied ways. That's because movement constantly

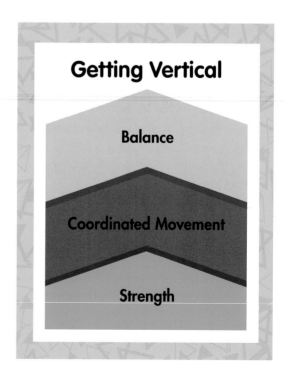

Getting Vertical

Balance

Coordinated Movement

Strength

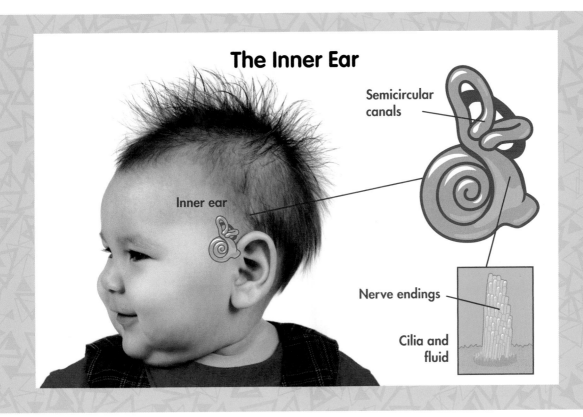

The Inner Ear

Semicircular canals

Inner ear

Nerve endings

Cilia and fluid

challenges the brain to adjust and record its understanding of what it feels like to be "in" and "out" of balance. And only when the brain has that understanding can it adapt to changing circumstances and help keep us from falling over.

In other words, without movement, there can be no balance. Here's how it works.

The vestibular system is centralized in the inner ear and mid-range region of the brain. Inside the ear are semicircular canals that contain cilia—tiny little hairs with tiny little nerve endings. The cilia (think seaweed) are bathed in fluid which, like water in a glass, washes back and forth in reaction to the body's movements. When the body moves, the fluid coaxes the cilia to stand upright, stimulating those nerve endings. This sends essential information to the brain about what the body needs to do to find, maintain, or regain balance.

For example, if you spin around many times, you may get dizzy. You feel as if your head is spinning. That's the fluid in your inner ear creating a tiny whirlpool effect. And that effect continues even after you stop, because it takes the fluid a while to stop whirling around. When the fluid comes to a rest, you feel back in balance.

Alertness and Concentration

Adults rarely think about balance, unless we start to lose it. When that happens, the vestibular system swoops in to save the day!

Imagine that feeling when you're about to fall off the curb. Your brain alerts to the situation. It instantly sends instructions to the muscles, which immediately jerk to attention. Your feet shift to center you, and your hands fly out to break your fall in case your feet don't make it in time. And all this happens without a conscious contribution from you.

This is your vestibular system at work, acting in coordination with other systems, such as the reticular activating system (RAS). The RAS signals the brain to matters that require immediate focus, shutting out everything else. Think of it as the brain's early warning system.[27]

In the curb example, the RAS helped resolve a potential physical danger. But equally (and more frequently), the reticular activating system helps the brain work through focused, cognitive tasks such as listening, reading, studying, and problem solving. And you can even *see* the RAS at work sometimes. It's called fidgeting.

Surprising as it may be, kids often fidget *because* they're trying to concentrate. During complex thinking tasks like schoolwork, the brain may begin to tire and lose focus. When that happens, the RAS activates the muscles to move (fidget) in order to wake up the thinking brain and bring it back on task. In other words, fidgeting can help concentration!

> Surprising as it may be, kids often fidget *because* they're trying to concentrate. Sitting still is one of the most advanced demonstrations of vestibular maturity, and the vestibular system is developed through movement. So if you want a child to learn to sit still, you've got to let him move.

Stillness

We all know sitting still is a big challenge for little ones. And unfortunately for kids, many adults perceive all that wriggling as a behavioral choice rather than a biological need. In fact, sitting still is one of the most advanced demonstrations of vestibular maturity. And as we've said, the vestibular system is developed through movement. So, as upside down as this may seem, if you want a child to learn to sit still, you've got to let him move.

As you encounter kids on the move, please keep these important points in mind:

- Kids don't learn to sit still by practicing sitting still. Kids develop stillness as their vestibular system matures, and that requires moving.

> ### Family Moves
> Print the "Cozy Cocoon" Motorvator from the digital file and share it with parents so families can have fun cocooning in and out as they help kids build their vestibular system.

- Insisting a kid sit still when it's not absolutely necessary will only lead to frustration and failure. His biological need to move will ultimately overtake his desire to please you.

- Not sitting still when you want him to is not necessarily misbehavior or "naughtiness." In fact, it may signal the child is trying to focus, listen, and concentrate.

Building the Vestibular System

Have you ever noticed how much young children like to turn themselves upside down? They do it because it feels good. And it feels good because it stimulates their vestibular system.

All children need daily vestibular stimulation—multiple times a day if possible. They get some of this through everyday active play, and in particular:

- Spinning slowly
- Rolling slowly
- Hanging upside down (when initiated by the child)

With all three of these activities, it's important to let the child take charge of the play. He will spin, roll, and hang upside down whenever it feels right to him, and he'll stop when he's had enough.

It's perfectly fine to suggest these activities, but let the child lead—with appropriate supervision from you, of course. Sometimes, you'll find kids resist this kind of play. If that happens, there are lots of ways to add vestibular activity into the day. For instance, if a child is not a big fan of the monkey bars yet, why not try reading upside down?

Speed matters. Doing vestibular activities slowly is essential to help the brain absorb and assimilate the physical sensations. Eight seconds per revolution when spinning or rolling is about right for building balance.

But going fast is important, too. It stimulates adrenaline and it feels good. What the child needs is to be able to go at both speeds. For instance, if a child tends to do everything quickly, he may lose his balance when he slows down. That suggests a need for more work on his vestibular system. It's probably a good idea to slow him down a bit.

Motorvator

Cozy Cocoon

Here's Why
Spinning is great for the vestibular system. Spinning slowly is even better to give the brain time to absorb the sensations.

Here's How
Have children form a long line and hold hands. Starting at one end, have children move so the line curls in to form a spiral. Be sure they move slowly. As they spiral together, the circle gets smaller and smaller while the giggles get bigger and bigger. When the cozy cocoon is as tight as can be, have the children slowly reverse their movements and open the spiral back into a straight line.

After children have done this a few times, add the "Cozy Cocoon" song. At the end of the song, have the kids break free and pretend to fly away like butterflies!

Cozy Cocoon
(sung to the tune of "The Wheels on the Bus")

The caterpillar spins
His cozy cocoon,
Cozy cocoon,
Cozy cocoon.
The caterpillar spins
His cozy cocoon,
So the butterfly
Can fly free!

Chapter Summary

- **The vestibular system** governs our internal sense of balance.

- **Balance underpins all aspects of our daily lives** and is critical for children's overall development.

- **Balance is learned.** Children aren't born with a sense of balance. They learn it through movement.

- **The vestibular system controls five aspects of everyday living:** posture, balance, alertness, concentration, and stillness.

- **Getting vertical is a biological drive** that requires strength, coordinated movement, and balance.

- **The reticular activating system (RAS)** redirects the brain for focus and concentration.

- **The highest form of balance is stillness.** But children can't learn to sit still by practicing sitting still.

- **Three ways to stimulate the vestibular system** are spinning slowly, rolling slowly, and hanging upside down.

For examples of some balance activities you can try, please see Part 6, pages 280–287.

CHAPTER 9

The Sense of Intuition: Proprioception

//

While the vestibular system provides your internal sense of balance, intuition manages your external sense of the world in which you move. Think of it as your personal global positioning system (GPS), helping you understand your body in relation to your environment.

Proprioception: The Body's GPS System

The technical term for the sense of intuition is proprioception. Proprioceptive sensors (proprioceptors) reside on nerve endings in all your muscles, tendons, joints, and ligaments and in the inner ear. They send information to the brain about your position in space, your relationship to that space, and the current conditions of the environment and objects you encounter. And this happens instantly and automatically every minute of the day, even while you're sleeping. As such, your sense of intuition plays a role in everything you do every day.

Intuition

Intuition is best described as your sub-conscious sense of you. In other words, your body knows where you are, even when you don't!

Proprioceptors measure and communicate to the brain the amount of flex, tension, and stretch in all the muscles, joints, ligaments, and tendons in the body. In addition, they work in concert with the inner ear to assess the body's orientation and position in space.

Proprioceptor

Intuition coordinates four interrelated navigation tools. It provides the brain with information for:

- Body awareness: What do I look like? What is my body made up of?
- Spatial awareness: How big am I? Do I fit in this space?
- Body subconscious: What is my subconscious sense of me?
- Strength management: What effort do I need to move through this space and use the objects in it?

Body Awareness

In order to use their bodies to explore and learn, children must first explore and learn about their bodies. And that begins with body awareness.

Body awareness is knowing the difference between your nose and your toes—and a whole lot more. It is made up of two critical understandings:

- **Body mapping** is an internal sense of what your body is, what it looks like, and where it begins and ends. As we've noted, at birth, a child doesn't understand she has a body. Strange as that sounds, she actually doesn't realize her hands and feet are connected to her. As a result, she cannot control them. In the early years, a young child is actually "mapping" her own body in order to learn how to control it.

- **Body design** is the innate understanding of how the parts of the body fit and work together. Once a child understands that she has a body, then the fun begins! She experiments with it like a new toy to see what she can do. Through that process, she learns that her body consists of different parts that do different things—together or independently.

The Body-Brain Relationship

As a child moves, her proprioceptive sensors are helping to create a relationship between her body and brain. Think of it as the body and brain learning to talk to each other. The more they talk, the more they discover.

For instance, it takes a while for a baby to find her thumb and get it into her mouth. Once she gets it there, she begins to suck, which often creates a sense of calm. This is the body and brain discovering what they can do together. And this new body-brain relationship creates a sense of body-brain confidence, contributing to her emotional well-being and emerging "look-what-I-can-do" self-esteem.

> The body is our most important reference point. It is our yardstick for judging our environment—whether it's big or small, wide or narrow, tall or short, empty or crowded.

There's just one catch. Children grow. Their bodies are changing all the time. And that necessitates learning and relearning their body map and body design.

For instance, you might see a child go through a clumsy phase or suddenly master something that seemed impossible a week ago. Phases of challenge and growth occur partly because the brain is adapting to changes in her growing body. And the only way the brain can adapt is through movement.

Spatial Awareness

While body awareness is the internal sense of unity between the body and brain, spatial awareness is the intuitive understanding of how the body fits within and moves through space.

In order to cross a crowded room, you might find yourself turning your body to squeeze through. You've learned that if you turn sideways you can squeeze through tight spaces, and you do this without thinking about it. But a child just learning to move on her own is also just beginning to understand what space is all about. That's why she often bumps into things or gets stuck. For instance, during circle time on the mat, she may misread how much space she has to sit down and accidentally sit on another child. Adults might think that a simple look would show her how much space she has to sit. But visual estimation of space is an advanced ability, in large part because the child is still mapping her own body.

The body is our most important reference point. It is our yardstick for judging our environment—whether it's big or small, wide or narrow, tall or short, empty or crowded, and so on. It's not a question adults have to think about, but it's a big idea for a little one: will I fit? And that likely explains why kids love to climb in, on, around, under, over, and through things. It's their way of exploring their place in our world.

This emerging understanding of her body in space not only helps a child avoid bumping into things, but also directly affects her ability to see relationships between objects and navigate appropriately. For instance, without this ability, she might struggle to put a letter in the mailbox or pour a glass of milk without spilling. These kinds of tasks require the ability to judge the size, shape, and mass of *both* things (the letter and the mailbox, the glass and the milk) and estimate how they will fit together.

Spatial awareness influences:

- **Handwriting:** A child with good spatial awareness will have an easier time learning how to write letters that are proportional to each other and space those letters to create words and sentences.

- **Critical problem solving:** Spatial awareness creates the foundation for understanding the concept of three dimensions, which is critical for grasping math and science concepts such as geometry and physics.

- **Sports:** Whether you're in or out of position on the playing field determines whether you catch the ball!

Body Subconscious

Body subconscious is your intuitive sense of you. In other words: your body knows where you are, even when you don't!

In fact, intuition never sleeps. For instance, as an adult, you probably never fall out of bed no matter how much you toss and turn. That's because your body subconscious has been finely honed over many years so that your sleeping body actually senses the edge of the bed and avoids going over it. The proprioceptors throughout your body keep track of where you are in space and enable your brain to work on a subconscious level to look after you.

In the wide-awake world, our sense of intuition, in coordination with our eyes and the vestibular system, helps us navigate space deliberately and safely. That navigation requires estimating the size, shape, scope, and mass of the landscape, architecture, and objects around us. How much space is there between the couch and the coffee table in the living room, or the book shelf and the art station at school? How far away is that toy over there? How (and when) do I change directions to avoid running into the wall? How high is that step?

When a child starts out, she won't know the answer to any of these everyday environmental encounters. She'll bump into things, knock things over, misjudge space, and, yes, fall down from time to time. In fact, to get a sense of what a child's body subconscious is like, try this little trick:

1. Put your left thumb over your head and be sure it's out of sight.

2. Touch your right forefinger to your left thumb.

Chances are, when you started you were certain you knew exactly where your thumb was. You took aim . . . and you missed! You see, you haven't practiced this trick, so your body subconscious isn't aligned for success. Try it a few more times, and finding your thumb will be a snap.

And that's exactly what a child is going through all day long with everything she encounters. She has an *assumption* of space with little experience to go by. But with plenty of trial (and more than a few errors) her emerging sense of body subconscious will help her move through her world successfully and intuitively.

Strength Management

Intuition helps you figure out how much energy you need for the job at hand. For instance, picking a dandelion seems easy enough. But when you pull, the flower is surprisingly resistant. Before you can even register this consciously, your proprioceptors have already communicated with your brain, which has commanded the muscles to use more energy. In response, your hand and arm pull harder and harder until the roots give up the flower.

Sometimes little ones just don't know their own strength. A child might break her pencil lead by pushing down too hard, or accidentally ram a toy truck into the wall, or hug a pal so hard she knocks him right over!

All of this might look like clumsiness—or even "naughtiness." But it's probably just her intuition-in-training.

> Intuition helps you figure out how much energy you need for the job at hand.

Motorvator

Weighty Matters

Here's Why
Varying experiences with different weights helps the proprioceptors learn to adapt to differing conditions.

Here's How
Whenever children are playing push-pull activities, such as pushing a baby carriage or a toy truck, add weight to the toy to vary the experience. Use anything you have handy, such as some books.

You can also vary experiences by having children push or pull things up inclines, through small spaces, over bumps, or through anything else that changes the terrain of the playing field.

Family Moves

Print the "Weighty Matters" Motorvator from the digital file and share it with parents so families can have fun helping kids adapt and grow in intuition.

Learning from past experiences to refine future actions is called motor planning.[28] And this is where repetition does some of its best work. With each new try, the proprioceptors work with the brain to get a feel for how much force is needed. Like Goldilocks, it may take many tries, but with each try, the brain adjusts its instructions to the muscles until together they've got it "just right."

Chapter Summary

- **Intuition, or proprioception, is our personal GPS system,** managing our external sense of the world in which we move.

- **Intuition is made up of four navigation tools:** body awareness, spatial awareness, body subconscious, and strength management.

- **Children aren't born with body awareness.** Through movement, they must construct their own body map and learn their body design—how the parts work, independently or together.

- **Body confidence is seamless communication between body and brain,** which leads to well-coordinated movement, emotional well-being, and positive self-esteem.

- **Spatial awareness is our understanding of how we fit into space,** which leads to a broader understanding of how objects relate spatially to one another.

- **Body subconscious is the body's ability to keep track of your position in space,** whether you're awake or asleep, derived from the constant communication between the proprioceptors and the brain.

- **Strength management helps us figure out how much force we need** to achieve a given task.

For examples of some intuition activities you can try, please see Part 6, pages 288–295.

CHAPTER 10
The Origins of Independence: The Motor Tools

///

As you can now see, we call the sensory tools the origins of learning because it's through the senses that children acquire information. But translating that information into *working knowledge* takes more than just collecting it. It takes *doing* something with it. Think of it as going someplace for the first time. You can get a map, ask for directions, or use GPS. But you don't really know how to get there *on your own* until you make the trip yourself. Indeed, Sir Edmund Hillary, the first person ever to reach the top of Mount Everest, once said, "It's not the mountain we conquer, but ourselves." And that is never more true than in early childhood.

And it's in the "doing" where three other essential tools—the motor tools of power, coordination, and control—come into play and seal the deal on learning. Because when a child puts learning into action, he *owns* it.

When a child has the opportunity and ability to investigate things in his own way, it supercharges early learning. Indeed, when a child is interested in something, he will seek it out, take time with it, and learn from it in a deeper, more meaningful way. That's because the learning is being served up on a platter of personal choice. He *wants* to know. And given the means (movement) to get to what he wants (experience), the quantity and quality of the exploration (learning) grows exponentially.

Now, what we're really talking about here is human nature. Self-motivated learning is far more effective at any stage of life. However, unlike grown-ups, young children are still developing the physical capabilities they need to free the mind to freely explore.

Beyond Gross and Fine

In the world of early childhood development, the word "motor" is often modified by "gross" or "fine." As you'll see in the following chapters, we hold a different view. But more than an academic debate over the semantics, let's examine how this commonly accepted terminology reflects our collective mindset and affects our practical approach to early childhood movement.

> Nothing happens in isolation. All muscles of any size are brought to bear in learning, formally or informally, indoors or out. You cannot separate "gross" and "fine."

First, by segregating the muscles into categories of "gross" and "fine," we ignore the essential early childhood truth that nothing happens in isolation. A more holistic, top-to-toe view recognizes and respects each child's individual needs.

Second, "gross" is often associated with playground shenanigans while "fine" is more commonly thought of as the stuff children need for the classroom. And along with that often comes an unspoken adult bias that "fine" is more important than "gross." As we'll discuss, all muscles of any size are brought to bear in learning, formally or informally, indoors or out. You cannot separate the two.

Likewise, "gross" is often associated with health and fitness. But small muscles need to be as healthy and strong as the big ones if children are going to get where they want to go and do what they want to do when they get there.

And perhaps most important of all, the idea of "gross" and "fine" relegates movement to just two among many items on the checklist of early childhood development, rather than recognizing it as the bedrock foundation that makes everything else on the list possible.

The Motor Tools

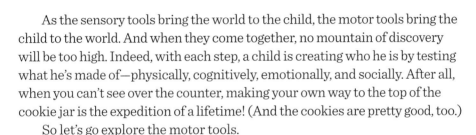

New ideas (which in this case are really nature's old ideas) call for new words. This is why we've adopted the term "motor tools" to describe the years-long process toward fully realized physical development as children slowly, naturally acquire:

- **The power** to move muscles with an appropriate amount of force and energy for a length of time

- **The coordination** to move different muscles in different ways simultaneously to achieve complex movement patterns

- **The control** to refine and adapt movements with precision for accuracy

As the sensory tools bring the world to the child, the motor tools bring the child to the world. And when they come together, no mountain of discovery will be too high. Indeed, with each step, a child is creating who he is by testing what he's made of—physically, cognitively, emotionally, and socially. After all, when you can't see over the counter, making your own way to the top of the cookie jar is the expedition of a lifetime! (And the cookies are pretty good, too.)

So let's go explore the motor tools.

Chapter Summary

- **Sensory tools and motor tools:** Sensory tools help children acquire information; motor tools help them translate information into *working knowledge*. As the sensory tools bring the world to the child, the motor tools bring the child to the world.

- **Beyond "gross" and "fine":** In early childhood development, nothing happens in isolation. All muscles of any size are brought to bear in learning, formally or informally, indoors or out. You cannot separate the two.

- **Years-long process:** Motor tools describe the years-long process toward fully realized physical development as children slowly, naturally acquire power, coordination, and control.

For examples of some motor activities you can try, please see Part 6, pages 296–315.

CHAPTER 11

Power: Beyond Gross Motor Skills

Power is a not a word usually associated with young children. Yet, if you think about it, it's the acquisition of power they're after—the physical, cognitive, emotional, and social power to stand on their own two feet, literally and figuratively. And in early childhood, power begins with the body.

Kid Power Calls on *Every* Muscle

But power is more than fitness. And it goes well beyond our traditional definition of gross motor skills. For our purposes, power is defined as the full and efficient use of the body's energy supply to do anything the brain needs done, as many times as needed, for as long as needed. And that includes every muscle, big *or* small. You see, pound for pound, the power the legs need to run across a field is proportionally the same to what the fingers need to run across a keyboard.

We've broken down the concept of power into four essential aspects:

- Strength
- Stamina
- Flexibility
- Agility

Strength

Muscles develop as needed, in response to stimulation. For young children, doing—or trying—many different kinds of movements offers the best opportunity for slow and steady strengthening of all the muscles.

In young children, muscle strengthening may not look like much at all. And it certainly isn't (and must *never* be) "exercise" in the traditional sense. For instance, when a baby kicks, those muscle contractions are exactly what she needs for building strength in the legs for crawling and walking later on. And in preschoolers, all that running around isn't just running for running's sake—it's their natural way of building power and strength for all the growing and learning that's to come.

Strength underpins virtually everything we do physically. Simply put, we're not going to get far without it. But more, strength is a mindset. It's that "look-out-world-here-I-come" invincibility that comes with feeling up to a challenge. Effort takes strength of body and will. And in early childhood, effort is everything. Adult precepts of "success" are far less important than a child's belief in himself and his own abilities, and the willingness to try and try again.

> Power is more than fitness. Power is the full and efficient use of the body's energy supply to do anything the brain needs done, as many times as needed, for as long as needed. And that includes every muscle, big or small.

Stamina

For adults, physical stamina is the ability to hold a position or sustain an effort without having to rest or revert to a position of comfort. The technical definition of stamina for young children is no different, of course. But how we measure it is. That's because a child's ability to hold a position, for example, is more likely to be influenced by other factors, such as her sense of balance.

Instead, for little ones, stamina is demonstrated through enthusiasm. You can see stamina in a child's disposition—upright posture, alertness, positivity, and willingness to try. For instance, when a child is learning to climb, she may not get to the top on the first try—or even the tenth. But she keeps on trying and having fun in the process. That's stamina in action and in development—persevering physically, emotionally, and cognitively.

When the muscles develop enough strength and stamina, they can repeat movements over and over again. As we've said, repetition yields muscle memory—automating movement and freeing the brain to think about other things.

Flexibility

Flexibility is defined as the ability to maneuver the body into different positions with ease. Now, it's easy to see that little ones are born flexible. And that actually has a lot to do with their bone structure. You see, babies have more bones (270–300) than adults (206).[29] Further, children's bones consist of more cartilage, which is suppler than bones. Over time, the bones will ossify and fuse together to create fewer, stronger bones for a more rigid structural frame.

This skeletal flexibility aids in birth and early growth. But more, it offers a child a critical window of opportunity to discover the full range of her body's physical sensations and at the same time explore what her body can do.

Agility

Agility is the ability to move the body quickly and nimbly. Agility takes a while to develop, but with it comes something essential to a child's self-esteem and self-confidence. We call it *body confidence*, the innate "trust" between the body and brain that comes with fully automated, coordinated movement. It is when the body and brain become one.

And in that "oneness" lies perhaps the most essential key to powering up young children: transferrable fitness—the development of muscles not for one or two specialized activities, but for the whole of life.

Transferable Fitness

The human body is designed for efficiency and to preserve energy. As such, we all have a natural tendency to do things in ways that feel comfortable and easy. Over time, these tendencies can become what others see as our natural gifts or talents. For instance, some children run like the wind. Others are great at hitting a ball with a bat. Still others dance joyously with ease and grace.

Adults (especially parents) want children to develop their gifts. And that's a great jumping-off point. But it's not everything a child needs for her development. If we focus only on the things a child is good at or particularly likes to do, we may be encouraging imbalances in her overall physical development—and with them, unexpected challenges in cognitive, social, and emotional development. In other words, just being good at soccer or ballet or running fast or any other single accomplishment does not necessarily signal a well-rounded, transferrable portfolio of abilities.

When a child excels at one or more specific things, be supportive, of course, but also take note of what the child is *not* doing and encourage her to try those things. For instance, if she loves to paint pictures but isn't keen on climbing monkey bars, suggest she paint a picture of herself sitting on top of the monkey bars. Talk about what it would be like to climb up. Say, "I wonder what you'd see from the top? I wonder if you'd like to paint a picture of that?" In other words, use the child's current interests to develop new ones. And by the way, if that's still not working, start smaller. Put a box near the monkey bars and invite her to climb up just a little to see what she can see. Any extension beyond her current boundaries gives her physical and sensory experiences she might not otherwise get, which is all fuel for her learning engine.

> ## Family Moves
>
> Print the "Splinter Skills" handout, the "Crazy Crab Crawl" Motorvator, and "Gill's Notebook: Born to Be Fit" from the digital file and share them with parents.

Then there's the opposite situation—when an activity *doesn't* come naturally and a child may try to work around it or avoid it altogether. In this case, try different ways at it. For instance, if she struggles to catch a ball, try a beanbag or bubbles. There are many ways to achieve the same developmental result, and variety makes the effort fun.

And again, effort is the key. Learning to push through difficulty promotes balanced physical development and often makes for great life lessons! Keep in mind, however, that pushing through should never mean repeating the same activity in the same way to the point of frustration and defeat (aka "drill and skill").

Motorvator

Crazy Crab Crawl

Here's Why
Develop transferable fitness by exploring the many different ways you can do one thing.

Here's How
Use children's natural curiosity to challenge their bodies. For this game, try finding all the ways you can crawl. Start by introducing the children to how a crab crawls. Have them sit on the floor with their hands behind them and lift up their bottoms and crawl like a crab. But this is Crazy Crab Crawling, so once they get the hang of it, introduce different fun challenges to navigate. For instance:

- Crab crawl around corners
- Crab navigate over small obstacles like a rolled up towel
- Crab limbo under a bar or table
- Crab zigzag through cones
- Crab tunnel through a hoop
- Crab mambo in a line with all the children
- Crab race across the floor or playground
- Crab treasure hunt
- Crab climb up the hill and roll back down like a snail

And any other crabby ideas the kids have!

Splinter Skills

Splinter skills are isolated, unrelated, and often unrelatable skills that may give the appearance of full physical competency but actually mask deficiencies. Often they involve muscle memory for specialized high-performance tasks, such as sports or dance. But there's no need to focus on high performance just yet. In fact, a well-balanced profile of physical capabilities in the early years can make it easier to develop specialized skills for high performance later on.

As adults, we can make the mistake of applying the "shortest distance" theory to children's development. For instance, give a child a pencil, show her the correct pencil grip, teach her how to write the letters, and have her go practice. Job done. But here's the thing: Practicing with a pencil is great if all you're ever going to do with your hand is write. But what about painting? Or the piano? Or sign language, ballet, or baseball? Practicing one specific skill over and over will fine-tune the muscles, tendons, and ligaments for that one thing. But it may not necessarily mean those muscles will be fully prepared for everything else they have to do.

> A well-balanced profile of physical capabilities in the early years can make it easier to develop specialized skills for high performance later on.

Rest

All muscles need time to rest. And children know this instinctively. One minute they're bursting with energy, the next they're slowing down for a quiet moment. Part of this ramp up/ramp down pattern is the child's own playfulness at work. And part is an internal sense of her own body's limits. That's because hardworking muscles build up lactic acid, which creates a burning, stiff, and uncomfortable feeling that tells us it's time to slow down.

Now, rest doesn't necessarily mean stopping the play. It might just mean using different muscles, switching from upper-body to lower-body activities—from hanging on the monkey bars to a game of leapfrog. Or it may mean adjusting the energy level from high to low for a while.

It's pretty easy to spot a child who needs rest; it's written all over her body language. She'll likely show less and less enthusiasm and effort. She may get distracted, restless, or forgetful. And of course, there's always the sit-and-pout-about-it strategy. Respecting when a child is tired is respecting the child. And let's face it. No matter how hard you try to engage her, chances are she's thinking about how she feels, not what you're trying to teach.

Gill's Notebook

Born to Be Fit

We are all born to be fit. But unlike adults, kids don't work out. They play out!

For little ones, fitness should only be measured in giggles because playing naturally maintains fitness. Just compare what you do at the gym to what a kid can fit into her average day and you might want to think about doing a few more reps.

Adults Work Out	Kids Play Out
Warm up	Wake up, stretch out, wiggle out of bed
The gym	The playground
The chin-up bar	The monkey bars
Sit-ups	Swinging
Push-ups	Wheelbarrow races
Resistance training	Tug-of-war ("Mine. No, mine!")
Free weights	Building blocks
Stair climber	"Race you to the top!"
Treadmill	"Race you to the door!"
Rowing machine	Rocking horse
Cardio	Skipping rope
Aerobics	Tag
Anaerobics	The hokey pokey
Exercise ball	Any ball
Cross-training	Skipping
Circuit training	Homemade obstacle course
Spin class	Biking
Reps and sets	"Again! Again!"
Glutes, abs, and thighs	Galloping on a hobbyhorse
Tai chi	Roughhousing
Yoga	Looking at books upside down
Stretching	Reaching for the cookie jar
Juice bar	Juice box
Cooldown	Bedtime stories and good-night kisses

Chapter Summary

- **More than gross motor skills:** Power is the full and efficient use of the body's energy supply in both the large and small muscles.

- **More than strength:** For optimal growing and learning power, muscles need strength, stamina, flexibility, and agility.

- **Transferable fitness:** A wide variety of activities each day ensures the best possible chance for balanced physical development and a wide range of experiences to fuel learning.

- **Splinter skills:** Children who excel at one thing may be missing out on essential developmental foundations they'll need for learning. Encourage a wide variety of physical activities each day.

- **Rest:** Muscles need rest at all ages. Watch for signs of fatigue and switch activities to use different muscles.

- **Kids don't work out; they play out:** Playing naturally—free to explore with their whole bodies—should never feel like work to kids.

For examples of some power activities you can try, please see Part 6, pages 296–301.

CHAPTER 12

Coordination: The Midlines, Body Rhythm, and Temporal Awareness

//

Like a well-oiled machine, efficient and effective movement depends on coordinated action involving every part of the body and brain.

Coordination is defined as the ability to move different parts of the body independently or together, at will (and automatically). It develops over many years through a kind of "bio-geometry" known as the *midlines* working in conjunction with our inherent sense of rhythm and timing to sync up all those moving parts.

And through this process, nature is not only aligning the body, it's optimizing the brain for the highest levels of thinking, reasoning, and creativity.

Meet the Midlines

The midlines are invisible to the eye, yet indispensable to advancing children's development.

Imagine the body divided by three lines. One line separates left from right. Another separates top from bottom. The third separates front from back. The midlines serve as the central pivot points for the body's sophisticated movement patterns.

Midline development is a slow, natural process that unfolds from birth to about the ages of seven to nine years (or beyond). As the midlines develop, they help children isolate individual body parts for independent movement, then work to coordinate movements involving multiple parts of the body.

As these complex movement patterns are forming, the child's brain is feverishly building neural pathways to keep up, and in particular, create and strengthen the pathways that cross the midline of the brain (the corpus callosum). These pathways or "superhighways" facilitate communication

The Midlines

Front-back midline

Left-right midline

Top-bottom midline

between the right and left hemispheres of the cortex. This integration of the two sides determines the speed, flexibility, adaptability, and depth of the brain's thinking.[30] (See Chapter 3 for more information on the cortex.) Think of it as doubling up on the brain's processing speed and power as it draws on the strengths of both its left and right sides.

Right Meets Left

There are many theories and much debate over the functions of the brain's left and right hemispheres. It's commonly understood that we each have a dominant hemisphere and that dictates how we think. Broadly we say people who are analytical, practical, and logical are "left brainers" while "right brainers" are creative, imaginative freethinkers. But that short-hand version of brain theory ignores the fact that in nearly everything we do, both the left and right sides are actively engaged. That's because the brain is most powerful when it uses both sides.[31]

> The midlines serve as the central pivot points for the body's sophisticated move-ment patterns.

In nature's wisdom, the brain builds its own unique network of neural pathways based on early childhood experiences. And importantly, that includes the development of the pathways that span the left and right sides of the brain. Of course, the brain has to start somewhere, and research suggests that start-ing point is the right hemisphere more so than the left.[32] Broadly speaking, the right side gathers and experiments with new sensations, ideas, and informa-tion, focusing on the here and now. The left side ana-lyzes and organizes information into reasoned thinking and future planning. As such, it makes sense that a young, inexperienced mind would be more right-focused at first, as the child is just beginning to gather material for the left side to consider, analyze, contrast, compare, and catalog.

But in order for a child to develop more sophisticated thinking, the two hemispheres must start working together more closely. That begins when he starts moving independently which requires vigorous and instantaneous left-right brain communication. As this process unfolds through midline development, body control increases, learning becomes faster and easier, and the ability to analyze and apply learning into actions and ideas increases exponentially. In other words, midline development is essential to optimiz-ing the "whole brain."

Brain Hemispheres

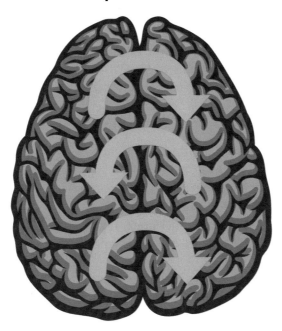

Corpus Callosum

Left Hemisphere

Uses logic
and analysis

Sees detail first

Contrasts differences

Controls feelings

Plans

Thinks sequentially

Is future-oriented

Right Hemisphere

Uses intuition
and estimation

Sees big picture first

Associates similarities

Is free with feelings

Is spontaneous

Thinks simultaneously

Is now-oriented

Movement and the Midlines

All three midlines develop through complex, coordinated physical activity including bilateral, homolateral, lateral, and cross-lateral movement patterns. Let's look at each of these more closely.

Bilaterality

Parents often wonder whether their child will become right- or left-handed. Experts agree handedness is predetermined from birth, and yes, some young children do show a preferred side early on. But that's different from developmental dominance, which does not emerge until the midline development stage. And for good reason.

In infancy, the vast majority of deliberate movement is bilateral or mir-rored movements—one side of the body doing what the other side does. For instance, you'll notice when a baby begins reaching for his bottle, he'll prob-ably use both hands. Later on he may use both feet at the same time to push himself on his ride-on. Using both sides helps develop body control, muscle strength, and coordination by allowing the body and brain to develop evenly on both the right and left sides. (And by the way, if a child does use one hand from time to time, chances are it's a matter of convenience, not handedness.)

For all of its advantages however, mirrored movement actually stands in the way of doing more complex things with the body. Until a child is able to alternate his arms and legs *intentionally,* crawling and walking won't be pos-sible. So around the time he is beginning to get up on all fours, nature is paving the way for the early stages of midline development.

Homolaterality

Homolaterality is the ability to move one part of the body while keeping the other parts still. Now, this might sound easy, but it's pretty tricky when you've been wired for mirrored movement your whole life.

A tell-tale sign of homolaterality emerging is when you see a child deliberately using just one hand. This will begin slowly, and he won't get it perfectly right for a while. For example, a toddler learning to wave bye-bye will wave one hand prominently, but the other hand is up and doing something, too. Or a child climbing a ladder might climb hand-hand-foot-foot (or right-right-left-left) instead of moving the arms and legs in opposition to each other.

Yet from the humble beginnings of single-handed bye-byes come essential capabilities for school readiness. For instance, homolaterality facilitates keep-ing one hand still while the other hand is writing, which in turn makes it easier for children to concentrate on what they want to express.

Switching Hands

When some children begin to write or draw, they may switch hands at the center of the page. This is nothing to be concerned about—but do take it as a cue that the child needs more work to develop his midlines.

To help him, give him two streamers or any other paired equipment. Encourage him to use one hand, then the other—but not both at the same time. Of note, you may need to help him at first by holding the inactive hand still for him.

Other homolateral movements include closing one eye and then the other, kicking balls while standing still, or riding a scooter.

Laterality

Lateral movement is when one part of the body does something in the opposite manner of another part, such as the way the legs and arms move when crawling.

Crawling is generally the first sign of laterality, and although adults may think of it as "baby stuff," crawling is a remarkably sophisticated movement pattern. You see, crawling engages all three midlines simultaneously, which not only gets baby where he wants to go, but also supercharges the growth of the pathways that span the left and right hemispheres and makes those pathways stronger and faster in the process.

> Crawling is generally the first sign of laterality, and is a remarkably sophisticated movement pattern that engages all three midlines simultaneously.

Independent movement demands—and develops—more whole-brain power because it requires something that hasn't been all that necessary up until now: planning. When a baby crawls, his brain has to map out which leg goes first and which arm goes with it. This is a major advancement for babies, because it's a whole new way of moving *and* a whole new way of thinking. By working through the process of planning motor activity, a child's brain prepares itself for another cognitive leap: understanding the concept of *future*—not what *has* happened or what *is* happening, but what *might* happen. In other words, deliberate movement awakens the notion of deliberate intent.

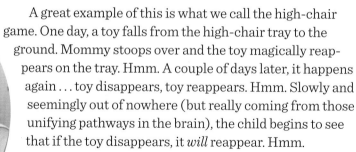

A great example of this is what we call the high-chair game. One day, a toy falls from the high-chair tray to the ground. Mommy stoops over and the toy magically reappears on the tray. Hmm. A couple of days later, it happens again . . . toy disappears, toy reappears. Hmm. Slowly and seemingly out of nowhere (but really coming from those unifying pathways in the brain), the child begins to see that if the toy disappears, it *will* reappear. Hmm.

So, thinks the child, what if I *make* the toy disappear? Deciding to test his nascent hypothesis, he shoves the toy over the side. And sure enough, Mommy retrieves it. He does it again. Toy returns. And slowly the idea that *if I do X, Y will happen* begins to dawn on him: cause and effect.

This is a milestone that may never make it into the family scrapbook, but it should. This child has just learned to reason.

Cross-Laterality

Bilateral, homolateral, and lateral movements all keep the arms and legs on their own side of the body. Cross-lateral movements use the arms or legs to cross over one or more of the midlines.

Deliberate cross-laterality is the most complex of the midline movements, requiring a high degree of coordination. If the midlines aren't fully developed, cross-lateral movements may feel unnatural to a child. For instance, if he needs to use his right hand to get something on his left side, he'll probably use his whole body to reach, twisting his torso to avoid crossing his midline. For him, it's easier to turn and face his body to the left than to reach across the right-left midline. This likely means he hasn't yet mastered cross-laterality.

Crossing the midlines not only streamlines movement, it supersizes those superhighways across the corpus callosum. As such, it plays a critical role in preparing young minds for formal learning.

For example, when children are just learning to write, they may reverse letters, such as transposing a *b* for a *d*. Adults might see this as a difficulty with writing, when in fact, it may simply mean the child is still working to sort out his midlines. After all, the only difference between *b* and *d* is which side of the line the loop falls on. If a child hasn't mastered the sides of his own body, the brain simply isn't ready yet to translate the concept of "sides" to other things.

As such, children need many different and active experiences with all of their midlines to achieve complex, whole-body movements and better understand the dimensionality of themselves and our world. That said, kids don't have to turn themselves into pretzels. As with most things, natural play and exploration should take care of the midlines over the course of all of the early years. And as that unfolds, the brain will be getting to know left from right, front from back, and down from up.

Motorvator

Gettin' Gluey (No Glue Required)

Here's Why
Cross-lateral movements are powerful tools for developing neural superhighways across the brain's corpus callosum. But crossing the midlines doesn't come naturally to little ones, so it helps to make a game of it.

Here's How
Wonder aloud how it would feel to have glue on your hands. Rub each child's hands as if you were applying glue.

Ask the children to show you what would happen if they put their gluey hands on their knees. Dramatize it for them: "Uh-oh. My hands are stuck on my knees!" Have the kids walk around with their hands "glued" to their knees.

Encourage the children to keep their hands on their knees while reinforcing the idea of stickiness. "This glue is really sticky. We'll have to pull really, really hard to unstick our hands. On the count of three: 1, 2, 3—pull!"

Try the glue game again with another body part—the sillier, the better!

Once the children get the idea, add cross-lateral movements. For instance, stick your right hand to your left shoulder. Or stick your left hand to your right knee. Or cross one or both arms behind the back.

The "Ugly Duckling" Stage

Motor Overflow

Often misinterpreted as clumsiness, awkwardness, gawkiness, or the age-old "ugly duckling" stage, midline development often produces a phenomenon called motor overflow.[33] Almost as if it's a bit confused, the brain compensates for the barrage of new, perplexing physical sensations by sending muscles commands unrelated to the task—unnecessary (and yes, clumsy, awkward, gawky, ugly-duckling-style) extra muscle movements. And like reflexes, the child probably doesn't even know he's making them.

For instance, you may notice that when a child is drawing a picture he may stand up, lean over the table, or strike an odd posture. He might fidget, wiggle his feet, or mirror his hand movements, all in an effort to keep the inactive hand still. Likewise, if he's learning to jump, both arms go up at the same time with his knees.

And then there's the tongue . . .

When the Tongue Sticks Out

Have you ever noticed when a child is concentrating hard that sometimes the tongue sticks out? There are lots of reasons for this, all perfectly normal and generally harmless.

1. **Motor overflow.** The tongue is the only muscle located precisely on the left-right midline, and it can pivot in either direction. That makes it a convenient candidate for motor overflow no matter which part of the body is moving.

2. **Balance.** The centrally located tongue sometimes helps the brain get its bearings. For instance, you might notice when a child draws with his right hand, his tongue sticks out to the left almost as if it's acting as a movement counterweight.

3. **Delayed release of the grasp reflex.** In Chapter 5 we discussed the reflexive link between the mouth and the hand. If a child does not release the grasp reflex, he may, when he begins to use his hands for more detailed

work, stick out his tongue or open and close his mouth, mirroring the original sucking motion the grasp reflex encourages. Note: If you suspect that reflex release may be an issue, find a mud pie for him to squeeze and smoosh. Gooey, sensory-rich play will help release the reflex. And it's fun, too!

4. Habit. The tendency to stick out the tongue should abate as the midlines mature, but if it doesn't, chances are it's simply turned into a habit.

And one last note: Through the years of midline development, you may see the clumsy, awkward, gawky, ugly-duckling stage come and go several times, as the child's body moves through its many phases. Adults often associate these phases with growth spurts, and yes, his body is growing and changing. But more, it's his brain that's growing, stretching, and sometimes letting off "motor steam" that trips up little ducklings from time to time.

Dominance: Righty or Lefty?

Complex systems require organization, specialization, and leadership to streamline activity, avoid confusion, and produce the best results. And that goes for the human mind and body as well. That's why during the years of midline development, handedness emerges.

> It doesn't matter whether a child is right- or left-handed, as long as he's allowed to follow the side nature has selected for him.

To control the body's more sophisticated abilities, the brain employs an efficiency strategy by triggering the emergence of a dominant hand. Think of this as appointing a field marshal to lead the body. Now, instead of sending out two sets of commands each time the brain needs something done, it begins talking more to the dominant side and less to the nondominant one. Streamlining communication in this way leads to smoother and more precise motor control, faster reaction times, and more effective use of energy. And of course, it answers the question: righty or lefty? But please note, it doesn't matter whether a child is right- or left-handed, as long as he's allowed to follow the side nature has selected for him.

Left-Handedness

About 90 percent of humans are right-handed. That majority status may explain why past generations often thought there was something wrong with left-handedness and tried to correct it.

We now understand that interfering with nature's plan for a child's handedness can cause physiological and cognitive confusion. This, in turn, can slow down progress in other developmental areas, such as concepts of print and letter formation.[34]

So when it comes to handedness, nature wants what it wants and the best course of action is to foster that plan.

Mixed Dominance

The brain craves efficiency and organization. So it not only selects a dominant hand, but also a dominant eye, ear, foot, and brain hemisphere. Some of these, like handedness, are easy to see. Others, like the dominant brain hemisphere, are harder to detect.

The Dominant Side of the Brain

Generally, each of us has a dominant side of the brain, but it's important to understand that this does not in any way restrict or limit whole-brain thinking. Instead, think of it as the brain's default mechanism. When learning new things or thinking new thoughts, the brain may tend to start with that hemisphere, but it may not stay there.

Generally speaking, handedness is a pretty good indication of the eye, ear, foot, and brain hemisphere dominance as well. But not always. For example, a child might be right-handed but left-eye dominant. That's called mixed dominance.

Ambidexterity

Ambidexterity, the ability to use the right and left hands with equal strength and precision, is often confused with mixed dominance. Even a child who exhibits high levels of ambidexterity still has a dominant hand, eye, ear, foot, and brain hemisphere. It may simply be harder to detect this by observation. And note, while ambidexterity can be a tremendous advantage in sports, dance, and other highly coordinated physical activities, it is not necessarily predictive of success in the classroom. Instead, it's more important to look to the child's underlying dominance profile in order to understand his unique learning processes.

Whether a child's dominance profile is single-sided or mixed, it is innate. And it's important to learning, because the brain is wired to automatically rely on the dominant side (hand, foot, eye, ear, brain hemisphere) over the nondominant side. As such, dominance determines the efficiency with which the brain acquires and processes raw information, and it plays an important role in determining a child's unique set of gifts and the potential challenges he may face as he grows.

The Journey of Mixed Dominance

Think of dominance as a train. A child with single-sided dominance has an "express train" that streamlines efficiently through the brain. But for a child with mixed dominance, the train may stop at different stations, and even choose alternative routes through the brain. When those two children approach new information, there's a chance they may perceive it differently, because their brains are taking different routes to process it.

In the case of mixed dominance, the circuitry through which information flows into, around, and out of the brain can sometimes follow routes that are not always the shortest or most efficient. And this can have both advantages and disadvantages. You see, the longer the pathway through the brain, the more "side trips" it may choose along the way. At times, this may result in confusion or misinterpretation. But equally, these side trips may yield new and original insights and innovations that are personally more meaningful, even if it does take a little longer to get there.

Mixed Dominance in School

Mixed dominance may never present any learning challenges. But if it does, they will usually show up when a child starts school, where a formal, comparative setting and calendar of learning outcomes determine whether a child is keeping up.

Children with mixed dominance may lag behind their classmates in some learning areas. This can cause frustration, self-doubt, and worry for the child and parents. In most cases, there's no real cause for alarm. So before sending a child through a battery of neural tests, it might be useful to check the child's dominance profile, which can easily be done at home or in school.

Gauging Dominance

A few quick, simple games can help you gauge hand, foot, ear, and eye dominance. But before you use them, remember that the midlines develop slowly throughout the early years.

For many children, the midlines aren't fully developed when school starts. So while testing for dominance may yield clues about what's happening *right now*, the child's profile may change next week, next month, or next year. Please do not apply a permanent label to a child just yet. For the most accurate dominance profile reading, wait until at least the age of seven, when most midline development should be mature.

If you want to have some fun and get a feel for a child's current dominance profile, here are a few quick games to try.

Hand Dominance: Play Ball! It should be apparent by the time a child gets to school whether he is right-handed, left-handed, or ambidextrous. If you're uncertain, have the child throw you a ball or beanbag several times, and see which hand he uses.

Foot Dominance: Backyard Soccer. Kick up a little game of soccer. You be the goalie. Have the child try to kick the ball through your legs. Have him try it from different angles and distances. The foot he uses most to kick the ball is probably his dominant foot.

Ear Dominance: Answering the Phone. Have the child sit down. Place your phone directly in front of him, equidistant from both hands. Call the phone and have him answer it when it rings. Note which ear he uses. Do this a few times to see if he consistently favors that ear. If he does, chances are that's his dominant ear. (And take the opportunity to practice his phone etiquette while you're at it.)

Eye Dominance: The Tube Telescope. Take an empty cardboard tube from a roll of paper towels and place it directly in front of the child, equidistant from both hands. Ask him to look through it, and note which eye he favors. Do this several times. If needed, add a game such as I Spy to keep it interesting for the child, spying for things up close and far away.

Now What?

If you suspect a child has a mixed dominance profile, here are several steps to consider taking:

1. **Don't panic.** Mixed dominance is part of a child's hardwiring and you may discover that it has little or no impact on formal learning. Even more, remember that mixed dominance can develop rich, vibrant, and unique insights that propel learning to places most kids can't go.

2. **Help the child get and stay active!** A physically active child will develop his midlines naturally, which will strengthen the brain pathways for optimal speed and efficiency. Active play—especially lateral, homolateral, and cross-lateral movements—facilitates brain processing power.

3. **"Snack" on midline activity throughout the day.** Children with mixed dominance who do show signs of learning challenges may benefit from midline activity before the lesson begins or regularly throughout the day. This warms up the brain for processing information with both hemispheres and keeps the thinking brain on task.

4. **Seek professional guidance.** If necessary, find a local professional who can test the child for learning difficulties due to mixed dominance or other issues.

5. **Respect the process.** Please remember: no matter what a child's innate talents or challenges are, there's no wrong way to learn. There is only that child's way.

Body Rhythm and Temporal Awareness

While the midlines enable all complex, coordinated movement, body rhythm and temporal awareness work together as our own personal "orchestra conductor" keeping all our moving parts moving in sync.

We've all got a sense of rhythm and timing. Even those of us with "two left feet" have got some, thanks to the steady beat of Mom's heart for nine months. Body rhythm is the *internal* sense of timing that effectively coordinates all body movements. Temporal awareness is the *external* ability to judge distance and timing in order to interact successfully with the world. And without them, two left feet would be the least of our problems! That's because these natural "pulse beats" underscore, regulate, and coordinate not only how we move but, in fact, how we think, communicate, and behave.

Physical Coordination

Walking: Walking requires an evenly paced left-right-left-right rhythm. Toddlers walk erratically partly because they are adjusting their body rhythm to big, new leg movements.

Running: Keeping a steady pace over extended time and space creates a graceful, effortless gait.

Speed: Speed isn't just about going fast or slow. It's also about controlling your pace, from slow to fast and back to slow.

Hopping and jumping: Sequential movements such as bunny hopping or skipping rope require an innate rhythm and tempo.

Communication

Talking: Like music, all spoken language has its own rhythm. Each syllable is a single beat in the symphony of sounds that makes up speech. Experiences with sounds, speech, and music build up a young child's auditory rhythm, readying him for the first word and all the words that follow.

Listening and comprehension: Rhythm and timing help a child understand the nuances of language and sounds. Inflections, pauses, accelerations—all contribute to the meaning.

Cognitive Development

Memory: Rhythm and timing help us remember things by bringing a sense of order and cadence to information. And when organized, information can be retained as a single unit rather than as individual bytes of information. For instance, when little ones memorize the rhythmical pattern of the ABC song, it makes it easier to remember 26 letters.

Social and Emotional Development

Time: Young children have only one concept of time: "Right now!" With little past experience to draw on, they are rooted in the present. And when now is all you know, it's impossible to understand the concept of waiting. A child's sense of time grows as he grows, and with it his ability to show patience.

Otherness: As we've said, children develop their own perceptions of the world using themselves as their principle point of reference. That's why children struggle with the idea of "otherness"—other times, other places, other people, and other ideas. As children come to know themselves in context to life around them, they begin to grasp this sense of otherness. And an important component in that awakening is their sense of rhythm and timing. Like jumping rope, you have to feel the rhythm before you can join in.

Object Permanence: Out of Sight, Still in Mind

The concept of "otherness" emerges over the early months of life, taking tangible (and actionable) root with a child's emerging awareness and understanding of the concept of "temporary." It's been well documented that young infants have no sense of object permanence—the understanding that what is out of sight still exists even though he can't see it.

Object permanence depends largely on memory. The child is just beginning to build the brain infrastructure required for short- and long-term memory, a reality that makes his days an out-of-sight, out-of-mind existence. This probably explains why peekaboo is an endless delight to young babies. Each time Daddy reappears, it's a new surprise all over again.

But around eight to ten months, things start changing. Baby's memory capacity grows, and after many months of routine, repetitive encounters, his brain makes a leap to realize that things can exist even if they aren't physically present. This leap is the concept of otherness fully awakening. Baby now understands that there are things outside himself and outside his control.

And you'll know this leap has occurred when baby starts to cry if you leave the room. Clearly, you're not forgotten anymore!

Temporal Awareness

Once a child begins to sense his internal body rhythm, he can use it to gauge the rhythms of the world around him. This process starts in infancy, as a child becomes familiar with his daily routine. Early physical encounters with time (feeding time, bath time, and so forth) give him an intuitive sense of rhythm and orderliness.

As he grows, he'll begin independently interacting with the world, discovering new rhythms and patterns in simple playtime pursuits such as banging a drum or playing hopscotch. These are the exact rhythms he'll one day need to navigate everyday life activities such as judging traffic or knowing when to politely interject in conversation. That's because temporal awareness is the ability to judge distance and timing developed through many, varied physical experiences with the dynamics of cause and effect. And as such, temporal awareness lays the groundwork for higher-level cognitive abilities such as analysis, anticipation, and prediction.

For instance, when playing with a ball, a child could be stationary and the ball could be rolled toward him. Or, he could be in motion and the ball stationary. Or, both could be in motion. These are complex dynamics in their own right, but then add the physics of speed, distance, and environment, and suddenly, catching a ball isn't as easy as it looks!

Even with a simple game of catch, it's impossible to "memorize" every which way the ball could roll. So in order to be able to position himself for the catch, a child must learn to estimate and anticipate what *might* happen. And when that happens, the concept of time—past, present, and future—comes into focus.

The Impatient Zone

"Are we there yet?" a child asks from the backseat. Uh-oh.

"In a little while," you answer, hoping that this will satisfy him. But you already know what's coming: fidgeting, fussing, fooling around, and falling apart. You have just entered the Impatient Zone.

Kids are impatient because *now* is all they know. With little life experience and immature memory processing, young children have no real concept of the past. Without understanding the past, they cannot understand the more complex concept of future. Without understanding future, children cannot understand waiting.

> For young children, time isn't real because it's not tangible. They can't see it, hear it, taste it, smell it, or touch it.

For young children, time isn't real because it's not tangible. They can't see it, hear it, taste it, smell it, or touch it. Ask any two-year-old what he did yesterday, and chances are you'll get a blank stare. Ask him if he went to the circus yesterday, and he'll tell you all about it. He remembers the circus. He simply doesn't relate it to the idea of yesterday.

For time-strapped adults, it's hard to imagine that the variable that rules our day could be so unreal to children. To understand this better, let's discuss how kids learn about time.

Learning About Time

Kids learn about time by moving through it. At first, a child may notice the difference between day and night. Next, he may begin to associate time with everyday routines. For instance, breakfast, lunch, and dinner are regular events that make time tangible for him.

Next comes the idea of time passing—of *before* and *after*. Putting on your socks *before* you put on your shoes is the very beginning of sequencing, which will later unlock abstract concepts such as *past* and *future*.

Actual increments of time—seconds, minutes, hours, days—are far more sophisticated concepts that will come to him with experience and language acquisition over time.

And then comes *telling* time. The ability to read the clock begins once the child understands numbers and number sequencing and, eventually, relating those numbers to the time-based events in his life.

> ### Family Moves
>
> Print the "Meet the Midlines" handout and the "Gettin' Gluey (No Glue Required)" and "Minute Moves" Motorvators from the digital files and share them with parents.

Talking About Time

For a young child, time concepts unfold naturally through everyday experiences and the words he hears. So it's important to choose your time words carefully.

Think about it: what does the phrase *in a minute* mean to a little one who doesn't yet understand what a minute is? Here are many time words adults use often in everyday conversation. Try to imagine what, if anything, these mean to a young child: *soon • as soon as • shortly • almost • just about • not long • later • in a second • in a moment • in a minute • in five minutes • in a while • just a minute • not now • until • not until • before • during • while • after • yesterday • today • tomorrow • next week • next month • last week • last month • since • once • never.*

No wonder kids get impatient!

To understand time, children need to get a feel for it. You can help that process by using time language that's specific, contextual, descriptive, and trustworthy. Here are a few examples.

- **"I'll play soon."** To be sure a child understands "soon," choose a specific time, then set a timer. When it rings, it will be time to play.

- **"I'll play later."** If you can't be specific, put time in context. For example, say, "I'll play later—when I've finished cleaning up."

- **"I'll play tomorrow."** If you're not sure the child will understand an abstract time concept, describe it. For example, say, "After you wake up in the morning, it will be tomorrow, and then I'll play with you."

How Young Children Learn About Time

Rhythm. While still in the womb, Mommy's heartbeat is the very first experience with the rhythm and beat of time. Later, this innate understanding of beat will help a child with the abstract concept of how time passes—how to count the minutes, so to speak!

Routine. As a newborn becomes accustomed to his daily routine, the orderliness and predictability of time creates a sense of comfort.

Sequence of events. As the routine of life settles in, the child will begin to get a sense of sequence, that one thing follows another. This is an early awakening to the idea that there is more than just "right now," which, of course, will eventually lead to understanding the passage of time— past, present, and future.

Time environment. At first, daytime and night-time will all feel the same, but over time, the predictable rotation of sunlight to darkness con-tributes to baby's sense of time.

Time language 101. Everyday, natural con-versation begins to mark time for the child. A bright and cheerful "Good morning" or a gentle, loving "Nighty-night" suggests the dif-ference between the two times of day. Later, parents and caregivers naturally introduce time concepts with the "Time to's . . ."

Time to . . . *Time to get up • time to have breakfast • time to go to school • time to go outside • time for play • time for dinner • time to get ready for bed.* Young children may not be able to read the clock yet, but every child knows what "Time to" means.

Number recognition and sequencing. Learning to recognize numbers and know how to say them is an essential precursor to telling time, as well as knowing the order of the numbers 1–12.

Time measurement. That things take time is an abstract concept until a child can begin to measure it for himself. Simple, timed games may help him understand time measurement, such as how many shovelfuls of sand can he put in his bucket in a minute.

Time language 201. Learning the words that describe time occurs throughout the early verbal years, including time parts such as minutes and hours, the days of the week, the months of the year, and so forth. As the child's vocabulary grows, so does his understanding of "How long?"

How long? The idea of waiting can present emotionally charged moments for both children and adults. As children's understanding of the length of time increases, so will their patience.

Numbers = time. As a child's experience with time and numbers comes together, he can begin to correlate how the numbers represent different times of day.

What time is it? Then the day arrives when he can "read" the clock. Now, he knows what time it is. But equally important, he knows what time it isn't. And, no, it's not time for ice cream.

Now, we can't promise that precision language will keep you out of the Impatient Zone entirely. But a little clarity and a lot of patience on your part may make those moments easier to navigate.

And one last note: When you say you'll be there "in a minute," be there in a minute. If you show up 10 minutes later, you run the risk of confusing the child. He may begin to sense that one minute is 10 times longer than it actually is.

But even more, when you show up when you say you will, you're teaching him the importance of keeping your word. And on that subject, every minute counts.

Motorvator

Minute Moves

Here's Why
Little ones learn about the intangible concept of time by moving through it.

Here's How
Set the timer for one minute (or whatever time increment you believe your child or group of children can manage). Use the timer to demonstrate how long a minute is, then challenge the children to see what they can do in that amount of time. Here's a list to get you started, but by all means, have the kids make up their own Minute Moves!

- How far can you run in a minute?

- How much sand can you scoop into your bucket in a minute?

- How many times can you roll over in a minute?

- How many blocks can you stack in a minute?

- Can you hang from the monkey bars for a minute?

- Can you wiggle your toes for a minute?

- Can you bounce a ball for a minute?

- Can you stay still for a minute?

- Can you brush your teeth for a minute?

- How many kisses can you give Mommy in a minute?

Chapter Summary

- **Midlines and coordination:** The midlines help children learn to isolate individual body parts so that they can move independently or together.

- **Three midlines:** These imaginary lines divide the body left from right, front from back, and top from bottom. The midlines serve as the pivots for sophisticated movement.

- **Midlines and the brain:** Midline development boosts essential neural pathways across the corpus callosum to facilitate whole-brain thinking.

- **Midline movements:** There are four types of midline development: *bilaterality* (moving both sides of the body in mirrored fashion), *homolaterality* (moving one side of the body while the other remains still), *laterality* (moving opposite sides of the body in opposition to one another), *cross-laterality* (crossing parts of the body over one or more of the midlines).

- **Motor overflow:** When the body and brain are working hard to coordinate with one another, sometimes extra muscle movements occur.

- **Motor planning:** Independent movement necessitates motor planning.

- **Dominance:** As children's movements become more complex, the brain needs to streamline communication with the body. This results in a dominant hand, eye, ear, foot, and brain hemisphere.

- **Dominance and learning:** The brain prioritizes information coming in from the dominant side, streamlining reception and information processing.

- **Body rhythm and temporal awareness:** These work together to create a sense of rhythm and timing, underpinning a wide range of physical, cognitive, social, emotional, and communication capabilities.

- **Object permanence:** Young babies do not yet understand that what is out of sight still exists.

- **Judgment and timing:** Temporal awareness is essential for interacting with our moving world.

- **Time concepts:** Kids don't learn about time by learning to read a clock. Time is intangible; the only way to understand it is by moving through it.

For examples of some coordination activities you can try, please see Part 6, pages 302–307.

CHAPTER 13

Control: Beyond Fine Motor Skills

What Is Control?

Up until now, much of our focus has been on the early childhood journey to automaticity—movement without conscious thought to unlock the brain for thinking tasks. Ironically, one of those thinking tasks is controlled movement.

In this context, control is defined as the ability to move deliberately and accurately to achieve whatever the brain intends. Now, it's easy to assume control applies only to older children, but in fact, it unfolds throughout the early years. For instance, a baby who consistently grasps her favorite toy is demonstrating precise control of her arms and hands—enough command to achieve this desired outcome. But that doesn't mean she's ready for handwriting just yet.

Control (aka fine and gross motor skills) applies equally to the small and large muscles. For example, a ballerina needs strong leg muscles to leap, of course. But she must also have precise control over those same muscles in order to leap with grace and artistry.

Self-Organization

When children begin to realize control over their bodies and understand their own power to accomplish things, a new concept emerges:

self-organization. For a child, self-organization means attending to her own needs independently within the frame of her current physical capabilities.

For instance, a baby feeding herself from her high-chair tray is show-ing the very earliest signs of self-organization. She can't prepare the meal yet, but she can get food into her mouth. As she grows, she'll learn to con-trol more of her own needs—using the toilet, dressing herself, washing her hands, waiting her turn—the dozens of everyday tasks that require her to think *and* act for herself. After all, knowing *how* to use the potty and knowing *when* you need to use it are two different things.

In a school or group setting, self-organization often goes unheralded, but without it time and energy can be taken away from learning. A self-organized child does not get distracted—or cause a distraction—while trying to put on her coat. But even the brightest child can be flummoxed by the wrapping on her snack if her self-organization skills aren't in place. And while she's working out her snack dilemma (with or without the assistance of the teacher), what else is she missing out on?

> Controlled movement is the ability to move deliberately and accurately to achieve whatever the brain intends.

Importantly, controlling her physical self and her physical needs not only helps a child get along in the world, but also builds the kind of confidence and positive attitude she'll need for learning—before, during, and after snack time.

Learning to Adapt

Now that the child is getting her body under control, it still doesn't guarantee that she is going to get it right every time. And that means she must learn to adapt—an essential aspect of control.

There are three basic ways to adapt or adjust movement for better accuracy:

- Positioning—changing direction
- Pacing—changing speed
- Pressure—changing force

Positioning

Because human movement is three-dimensional, we can change the position of our movements in any direction.

For instance, in a game of hopscotch, the player throws her marker to land on a specific space. She may hit the mark or miss to the left or right or go beyond her target or fall short of it. The next time she throws her marker, she'll adjust accordingly.

Now, in hopscotch, the target is known. But breakthroughs in learning (and life) sometimes don't come with prefabricated end goals. This is perhaps where controlled movement contributes most to early learning readiness. By empowering children with the physical sensation of change—a little to the left, a little to the right, a little higher, a little lower, and so forth—we are helping them learn the principles of incrementalism and experimentation, no matter who decides what the end goal is.

Pacing

Most preschoolers seem to have one speed: fast! We often attribute that to innocent exuberance. But there's another reason, too: slow is difficult. Going slow is physically demanding. It requires concentration, patience, and control—all in short supply with preschoolers.

Pacing—the ability to ramp up and ramp down—is essential for activities that take an extended time to complete, such as a long-distance run or a full day of school. But more, the physical sensation of controlled speed helps children begin to understand the concept of modulation—that different tasks require different levels of intensity. And in the process, this may give children a clearer understanding of those words they hear every day: "Be careful."

From modulation comes the even more sophisticated concept of moderation. "Enough" is a very difficult concept for young children, who don't yet understand their own limits—from how far they can run to how many cookies will give them a tummy ache. Parents, teachers, and caregivers often play the role of "Enough Cop," setting and enforcing limits. And of course, children need that kind of guidance. But if a child never goes to the edges of "too much" or

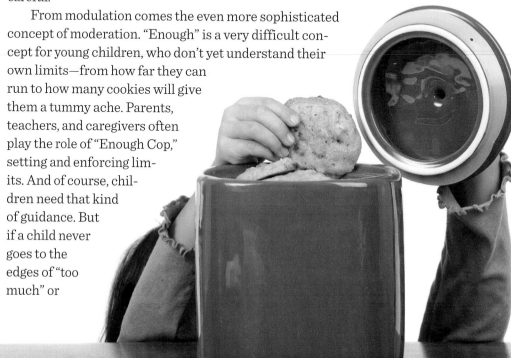

Traffic Cop

Here's Why
The more practice children get at modifying their movements in different ways, the better they get at controlling their bodies—and themselves.

Here's How
Start the game by playing the role of traffic cop. As the game progresses, look for opportunities to let each child lead.

Choose a basic movement pattern children can do easily. For this example, let's say the children are all preschoolers who have mastered jumping with two feet.

Start the game by explaining that there's a terrible traffic jam, and the cars must get moving again. Have the children line up like cars on a road. When the traffic cop gives an instruction, the cars all have to move in that direction.

For instance: "Junky jalopies are very jumpy. Can you show me how you jump in place? Good. Now, can you show me how you jump forward?" As the children get good at jumping forward, stop the traffic and change the movement. (If you've got one, use a whistle, just like a real traffic cop!) "Now can you show me how you jump sideways?" Continue the game until the children have had a chance to jump in many different directions and ways. Here's a list of ways to get you started:

Forward	High	Straight	Between
Backward	Medium	Curvy	In front of
Right	Low	Zigzag	In back of
Left	Strong	Feet apart	Below
In a circle	Light	Feet together	Follow the leader
Fast	Smooth	Over	As a team
Slow	Jerky	Under	One at a time

When the children get the hang of the game, trade in the junky jalopies for race cars and running, dump trucks and crawling, or whatever the children come up with. With each vehicle, change directions, styles of movement, and pacing so children have many chances to control their movements in different ways.

If the children get really good at the game, try giving two-part instructions. For example, "Move forward, then to the right."

"too far," she will never come face to face with her own limits. And that lack of self-understanding might one day lead to struggles with self-control and the emotional maturity and critical reasoning it brings—no matter how good those cookies look.

> Knowing their own strength is one of the first physical experiences children have with cause and effect, estimation, and prediction.

Pressure or Force

Adjusting the application of pressure or force is the third way we modify our movements for accuracy. As we discussed in Chapter 9, this can be intuitive or it can be deliberate.

For instance, when a child is first learning to use a pencil, she might break a lot of lead as she gets a feel for how much pressure she needs to use to write. Later, she'll use that sense of appropriate force as a reference point. She'll draw lightly to create delicate lines or press hard to create bold strokes.

Knowing their own strength is one of the first physical experiences children have with cause and effect, estimation, and prediction. "If I push this hard, X will happen. If I push that hard, Y will happen."

And from this early understanding of cause and effect comes a big leap to planning and strategizing. Knowing what can be done and having a sense of what might happen leads naturally to the question: "What do I *want* to do?" When a child reaches that level of control, she is not only ready to learn what you have to teach, but able to start learning through her own self-directed experiments.

Gill's Notebook

M Is for Monkey Bars

Fine Motor Development: A Job for the Whole Body

A child's hands are powerful learning tools. With her hands, a child can control the world around her, build and create what she imagines, and express herself—first with gestures, then with scribbles, and eventually with pictures and written words.

Parents and teachers know the importance of fine motor control—especially when it comes to handwriting. That's probably why they frequently ask me for advice on this subject.

Here's what I say: Put your pencils down and go play on the monkey bars.

The Natural Order of Motor Control

A child's understanding of her body and her muscle control and coordination develop in a natural, orderly way—from the top down and from the inside out. It starts at the head and works toward the toes while building out from the torso to the arms and legs.

This order of priority, established by the brain, ensures that the large muscles necessary for coordination and locomotion are well developed first. They can then support the complex mastery of the small muscles. The hands alone have more than 60 muscles, dozens of bones, and hundreds of ligaments and tendons.

So you see, on the developmental timeline, the hands (and feet) come last.

What Are Fine Motor Skills?

This doesn't mean that a child's hands aren't active as she grows. Very young hands begin moving with simple, reflexive, whole-hand grasping. Over time, early reflexes release and the pincer grip kicks in, letting the child use her forefinger and thumb in unison. Each day, more deliberate hand and finger movements emerge.

But none of these movements are fine motor skills yet. Fine motor refers to the highly precise, controlled, almost imperceptible movements necessary to do detailed work, such as using a pencil to write. But even writing isn't all fine motor skills. In fact, it involves much of the body:

- The core muscles hold the body in an upright position.
- The shoulder muscles bear the arm's weight and rotate freely to position the arm.
- The upper arm holds the weight of the lower arm and hand, delivering the hand to the page.

- The lower arm provides the fulcrum on which the wrist rotates.
- The wrist holds the hand steady and rotates to the appropriate position.
- The fingers fold around the pencil, which the thumb holds in place.
- Together, all five fingers place the pencil at the correct angle to meet the page, press down and maintain the right amount of pressure to leave a mark, and make tiny left, right, up, and down movements across the page.

If any of these muscles don't do their job, writing will be very hard indeed. This is whole-body learning, and it brings us full circle back to the monkey bars.

Climbing, hanging, swinging, and other high-energy activities that build strength in the upper body and core muscles are vital to developing fine motor skills. Twisting, turning, dangling, and swinging develop flexibility and agility in the shoulders, elbows, wrists, and fingers. Pushing, pulling, tugging, and lifting build strength and an intuitive understanding of simple physics such as weight, pressure, and resistance.

Messy play, too, is ideal for building strength and dexterity in the hand and finger muscles. Play dough, sand, water, mud, and other tactile materials provide sensory experiences for the brain and hands and might even mean neater handwriting someday.

"Eye-Everything" Coordination

The eyes may well be the body's best partner for insuring accuracy. They often play a directorial role in how, when, and where we move. But when a child can move her body without having to look directly at her movements, she's using her brain and body more efficiently. That's why eye-hand coordination is defined as a child's ability to direct her hands to an object *without* looking at her hands.

Family Moves

Print the "Traffic Cop" Motorvator and "Gill's Notebook: M Is for Monkey Bars" from the digital file and share them with parents.

This level of control is possible only after the eyes and hands have formed a partnership. For instance, sometimes the hands need help getting to where the brain wants them to go, so the eyes point the way. A baby sees the toy before she reaches for it. Conversely, sometimes the eyes struggle to track a moving object, so the hand points the way. A child keeps track of the floating balloon by pointing at it.

The eye-hand relationship is critical to early learning. But the eyes must also be good partners to the rest of the body.

For example, a good soccer player knows how to dribble the ball without having to look at it all the time. She'll look toward the goal and then back to the ball many times without stopping. And she can do the same thing with her knees, chest, and head. In other words, keeping her "eyes on the ball" means *more* than keeping her eyes on the ball. It means controlling the ball and controlling herself to get to her goal.

Gill's Notebook

In Defense of Reading with Your Fingers

Adults often ask me if there's anything wrong with young children using their fingers to follow words on a page when reading. Here's my one-word answer: no.

Common wisdom says that children should read and count with their eyes only. But this rule ignores the fact that young children learn nearly everything else kinesthetically. Why should reading or counting be any different?

For early readers, the fingers often form a scouting party for the eyes, keeping the eyes on track and flowing word to word. This helps a child focus on the *meaning* of the words rather than on the physical mechanics of moving her eyes from one word to the next. As the eye muscles mature, they'll grow in proficiency and the fingers will no longer be needed.

Similarly, counting on the fingers is the brain's way of physicalizing numeracy—a natural, multisensory entry into the world of mathematics. When she's mastered counting, chances are the child won't need her fingers anymore. And even if she does from time to time, it's just her way of adding dimension and deepening the learning.

Chapter Summary

- **Control** is as the ability to move deliberately and accurately to achieve whatever the brain intends.

- **All muscles**—large and small—require control.

- **Self-organization** is a child's ability to attend to her own needs within the frame of her current capabilities. In early learning environments, self-organization is essential for optimizing learning time and energy.

- **Controlled movement** is the ability to adapt and adjust through changing position, pace, or pressure.

- **Control and conceptual development** are intricately linked. Physical control unlocks essential intellectual concepts, such as incrementalism, experimentation, modulation, intensity, moderation, estimation, and prediction.

- **"Eye-everything" coordination** is the ability to direct any body part *without* looking at it.

- **Fine motor development** begins with the large muscles.

- **Whole-body learning** invites a child to use her body to assist her brain in learning.

For examples of some control activities you can try, please see Part 6, pages 309–315.

PART 3

Language: The Bridge to Formal Learning

CHAPTER 14

Verbal and Physical Language

//

So far, we've explored how movement underpins all of early childhood development and creates deep and lasting foundations for learning. Returning to the Kinetic Scale for a moment, we've described how the reflexes kick-start movement and support the development of both the sensory and motor tools. Now let's turn our attention to translating those early physical and sensory realizations into the higher levels of human thinking, reasoning, and creativity needed for the classroom. And for that job, our translator is language.

What Is Language?

Traditionally, we think of language as the spoken or written word. But in fact, our capacity to communicate is far more expansive. Language in all its forms includes communication that is:

- Verbal (speech or singing)
- Physical (expressions, gestures, movements, touch, and dance)
- Musical (beat, tempo, melody, and harmony)
- Symbolic (written word and art)

Now, it comes as no surprise that language is pivotal for learning. But just knowing words or lyrics or letters isn't enough. Real learning happens when language is put in experiential context, resulting in a simple, dynamic, and endlessly repeatable formula:

Experience + Language = Understanding

The Kinetic Scale

The Senses	Balance (Vestibular)	Intuition (Proprioception)	Power	Coordination	Control
Sight	Posture	Body and spatial awareness	Strength	Midlines	Positioning
Hearing	Balance	Body subconscious	Stamina	Dominance	Pacing
Smell	Alertness	Strength management	Flexibility	Body rhythm	Pressure or force
Taste	Concentration		Agility	Temporal awareness	Eye-everything
Touch	Stillness				coordination

Sensory   **Reflexes**   **Motor**

Language
Verbal
Physical
Musical
Symbolic

Language bridges the divide between the physical and tangible world children are getting to know and the promised horizons of higher reasoning, critical problem solving, creativity, and invention. In short, language transforms life experiences into the conceptual abstractions that are the tools of a thinker.

Learning to communicate is a busy two-way street—figuring out how to understand others and how to make yourself understood. If that's not enough, it requires mastering all forms of language—verbal, physical, musical, and symbolic. And throughout it all, the whole point of language is coming into focus, navigating the subtleties, complexities, and mysteries of human relationships.

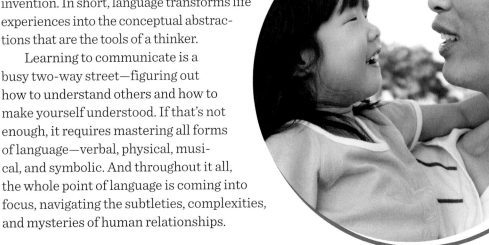

Many adults think language development means growing a talker. So let's begin there.

Verbal Language

Words! Words! And More Words!

It's common wisdom that children exposed to language are better prepared for the verbal and written world. More specifically, children need lots of real-time language in many different situations with as much sensory and motor stimulation as possible.

And the reason is simple: what he hears is what he'll say.

A child's ears are more sensitive to sound and frequency in early childhood than at any other time.[35] At first, words are just noise to a baby. But when he hears the same words over and over, he eventually figures out that the noise has meaning.

Meanwhile, control over the muscles in his mouth is sharpening. He begins mimicking the mouth movements he sees and the sounds he hears, until one day, there it is: the first word! Chances are it's more a sound than a word, but still, it's a wondrous thing. And before you know it, he's babbling a blue streak.

Then comes an amazing moment in a child's verbal journey—the day it's clear he knows what he's talking about. The first time he utters, "Da!" and points to Daddy marks his first deliberate use of verbal language.

Vocabulary Acquisition

From there, the sounds get easier to mimic, and soon the child has a handful of words down pat—with more on the way. This is the beginning of vocabulary acquisition, labeling the familiar tangibles in his world: *mama*, *dada*, *ba* (bottle), and so on.

Caregivers can enhance his vocabulary acquisition by surrounding the child with words. Daily, eye-to-eye conversations urge him toward the verbal world. Narrating his everyday experiences gives him labels for people, places, and things. And this can happen anytime, or anywhere, while doing chores or on a trip to the zoo. Every experience feeds his hungry brain with sensory inputs, physical experiences, and—with your help—words, words, words!

Simple songs and rhymes also offer great opportunities for expanding a child's verbal reach. The rhythmical patterns support his emerging sense of language while giving him new words and sounds to play with.

And along the way, without even trying, you are giving him cues for modulating his voice through intonation, inflection, and pacing. When you speak in a high tone to express excitement or whisper in a quiet moment, he may not understand your words, but he's beginning to see your intent. And he'll put that to good use in his own verbal world down the road.

Transferable Language

With some vocabulary under his belt, a child can take the next step: transferring the language he's learned to new situations. For instance, sand on the beach is similar to sand in the sandbox. After many experiences with sand in both places, the child begins to understand that sand is called sand no matter where it is. That's the beginning of transferable language.

> Children need lots of real-time language in many different situations with as much sensory and motor stimulation as possible. And the reason is simple: what a child hears is what he'll say.

From there, the next leap is associating the color and texture of sand with other things. Sand castles are made of sand; sandpaper feels rough like sand; Mommy's hair is sandy-colored; and so on. His ability to learn, understand, and communicate multiplies exponentially when he begins to associate. And while these early experiences with transferable language will center around his physical and sensory world, this is, in fact, the earliest manifestation of metaphor and the launching pad for higher, abstract thinking.

Gill's Notebook

Making Every Word Count

When it comes to young children, not all words are created equal. That's why I like to tell parents and teachers to pack their words full of calories for children to chew on. Here's what I mean.

Specificity: Use Nutritious Language

Young children have a tough enough time working out one word from the next, so my first rule of thumb is: *Think in specifics*. Be as literal as you can. For instance, when presented with a child's painting, saying "That's beautiful" might make him feel good, but it won't give him more information about his painting. Instead, be specific with your praise: "I like the way you used yellow to create that circle." Now his understanding of yellow and circles is more complete.

Variety: Use Many Different Words

No matter where you are, take time to point out the rich details that surround you. For instance, in the garden there are lots of different flowers, so take a word tour. "This is a daisy. See how the petals are white?" Use simple comparisons: "This is a flower, too. It's called a rose. See how the petals are red?" Use lots of different words in many different ways to help those words sink in.

Personalization: Make It Meaningful

Experience has more learning punch when it has personal meaning. Get down on the floor with the child so the learning is at his level, and stay close through the experience so you are sharing it together. Use the child's name to make it about him, and relate it to things he already knows. And of course, let him get his hands into the learning while you narrate the action.

Be a Good Verbal Model

Model proper pronunciation and grammar. The child won't know the difference, but he will imitate you.

Use Context

Select words that you can use in different contexts, so the child will learn that words can have multiple meanings. (We'll discuss this more in Chapter 16.)

Make It a Conversation

Show him how much fun words are. Invite discussion. Stay open to questions. And whenever you can, let the child teach you. After all, nothing's more empowering than a listener interested in what you have to say.

The Evolution of Communication

Learning to verbalize your thoughts is a continuous process that happens throughout the early years (and some would argue over a lifetime). But it's more than just knowing the words. On pages 146 and 147, we've drawn a map of the key steps children take toward successful communication. Notice the interplay of verbal and nonverbal communication. And remember, it's a two-way street of understanding and being understood.

Physical Language

Grown-ups tend to focus on children's verbal language. But the first language kids learn is actually nonverbal (physical) language—what we often call body language. It begins in the first moments of life when a gentle touch, soothing tone, and a smiling face welcomes baby into the world. No words are necessary for a newborn to understand what love feels like.

When you talk to a child of any age, he not only hears your words, but also sees and feels your body language. Physical language turns your message into a multisensory experience, tripling your communication power and his chances of understanding. This triggers intellectual and emotional connections in the brain that leave lasting impressions and provide a model he can use to express himself someday. In other words: verbal language (voice, intonation, words) + nonverbal language (posture, gestures, expressions, touch) = maximum emotional interaction.

Our First Language

Research shows that body language accounts for more than 50 percent of all human communication.[36] Posture, gestures, facial expressions, and touch all contribute to communicating our emotions, intentions, and beliefs. Since words of their own are not available to children at first, body language is the first language they learn.

The Evolution of Communication

Sounds like fun out there!

Before Birth
Becomes familiar with the everyday sounds of his soon-to-be world.

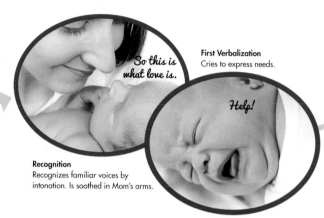

So this is what love is.

Help!

First Verbalization
Cries to express needs.

Recognition
Recognizes familiar voices by intonation. Is soothed in Mom's arms.

I get it!

Mama. Dada. Nana.

Look what I can say!

Understanding Deepens
Regularly responds to familiar and situational words, such as *diaper*.

Vocabulary Acquisition
Begins acquiring vocabulary rapidly and with increasing ease. Speaks one word at a time.

The First Word
Clearly articulates a recognizable word—usually *dada* or *mama*.

Me cookie.

E-I-E-I-O!

Train.

Train.

Early Sentences
Can put two or three words together in context.

Complexity Increases
Demonstrates more complex language skills, such as completing sentences or lyrics: "Old MacDonald had a farm . . ."

Transferable Language
Able to understand and use the same word in different situations, such as a toy mailbox and the mailbox outside.

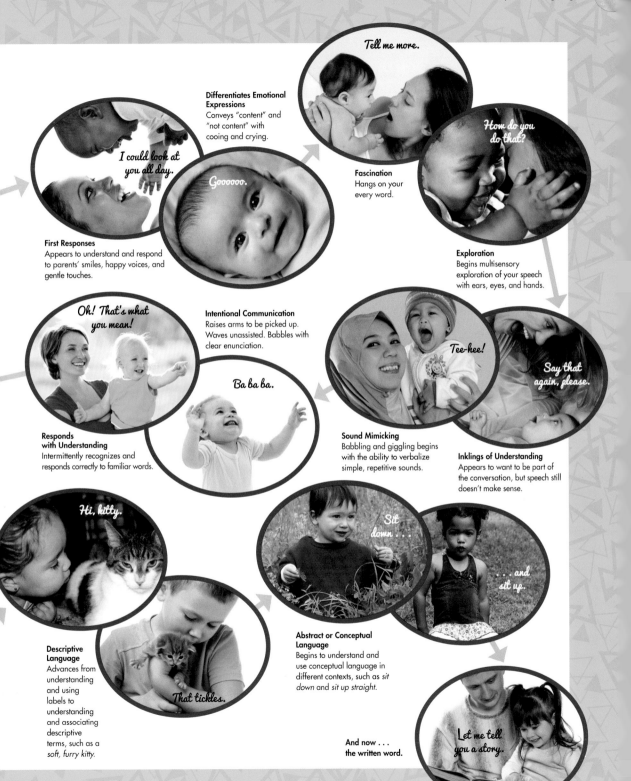

Tell me more.

Differentiates Emotional Expressions
Conveys "content" and "not content" with cooing and crying.

Goooooo.

I could look at you all day.

Fascination
Hangs on your every word.

How do you do that?

First Responses
Appears to understand and respond to parents' smiles, happy voices, and gentle touches.

Exploration
Begins multisensory exploration of your speech with ears, eyes, and hands.

Oh! That's what you mean!

Intentional Communication
Raises arms to be picked up. Waves unassisted. Babbles with clear enunciation.

Ba ba ba.

Tee-hee!

Say that again, please.

Responds with Understanding
Intermittently recognizes and responds correctly to familiar words.

Sound Mimicking
Babbling and giggling begins with the ability to verbalize simple, repetitive sounds.

Inklings of Understanding
Appears to want to be part of the conversation, but speech still doesn't make sense.

Hi, kitty.

Sit down . . .

. . . and sit up.

Descriptive Language
Advances from understanding and using labels to understanding and associating descriptive terms, such as a soft, furry kitty.

That tickles.

Abstract or Conceptual Language
Begins to understand and use conceptual language in different contexts, such as sit down and sit up straight.

And now . . . the written word.

Let me tell you a story.

Indeed, at any age, body language is often the best communication tool a child has. Babies don't take long to figure out how to get what they need—from pointing to the toy they want to a full-bodied tantrum. Toddlers and preschoolers lean forward with excitement when they're engaged. They slump and pout when they're bored.

Learning to Relate to Others: Dialects of Adult-Child Communication

Children may not yet understand all the words you use, but they are sensitive interpreters of body language. That's why it's important to pay attention to what your words *and* your body are saying.

The ability to interpret the entire message—verbal and nonverbal—is the first step toward understanding the complexities of human relationships. And for that, children's reference point is us. There are many "dialects" of adult-child communication. Let's take a look at just a few.

Engaged and Playful

Active listening is one of the most important ways you can send the message *you're important to me*. Get down on the child's level, lean in, and make eye contact. Hang on his every word. React with positive verbal and nonverbal cues such as nodding, smiling, and hugging. And show broad emotions as he speaks so he knows what it feels like to be understood. These simple messages foster self-esteem in powerful ways while encouraging him to communicate even more.

And remember, a young child is a talker-in-training. He may need time to think things through and find the right words. Try not to anticipate his words or step in and speak for him. Instead, apply the WAIT principle: "**W**hy **A**m **I T**alking?" When you speak before the child has a chance to form his own ideas into words, you may miss out on one of the most important parts of active listening—learning something!

Protective and Assertive

Sometimes it's important for children to listen very carefully to you—especially if there's a safety concern. In such cases, without thinking about it, you likely go into protective-assertive overdrive. The pitch of your voice changes, you stand taller, you adopt a wider stance, and your muscles tense in readiness for action. Children will sense this change in you—but only if you don't overuse this dialect.

Aggressive and Dominant

A fine line separates protective-assertive body language from aggressive-dominant. Aggressive and dominant dialect says, "Because I said so!" Frustration or anger can be costly to your relationship with a young child. Showing aggression can damage his trust in you, leaving him confused and frightened. Now, everyone gets angry from time to time. But remember: there's a big difference between feeling anger and showing it. When you feel angry, step away for a moment, relax your muscles, and regroup before you speak.

Nurturing and Empathetic

Empathy is foundational for a child's healthy social develop-ment. But children can't learn to understand how others feel unless they feel understood by others first—and especially by those they look to for guidance and support. Communicating "I understand" with open, accessible body language pro-vides the reassurance a child needs in good times and bad. A hug says more than "You're safe." It says, "I understand how you feel, and I care about you." A broad smile and a pat on the back say more than "I'm proud of you." They say, "You're important to me. I'm paying attention to you."

Distracted and Disengaged

Little ones sense when your head's not in the game. Of course, as teachers, caregivers, and parents we're constantly juggling priorities. But children need and deserve to feel valued by us. Their self-esteem depends on it. And so does their ability to value others.

Verbal and Physical Language: The Gateway to Socialization

The point of language is to interact with others. Language—in all its forms—is the common ground upon which humans form relationships.

Situational Language

Like having a new toy, once children start to talk, it's often difficult to get them to stop. That's because they haven't yet learned there are different "voices" for different occasions, including when it's time to be quiet. And as

"That's So Rhinoceros"

"Oh, that's so rhinoceros, Mommy," said a three-year-old when his mommy made a funny face.

Rhinoceros? Where did he get that?

With a little detective work, Mommy figured out that he must have meant *ridiculous*, a word Aunt Milly said the other day. But there's a rhinoceros in his favorite book, so he must have mixed up the words.

While this makes for a cute kid story, this child was actually demonstrating a sophisticated and socially savvy use of language. He correctly remembered the word *ridiculous* in context to a silly situation. He also remembered the word *rhinoceros* from his storybook. He chose the wrong word, but still made himself understood.

This is the very point of language: to facilitate human interaction. But as this example proves, there's more to language than just knowing the words.

complex as it is to learn how to speak, learning to adapt your words (and volume) to different situations requires experienced social processing.

For most children, this likely starts with *"Shhhh,"* and mimicking a grown-up's whispers. They soon grasp that they can control their own volume, and with a little practice, most oblige. This helps little ones understand that language has subtleties and nuances that will graduate them from articulating words to delivering words in context.

Good Manners

It's never too early to introduce simple etiquette expressions like *please, thank you,* and *excuse me*. These expressions lay the foundations of genuine respect for others. At the same time, understanding the need to use different words and strike a different tone when speaking to different people—for example, a teacher versus a playmate—is great practice for emerging social skills.

Family Moves

Print "Gill's Notebook: Making Every Word Count" and the "How Many Ways Can You Say _____?" Motorvator from the digital file and share them with families to support stimulating language development at home.

You'll likely find the easiest way to help a child get on board the Good Manners Train is to lead by example.. When you model good manners toward him and others, he will be more likely to pattern his behavior after yours as your values become his values. But of course, like everything else, patient coaching is all part of your role modeling.

Motorvator

How Many Ways Can You Say _____?

Here's Why
A child's voice and body are instruments for helping him communicate his thoughts. Learning to express ideas in different ways helps him master situational language.

Here's How
Start by asking the children to find different ways to say a single word—for example, the word *please.* Then prompt the children to experiment with their voices, For instance: "I wonder what *please* would sound like if you were very, very quiet? Loud? Happy? Sad?"

Encourage the children to use their full range of pitch and body language. For example: "I wonder what *please* sounds like when you're really tall? Or really short? I wonder what *please* sounds like if you're sliding down a slide?" Add silliness: "How does a cow say *please?*"

Other languages are often fascinating to little ones, too. Explain that children in Mexico don't say *please;* they say *por favor,* and in France they say *s'il vous plait.*

Confident Language
While respect for others is essential, the ability to exhibit self-respect is, too. And that means learning to speak for yourself.

Sometimes, adults speak for children in social situations—especially around other adults. When that happens, it excuses the child from finding his own words. This is more than a lost learning opportunity, because he might come to think grown-ups don't believe he can speak for himself.

Whenever possible, avoid putting words in a child's mouth. Instead, show respect for his point of view by staying quiet while he's finding his own words. This will go a long way toward developing his vocabulary, grammar, and syntax, as well as social navigation tools such as self-confidence, compassion, empathy, teamwork, and negotiation.

Chapter Summary

- **Language takes four forms:** verbal (speech or singing), physical (expressions, gestures, movements, touch, and dance), musical (beat, tempo, melody, and harmony), and symbolic (written word and art).

- **Experience + language = understanding:** Young children need experiential context to make words their own.

- **Two-way street:** Mastering language in any form means learning to understand others and make yourself understood.

- **Vocabulary acquisition** is enhanced by a rich environment of conversation and narration.

- **Expressive communication:** Children learn the subtleties of language by listening to our intonation and inflection and by watching our body language.

- **Transferable language:** Learning how to transfer words from one context to another is the earliest form of metaphor and abstract thinking.

- **Make every word count:** Use concrete words. Use a variety of words. Relate words to something the child already knows. Be a good verbal role model. Engage the child in conversation.

- **Physical language (body language)** is the first language children learn to understand and speak.

- **Verbal language + nonverbal language = maximum emotional interaction:** Body language amplifies your message by making it multisensory, which in turn makes it easier to understand and assimilate.

- **Body language "dialects":** Be aware of what you're saying with your words and your body.

- **Gateway to socialization:** Children often learn the subtleties of human interaction by following your example.

- **Good manners** begin early. Model the *please* and *thank you* that you want to hear.

- **Confident language:** Encourage children to speak for themselves and respect what they have to say.

CHAPTER 15
Music and Movement

Growing a talker takes both verbal and physical language. But two other forms of human communication develop in the early years, as well: music and symbolic language. Let's take a look at music next.

Music Rocks!

Studies have shown that music has huge, positive effects on early childhood development.[37] Exposure to music—listening, singing, dancing, or playing—fosters many essential early learning capabilities, including:

- Speech development
- Listening skills
- Patterning and sequencing (math skills)
- Rhythm, beat, and timing
- Social skills
- Emotional development
- Memory
- Physical coordination

Music alone is a powerful force for learning and growing. But when you add movement to music, from toe tapping to hand clapping to ballet dancing, the benefits multiply manyfold.

The Elements of Music

For our purposes, let's examine the elements of music (beat, rhythm, tempo, pitch, dynamics, melody, harmony, intervals, and lyrics) to better understand why it serves up learning in such a powerful way for children, and what happens when movement partners with music to amplify those effects.

Beat

Beat is the master timekeeper for a musical piece. Its constant pulse is the guiding force keeping all the elements working together. The beat may remain steady or it may speed up or slow down to create different effects within the song.

Rock-a-Bye-Baby

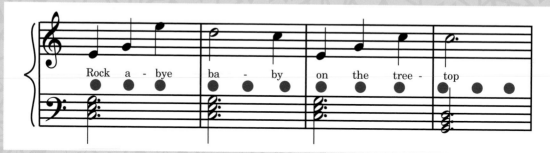

To understand beat, note the red dots on the music score for a line from "Rock-a-Bye Baby." Notice how the dots are evenly spaced, regardless of how the words and music flow.

When we hear music, we instinctively register the beat (as illustrated by the red dots). If you've ever found yourself tapping your foot, nodding your head, or clapping to music, chances are you're following the beat. Some experts believe we respond this way because we begin life to the beat of our mother's heart.

Beat underscores a child's movement development in many ways, including body rhythm, coordination, balance, and spatial reasoning. Of course, beat underpins the speech patterns that become our way of talking. And more, this intuitive sense of beat we all share underscores a child's sense of belonging—of being in sync with the rest of the world.

> **While beat creates a sense of unity, rhythm opens the door to individuality.**

Rhythm

Rhythm describes the length each note is played or sung, creating points of interest and emphasis that give each song its unique quality. In this way, rhythm begins to tell the "story" of the song, much the way we pace our words to make a point when speaking.

Note the difference between beat and rhythm in "Rock-a-Bye Baby." Look at the blue bars in the music, representing the song's rhythm. As an experiment, sing the song to the beat, then again to the rhythm, and you'll feel the difference.

Rock-a-Bye-Baby

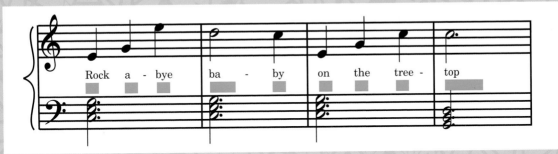

We all have a sense of rhythm unique to ourselves—an awareness of and responsiveness to the flow of music and, more broadly, the rhythms of our world. Though we're not consciously aware of it, rhythm ebbs and flows through everything we do, from the way we walk and talk to the way we feel and think. As such, while beat creates a sense of unity, rhythm opens the door to individuality.

Tempo

Tempo is the pace and timing of the music used to underscore the emotional quality of the piece. A fast song is usually exciting and energizing, while a slow song is usually more soothing and thoughtful. Tempo can change throughout the song to build momentum—from fast to slow or slow to fast depending on the story the song is telling.

And in that, tempo is a learning tool. Children experience time in the music as they intuitively regulate the pace of their movements according to the tempo. But more, as a temporal art form, music exists along a continuum of time, expressing the fundamental time concepts of beginning, middle, and end. As we've noted, this is one of the first conceptual foundations for developing anticipation and prediction.

For instance, in the song and finger play "Itsy Bitsy Spider," the story of the spider occurs before, during, and after a rainstorm. By combining the simple melody, lyrics, and movements, the song creates a tangible experience with time.

Pitch

Pitch describes the relationships among notes as they go up and down the scale. The pitch of the notes is like the words in a sentence, selected and arranged to communicate an idea. With or without lyrics, the pitch of the notes tell the story of the song.

To understand how pitch facilitates musical storytelling, hum the tune of "Twinkle, Twinkle, Little Star" without the lyrics. Notice how the notes take you up to the sky, then back down to Earth.

Now add movement. As you sing, most likely your facial expressions and body language naturally react to the pitch. The changes in pitch combined with the changes in your body language help the child understand that each note conveys a different idea. In addition, changes in pitch convey the ideas of high and low, which will naturally influence inflection, intonation, and accent in her speech and body language—all great contributors to her language toolbox.

Sing-a-Word Sing-Along

Here's Why
Music is a great tool for sharpening listening skills and understanding the concept of time.

Here's How
The object of this activity is for each child to sing only one word of the song, but to sing the whole song in tempo together. Any song the children know well will work. Have the children sit in a circle and decide who goes first. Take turns going clockwise around the circle.

Child 1: The	Child 1: up
Child 2: itsy	Child 2: the
Child 3: bitsy	Child 3: water
Child 4: spider	Child 4: spout
Child 5: went	And so forth . . .

Once the children get the hang of it, have them reverse direction and sing counterclockwise. Next, add a surprise element. Each time you ring a bell, they must change direction.

Dynamics

Dynamics are the variation in volume (loud and soft) and emphasis (strong/aggressive, soft/sweet, playful/sad or mournful) within the music that express the emotional intent. For instance, the action-packed "Grand Old Duke of York" is a rousing preschool march. But imagine what would happen if we sang a march like a lullaby. It might be funny, but the intent of the song would be lost.

> Dynamics help young children understand the full spectrum of human communication, relationships, and emotions.

Dynamics help young children understand the full spectrum of human communication, relationships, and emotions. Then add movement to the music, and they play out those feelings and relationships physically. By example, when children act out "The Grand Old Duke of York," they march in unison (or at least try to), creating a sense of structure and belonging. They stand straight and proud, marching up and down the imaginary hill, physically experiencing the concepts of up and down. And when the song introduces the idea of "neither up or down," children begin to understand the nuanced concept of in-between.

The Grand Old Duke of York*

The grand old duke of York,
He had 10,000 men.
He marched them up to the top of the hill,
And he marched them down again.

And when they were up they were up.
And when they were down they were down.
And when they were only halfway up,
They were neither up nor down.

Melody

Melody is a sequence of individual notes strung together to a specific beat, rhythm, tempo, and dynamics. This is the tune we hear—the basic recipe of all music.

Music is no random or careless assemblage of parts. All good music—even the simplest children's song—is the product of technical skill and creative eloquence. It fully engages the listener, both cognitively and emotionally. In fact, brain scans of people listening to music show that it stimulates multiple regions of the brain simultaneously, which probably explains why music and lyrics are so memorable.[38] And it's this effect that makes music one of the best teaching tools for young children. You see, when all the

---

*If you're not familiar with this song, type the title into the search box on YouTube and you'll be able to hear it sung.

pieces of a melody come together, it creates a vivid physical, cognitive, and emotional response. And when that happens, music plays a "magic trick" on memory, compressing or "chunking" individual bits of information (such as 26 letters in the ABC song) into a single, easy-to-remember unit.

Harmony

Defined as many different sounds blending into one, harmony plays the role of the musical coordinator, much the way midline development helps us coordinate our movements. And like coordinated movement, when you get it right, it's a rich, compelling, harmonious weave. Get it wrong, and it's a discordant disaster in more ways than one.

Think about what happens when your national anthem is played, or a favorite pop song comes on at a party. Without realizing it, people unite around the music.

For children, it's even more true. The concept of harmony—adding complexity for a richer result—is an early lesson in the intricacies and subtleties of life for the simple reason that life doesn't happen one thing at time.

Consider the art of conversation. In order to communicate with just one other person, you must be able to harmonize your speech with his. That requires knowing when to listen and when to speak, knowing how to relate your ideas to his, and knowing how to respond to his ideas while looking for cues in his responses to you. But little ones, of course, are just beginners. Harmonizing with music is a first step toward learning to manage the tricky waters of social situations.

Intervals

Nineteenth-century composer Claude Debussy is believed to have said, "Music is the space between the notes." That space is called an interval—the difference in pitch between two notes. In other words, intervals are the tiny bridges that take the listener or performer from one idea to the next.

In music, an interval can be the tiny waver in a trilled note or a multi-octave jump in pitch. In speech, an interval is the breath between sentences or a dramatic pause for effect. Movement has intervals, too. Muscles flex and relax depending on the situation. Complex movements require many changes in speed, direction, and force involving many muscles flexing and contracting all at once.

Intervals mark change. They are the spaces—physical and temporal—that allow us to consider and react to what has happened while preparing for what's next. Intervals are the opportunities between ideas to take it all in. And we all need that, especially children.

Family Moves

Print the "Sing-a-Word Sing-Along" Motorvator and the "Music and Movement" handout from the digital file and share them with parents to encourage families to enjoy music and musical play at home.

Lyrics

Even without lyrics, music is a powerful communication tool. With lyrics, music becomes a bilingual experience.

Lyrics reinforce language skills through rhyming and repetition. As we discussed in Chapter 3, repetition is key to embedding information in young minds. Rhyming serves a similar purpose by creating predictable patterns in the language. "Old MacDonald Had a Farm" is a great example. The lyrics rhyme and repeat in each verse, with one small change per verse: the animal and its sound. The combination of music, repetitive language, familiar animals, and fun sound effects is ideal for building comprehension.

Singing and Dancing

At first, many young children struggle to sing and dance simultaneously. That's a signal the child hasn't fully automated the movements required for the dance. As we discussed, when the brain is confronted with two thinking tasks (in this case, lyrics and dance), it has to make a choice. Given the brain's priorities in the early years, chances are dancing will win.

If this happens, have the child focus on dancing while you sing the lyrics. In this way, she will still get the triple benefit of music, lyrics, and movement. Soon enough, you'll find she'll be able to sing and dance with E-I-E-I-O ease.

Now add movement to the music and lyrics and the experience is trilingual! By acting out the words to the song—dancing like a "moo moo" cow or a "quack quack" duck—children not only sing the words, but also *become* the words, all set to a memorable melody that sings in their memory, often for the rest of their lives.

Playing Music

When little ones make music with their own bodies or instruments, they are physicalizing and internalizing the powerful lessons it has to teach, and learning about their auditory world in the process:

- What is sound?
- Where does sound come from?
- What can I do to influence the sound?
- What sounds can I make all by myself?
- What happens if I use different instruments?
- Which sounds do I like and dislike?
- Can I hear the differences in sounds?

Body Percussion

A child's first musical instrument is her own body. Body percussion—clapping, stomping, snapping, and so forth—helps children literally *feel* the music on a deep, personal level. And since no instruments are required, body percussion is available anytime, anywhere.

Of note: For babies who can't yet clap or stomp on their own, gently tap on their arms, legs, or backs to the music. Babies love the feel of your touch, and it will awaken in them the concepts of beat, rhythm, and tempo.

Silly Sound Effects

Kids love making silly sounds. From the classic raspberry *(pfffffffft)* to mouth pops, snorts, burps, and more, kids roar with laughter at these silly discoveries. And while it's easy for adults to chalk it up to "kid stuff," in fact, silly sounds offer a great way for them to discover what their bodies can do.

Mimicking familiar sounds—from *woof* to *vroom* to *pfffffffft*—is a sign that the brain is working hard to distinguish details in sound. As we discussed in Chapter 7, auditory discrimination is essential for building strong listening skills, enunciation, vocabulary acquisition, and eventually for learning phonetics for spelling and writing.

In other words, never underestimate the power of *pfffffffft!*

Music with Everyday Objects

Everyday objects make great musical instruments. A child's first instrument might be a simple rattle. But pretty much anything can create music: cooking pots and wooden spoons, drinking cups, jingling keys, plastic containers, and so on. Anything that allows children to make their own sounds—no matter how noisy—opens up the world of musical possibilities and empowers them to communicate.

Musical Instruments

A wide body of research suggests that learning to play a musical instrument benefits children's development in many important ways.[39] That said, it's important not to push children into formal lessons too early. Many instruments require sophisticated physical capabilities. Trying to play when they don't yet have these capabilities could thwart children's efforts and dampen their enthusiasm for music. Even if a child shows interest and aptitude early, be sure her motor development is ready for this step. Then, when she *is* ready, playing music becomes a powerful learning tool that supports development in a range of areas:

- **Muscle strength (power).** Playing an instrument leads to discoveries such as loud and soft; continuous playing helps with sustainability and perseverance.
- **Mood.** Different instruments help express different emotions.
- **Midlines (coordination).** Many instruments require arms, hands, and fingers moving in different ways at different times, which of course, encourages midline development.
- **Individuality.** Improvisation using different instruments enables a child to make up something that is entirely his own.

And of course, playing an instrument with others helps children to understand important social concepts including:

- **Cooperation.** Playing together teaches cooperation in order to create harmonious sound.
- **Listening (the senses).** Paying attention to the other instruments is as important as hitting the right notes.

- **Rhythm and timing (coordination).** Rhythm and timing are made more complex by the coordination of multiple instruments. Children need to be in sync with the beat and rhythm of the song as well as be able to anticipate when their part starts and stops.

- **Teamwork.** Playing together, children learn how to play their part as part of a larger team effort.

Chapter Summary

- **Music fosters early learning** by helping develop speech, listening skills, patterning and sequencing skills, rhythm, beat, timing, social skills, emotional skills, memory, and physical coordination.

- **Beat** is the master timekeeper, engaging listeners in a common experience.

- **Rhythm** describes the timing of each note in a song. We each have a unique sense of rhythm that influences our style of moving, communicating, and thinking.

- **Tempo** describes the pace and timing of the song (fast or slow) and serves as the listener's guide on the emotional journey of the music. Tempo underpins an innate understanding of order, sequence, and the passage of time.

- **Pitch** tells the story of the song as the notes go up and down, much like words selected and arranged in a sentence to convey an idea.

- **Dynamics** are variations in volume and intensity. They express emotion and offer clues about the overarching message of the music. Dynamics offer children the opportunity to explore feelings.

- **Melody** brings pitch, beat, rhythm, tempo, and dynamics together to create music and make it memorable.

- **Harmony** introduces complexity to the music and mirrors important social skills.

- **Intervals** mark the changes in music. They build anticipation for what's next while giving the listener the time she needs to follow along.

- **Lyrics** multiply the language development value of music for young children.

- **Playing music** offers many benefits to early learning and can be done with the body or with an instrument.

CHAPTER 16

Directionality: The Road to Symbolic Language

Symbolic language—literacy, numeracy, and the arts—are the last forms of communication children adopt, yet the foundations for these all begin long before a child can control a pencil. And once he has that pencil in hand, the next challenge is to know where to go with it.

Now, the cognitive processes for learning to read and write are the subject of many scholarly volumes. We will leave those topics to the experts. Instead, let's examine how early movement and sensory experiences lay the groundwork for schoolwork.

Directionality: Where Is *On*?

The kindergartners wriggled and squiggled, making it hard for the frazzled bus driver to get a head count. "Will everyone please sit down and sit up straight so I can count the children on the bus?"

Little Daniel knew how to help. He jumped off the bus, stood back, and surveyed the roof. Pointing to the top of the bus, Daniel reported to the bus driver that there were no children on the bus.

Was Daniel correct?

Yes, he was, actually. You see, Daniel's definition of the word *on* was things that are found at the top of other things (in this case, the roof of the bus). Which *is* correct. Just not all the time.

> Directionality acts as the brain's tour guide to understanding our three-dimensional world.

OVER TOP ON
UNDER OFF
IN UP AROUND SIDEWAYS
OUT DOWN
NARROW
WIDE
BEFORE BETWEEN BIG
AFTER SMALL
BACK MORE LESS RIGHT
FRONT FAR
BESIDE ACROSS
HIGH NEAR LOW
LEFT THROUGH
BOTTOM

Daniel wasn't experienced with the term "on the bus," which actually describes the state of being "*in* the bus."

Words such as *on*, *top*, and *in* are directional concepts (and idioms of language) that require context to determine their immediate meaning. And context comes from experience. For instance, Daniel seemed confused by *on*. So what would happen if we asked Daniel to put on his coat or to step on a line? Where is *on,* now?

Directionality acts as the brain's tour guide to understanding our three-dimensional world, making it much more than a matter of semantics for young children. Think about it. The bus driver asked the kids to both sit *down* and sit *up*. What do you do with that if you're four?

Success in a formal learning environment (or other social settings) is often dependent on understanding what's being asked of you: "Stand *in* a circle." "Sit *across* from your neighbor." "Read from the *top* of the page." "Sit

What's ON?

Move ON
Walk ON
Run ON
Tug ON
Put ON
Pull ON
Push ON
Pour ON
Take ON
Pile ON
Climb ON
Build ON
Pick ON

Think ON
Get ON
Jump ON
Dump ON
Hop ON
Carry ON
Drive ON
Step ON
Spot ON
Slap ON
Stumble ON
Reflect ON

Grow ON
Live ON
Open ON
Close ON
Stop ON
Start ON
Turn ON
Hold ON
Set ON
Add ON
Work ON
Drag ON
Call ON

Stay ON
Stick ON
Sit ON
Stand ON
Come ON

Bank ON
Rely ON
Land ON
Big ON
Keen ON
Trip ON
Try ON
Tie ON

You're **ON** a roll!

down and sit *up* straight." These directional concepts begin with an understanding of our own, personal orientation—the answer to the question, "Where am I in relation to other things?"

Laying the Groundwork

Orientation and directional reasoning lay the foundations for symbolic language. First, let's look at orientation.

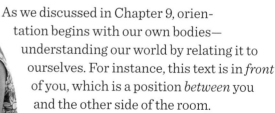

Orientation

As we discussed in Chapter 9, orientation begins with our own bodies—understanding our world by relating it to ourselves. For instance, this text is in *front* of you, which is a position *between* you and the other side of the room.

For a child, his sense of orientation increases dramatically when he begins to move for himself. But it will be a while before he masters the words. That's where everyday conversation comes in. A simple invitation, "Come *over* here and sit *on* the couch *next* to me," plants deep seeds of directional concepts and contexts. But what's most important early on is that the child be actively—personally—engaged in experiencing space. Why? Because spatial orientation begins with the body.

Directional Reasoning

As a child is mastering orientation, he's laying down critical foundations for conceptualizing relationships. Only when a child understands how he relates to his surroundings can he grasp the abstract concept of how things *un*related to him relate to each other. For instance, when playing soccer, a child first learns the ball is in *front* of him when he kicks it—a situation where he uses his own body for orientation. From there, he's ready to grasp that the ball is also in *front* of the goal—the spatial relationship of two things unrelated to himself.

It's hard to imagine how a child doesn't "get" this. But in fact, only when directional reasoning comes into focus will it be possible for him to understand that *front* can be in a lot of different places all at once.

Orientation Begins with the Body

Directional reasoning begins in earnest as the midlines develop, providing a kind of organic geometry necessary to establish a three-dimensional understanding of space. And with that in place, the brain can begin to triangulate the position and orientation of objects in any situation, related or unrelated to the body, along with the language the child needs to describe any circumstance.

Changing Planes

Orientation and directional reasoning also support the ability to transfer information from one location to another, including different planes of orientation. For example, the teacher writes an "A" on the board—a vertical plane—and asks the students to copy it onto their paper—a horizontal plane. Moving that information from one plane to another might seem simple, but it is actually an intricate piece of cognition. The brain must be able to transfer the information presented to it vertically (the board on the wall), process it, hold it in working memory, and then reinterpret it onto a horizontal plane (the paper on a table or the floor) with accuracy and without losing meaning (comprehension). And if things are going really well, not only will the accuracy remain intact, but the meaning will also connect with prior knowledge ("apple") to inspire new ideas and new thinking.

This simple act of moving information from one location to another presents opportunities for deeper understanding and comprehension, but it also opens up opportunities for misinterpretation and lost meaning if a child doesn't have a strong foundation in interpreting, managing, and processing his world in 3-D.

Motorvator

In and Out

Here's Why
Experiencing directional words using your own body is the starting point for understanding that words can mean different things in different contexts.

Here's How
Give each child a floor tile, a hoop, a rope, or anything else that creates a defined space on the floor. Now challenge the children to put parts of their body in the space and leave the rest of their body out of the space. For instance:

- Can you put both hands *in* the space, but leave the rest of your body *out* of the space?

- Can you put one knee *in* the space and leave the rest of your body *out* of the space?

- Can you put your bottom *in* the space and leave nothing *outside* of the space?

Gill's Notebook

Learning Left and Right

Almost by osmosis, and with no formal training, young children acquire simultaneous command of multiple directional concepts. Through interacting with their world and hearing words to describe it, they piece things together pretty well all by themselves. And that's remarkable, because directional reasoning is pretty tricky stuff.

Learning left from right would be a snap if everyone's left were your left and everyone's right were your right. But of course, that's not always the case. Left and right depend on which way you're facing (orientation) in relation to others (directional reasoning). Ask two children to face each other and raise their right hand. *Right* is not on the same side. "My right" and "your right" are two different things. Yet both are right (and correct) . . . for now. Have those same two children stand in front of the mirror and raise their right hand, and *right* is now on the same side. "My right is your right."

Let's face it. That's just plain confusing.

The concepts of left and right actually require advanced directional reasoning. That's probably why they take a long time (or a lifetime) to master. So here's how I handled teaching left and right when I was an early childhood teacher:

For the first 10-week term of the school year, I would focus on the concept of *left*. When a child earned a sticker, I put it on his left hand or foot. When children wanted to participate or ask a question, I had them raise their left hand. I had them write their names on the left side of their paper, stand to the left of me, jump to the left, shake hands with their left hand, and so on.

And I constantly reinforced the concept with the word. "I'm putting this sticker on your *left* hand. You did a good job of writing your name on the *left* side of your paper." In other words, I employed the principle: Experience + Language = Understanding.

> Young children acquire simultaneous command of multiple directional concepts through interacting with their world and hearing words to describe it.

And when the kids returned from vacation for the next term, we'd do the same, only on the right.

Over time, and with lots of practice, left and right became firm, fixed concepts. And with those foundations, the children were then ready to apply left and right to other things, such as putting their left shoe on their left foot.

Developing Symbolic Language

Orientation and directional reasoning underpin every aspect of formal learning, including the traditional three Rs. Let's take them one at a time.

Mathematics: From 3-D to Numeracy

Before children can grasp 1 + 1 = 2, they must understand the simple concepts of *more* and *less*. Until they understand that, putting two things together to make something bigger won't make any sense.

The following is a list of directional concepts in relation to mathematical constructs. Of course, many math concepts will apply to much of this list, but for this demonstration, we're showing only one here. Note how the physical experiences children are gathering in the early years are described by mathematical concepts:

- Before and after: counting
- More and less: addition, subtraction, multiplication, and division
- Big and small: sequencing
- Up and down: greater than and less than
- Beside and between: relationships
- High and low: comparisons
- Near and far: estimation and prediction
- Over and under: measurement
- Left and right: horizontal

- Top and bottom: vertical
- On and off: positive and negative
- In and out: sets and subsets
- Back and front: dimension
- Through and around: diameter and circumference
- Across and sideways: angles
- Narrow and wide: minimum and maximum
- Middle: midpoint and half
- Partway: fractions and percentages

Writing: Forming Letters

Children lacking experience with directionality may struggle with writing. For instance, to explain how to write the lowercase letter "p," a teacher may say, "Draw a line *down,* then *up,* then *around,*" using three directional concepts. The teacher might also say that the straight line extends *below* the baseline before coming back *up* and that the loop needs to go *around* to the *right*. Got it? Okay. Now when you write the letter "b," draw the line *down-up-around,* only this time, the line stays *above* the baseline. Lowercase "q" is a *backward* "p," and the letter "a" is a "q" whose line doesn't dip *down below* the baseline.

Writing the letter "p"

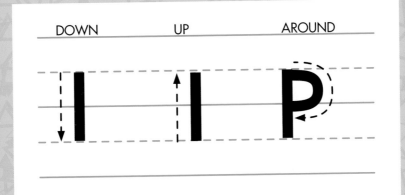

DOWN   UP   AROUND

See the challenge?

Now of course, the teacher will also use visual cues, drawing the letters on the board or on the child's paper. This may help the child write one letter properly. But if the child still doesn't fully grasp these directional concepts, he'll be starting from scratch when he gets to the next letter in the alphabet.

Reading: Concepts of Print

Before a child can read successfully, he needs to master the mechanics of reading. These mechanics are called concepts of print, and directional reasoning underpins them all.

- Print *begins* and *ends* in different places.
- Books have a *front* and *back*.
- Pages turn in a specific direction—to the *left* for some languages and to the *right* for other languages.
- Print is always read in the same direction—*left* to *right* or *right* to *left*, and *top* to *bottom* or *bottom* to *top*, depending on the language.
- At the *end* of the line, the print skips *down* (or *across*) a line and starts again.
- When read aloud, each word *on* the page represents a spoken word.
- One side of a two-page spread is read *before* the other (the *left* side for some languages and the *right* side for others).

- Print is more than letters. It also contains punctuation marks and sometimes numbers.
- In Western languages, letters make up words, words make up sentences, sentences make up paragraphs, and paragraphs make up chapters or stories.

Family Moves

Print the "In and Out" Motorvator and "Gill's Notebook: Learning Left and Right" from the digital file and share them with parents.

In so many ways, reading, writing, mathematics, and all the other learning children encounter in school and in life start in the physical world of movement. When you look underneath the abstractions of academics and relate them back to children's natural, kinetic state, now you're speaking to them in their native tongue.

Chapter Summary

- **Symbolic language:** Symbols are the last form of language children adopt, but their foundations begin in early childhood.
- **Directional language** can have many different meanings depending on the context. Directional language can be confusing, yet is essential for navigating our physical, cognitive, and social world.
- **Directional reasoning** is the understanding of how two objects relate to each other in space.
- **Directional reasoning underpins academic skills** such as mathematics, writing, and reading.

PART 4

A Learning Child

CHAPTER 17

Kinetic Development: A Balancing Act

///

To this point in our story, we've explored the raw ingredients that unlock movement and prepare the brain for everything it needs to do. So now comes the next big question: how can we be sure each child is getting the kind of movement she needs in today's containerized world?

One-Size-Fits-All Fits No Child at All

Before we go any further, let's dispense with the notion that any one-size-fits-all approach is going to fit each child's unique needs. And the reason is simple: no two children are alike. Genetic makeup, personality, disposition, environment, nutrition, experience, and likely dozens of other factors contribute to human individuality. But more, kids are growing and changing all the time, and so are their needs.

As we've said, milestone timelines can be misleading—even frightening—if held up as mandates rather than broad guidelines. After all, some children walk at 8 months, others at 16 months. Some children can catch a ball when they're two years old, while some four-year-olds still can't. Nevertheless, comparing children by chronological age persists.

Given all the "moving parts" in the early years, a child's age is perhaps the most misleading variable to consider in assessing a child's movement needs. Instead, we prefer to be guided by something that's simple and easy-to-see: What can the child *do*?

The Kinetic Scale

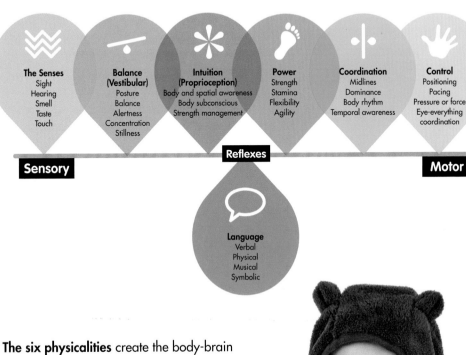

The Senses	Balance (Vestibular)	Intuition (Proprioception)	Power	Coordination	Control
Sight	Posture	Body and spatial awareness	Strength	Midlines	Positioning
Hearing	Balance	Body subconscious	Stamina	Dominance	Pacing
Smell	Alertness	Strength management	Flexibility	Body rhythm	Pressure or force
Taste	Concentration		Agility	Temporal awareness	Eye-everything coordination
Touch	Stillness				

Sensory   Reflexes   **Motor**

Language
Verbal
Physical
Musical
Symbolic

The six physicalities create the body-brain relationship that wires the brain for everything else. Three sensory tools and three motor tools strike the right balance for optimal development.

Primitive and postural reflexes underpin and enable all early movement.

Language transforms experience into understanding by translating the concrete into the conceptual.

The Journey of Can-Do

Turning back to "The Evolution of Independent Movement" (see Chapter 4, page 33), we identified many of the observable, developmental changes in young children as they move through the early years, all marked by increasing capabilities—or "can-dos"—children acquire along the way. And while the exact progression of these can-dos may vary a little or a lot from child to child, in nature's wisdom there is an orderly and cumulative sequence of events that occurs broadly across six stages of movement development:

Snugglers (birth to rolling over). The snugglers stage spans the time infants move from nonmobile, full dependence on others to the first glimmers of **intentional, self-directed movement.**

Squigglers (rocking, crawling, sitting up). Children discover **mobility independence** throughout this period, unlocking a wide range of early investigative explorations—the seeds of curiosity.

Scampers (pulling up to walking). The final evolutionary steps from prone to upright occur in this period, bringing children to steady-on-their-feet vertical—and along with it to an explosive period of **new perspectives** and capabilities all now within reach.

Stompers (running and jumping). Full of experimental energy, a larger sense of **confidence** emerges as children test the limits of what their bodies can do. Speed, strength, and daring define this period, as stompers redefine what's possible and quite literally learn to defy gravity.

Scooters (hopping and climbing). Ever more complex and sophisticated whole-body **coordination** is emerging, sparking huge advancements in physical, cognitive, social, emotional, and communicative capabilities.

Skedaddlers (skipping, leaping, cooperative games, and dance). As the body and brain now become one, **self-control** comes easier.

Tilting the Scale

Now that we know how children's can-dos unfold, we're ready to explore how the Kinetic Scale enables this progression. Over the next few pages, note how the Kinetic Scale rebalances the physicalities children need as they progress through each of the can-do stages of early childhood movement. You'll see that for very young children, the Kinetic Scale tilts toward the sensory tools—the senses, balance, and intuition. As the child grows, the Kinetic Scale tilts toward the motor tools—power, coordination, and control.

> The Kinetic Scale rebalances the physicalities children need as they progress through each of the can-do stages of early childhood movement.

Please note, the operative word here is *tilt*. This is *not* an on/off switch. Nor is the Kinetic Scale a checklist. At every stage of development, reflexes, physicalities, and language are all at play helping to develop the whole child as nature intended. The Kinetic Scale simply adjusts the balance and proportion of these elements as the child grows. To express this balancing act, you'll note that the can-do stages overlap.

As we've said, the Kinetic Scale is guided by what the child can do, not by her age. But for clarity, we have indicated approximate ages when these stages generally occur. For instance, we've identified the squiggler stage at approximately 6–14 months, which overlaps with the scamper stage at 9–24 months.

The Kinetic Scale is only a tool. It's meant to help you create a balanced movement diet that is developmentally appropriate and tailored to each child. Be guided by this, but more importantly, be guided by the child. What she's doing with her body tells you what her brain is trying to figure out. That is nature's course, and working "with the grain" of nature is the best course you can take.

The Journey of Can-Do

Prenatal
primitive reflexes:
involuntary movement

Snugglers

Primitive reflexes in
place at birth

Head control:
first attempts

Awakening of senses with touch,
massage, and skin-to-skin contact

Hand and foot
recognition

Pincer grip

Crawling

Changing hands

Releasing grasp
voluntarily

Sitting
independently

Scampers

Navigating small
spaces

Pulling up
to stand

Cruising

Marching

Balancing on one foot

Handedness:
early signs

Scooters

Temporal
awareness

Hopping

Climbing in opposition

Galloping

Midlines developing

Hand and foot
dominance developing

Skedaddlers

Hip tips:
attempting to roll over

Sensory discoveries:
especially mouth

Rolling over onto
tummy

Pushing up from
tummy

Squigglers

Postural reflexes
emerging

Rocking

Up on all fours

Commando crawling

Mouthing things

Grasping

Studying facial
expressions

Bobbing up and
down, aided

Standing, unaided

Climbing up
furniture or stairs

Eye-hand
coordination:
self-feeding

Walking
unaided

Stompers

Manipulative skills
emerging

Jumping forward
on two feet

Upper body
strength
developing

Jumping on
two feet

Bobbing up and
down, unaided

Running

Leaping from standing

Crossing the midline

Leaping from running

Skipping

Automated coordinated
movement

Snugglers

Infants learn about the world largely through ingesting sensory information. Providing snugglers with a gentle, rich, and steady diet of **sensory** experiences gives them the jump start they need.

Balance underpins all current and future movement and aids the development of the other sensory tools. Rocking and gently tipping snugglers stimulates the vestibular system and gives them an early sense of orientation. These movements also soothe and comfort snugglers, because they mimic the sensations of the womb.

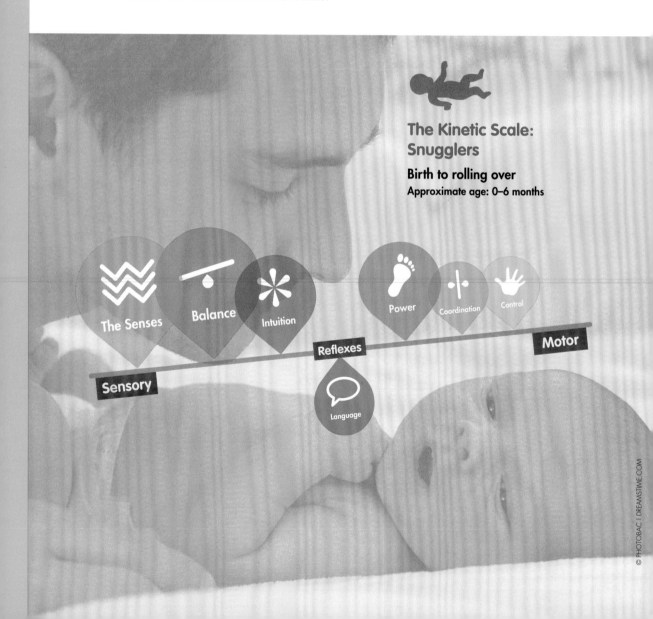

The Kinetic Scale: Snugglers

Birth to rolling over
Approximate age: 0–6 months

The Senses · Balance · Intuition · Power · Coordination · Control · Reflexes · Motor · Sensory · Language

Squigglers

Squigglers continue to understand their world principally through their **senses**. They are sharpening their sight and hearing, exploring more with their mouths, and are interested in textures and scents. Continued sensory experiences—especially multisensory ones—should be part of their daily play.

Squigglers can now roll over at will—the first self-directed **vestibular activity**. As they grow through this stage, they enjoy increasing—yet still gentle—levels of vestibular stimulation, such as "airplane rides" on an adult's knees or gentle, slow, supported tipping upside down.

Helping the child explore her body in space is important during this stage, as both **body and spatial awareness** serve as essential tools for developing independent movement.

The Kinetic Scale: Squigglers

Rocking, crawling, and sitting
Approximate age: 6–14 months

The Senses Balance Intuition Power Coordination Control

Sensory   Reflexes   Motor

Language

Scampers

On their feet and ready to go, scampers have so much more to explore and take in. The **senses** now act even more as the fuel for movement, and movement the fuel for the senses. Encourage **self-directed exploration** by providing a sensory-rich environment that includes both familiar favorites and new experiences.

Independent movement (from crawling to walking) requires **dynamic equilibrium**. That means scampers need to experiment with different orientations that help the brain recognize and adjust its internal sense of balance.

The world feels different when you stand up. And it requires a whole new set of **intuition** tools. Scampers need lots of time exploring space and objects like play tunnels, slides, and even cardboard boxes, which give children a sense of how they fit.

Scampers are just beginning to learn their own **strength**. They need to test their ability to move their own bodies and the things they encounter in their world, including toys, furniture, pets, parents, and teachers! And scampers have seemingly inexhaustible energy as they discover the power of their own will.

The Kinetic Scale: Scampers

Pulling up to walking
Approximate age: 9–24 months

The Senses · Balance · Intuition · Power · Coordination · Control

Sensory · Reflexes · Motor

Language

Stompers

Pushing boundaries is key for stompers. They're not ready for delicate, graceful movement, but they are picking up **speed and endurance**. High-energy activities and plenty of room to move builds stompers' self-confidence, strength, and ability to make big, whole-body movements.

Stompers need more advanced **coordination** to carry out all they want to do with their bodies. This need may lead to some frustration, as they are only beginning to refine lateral and homolateral movements. Give stompers opportunities to make whole-body movements and lots of room to run, jump, and be goofy.

The Kinetic Scale: Stompers

Running and jumping
Approximate age: 20 months–3½ years

The Senses | Balance | Intuition | Power | Coordination | Control

Sensory | Reflexes | Motor

Language

Scooters

Big, whole-body movements are the jet fuel for this stage, building **power** in the muscles to climb ever-more-challenging movement mountains.

Scooters are gaining more coordinated control over their **midlines**, so they can now isolate the movements of different body parts. More challenging movement experiences foster advancements such as learning to ride a tricycle, playing simple throw-and-catch games, and tackling the monkey bars.

Because scooters have more strength, endurance, patience, and determination to try things more than once, controlling their movement is getting easier.

**The Kinetic Scale:
Scooters**

Hopping and climbing
Approximate age: 3–4 years

The Senses • Balance • Intuition • Power • Coordination • Control

Sensory • Reflexes • Motor

Language

Skedaddlers

The **three motor physicalities** are in full focus for skedaddlers, who are nearing the finish line of movement development and achieving full automaticity.

Skedaddlers engage in more **imaginative**, involved role play and make-believe with and without playmates, as well as playground games with simple rules and reaching for the next rung of the monkey bars. These are all signs of a child who's in command of her body while making big leaps in **independent thinking.**

The Kinetic Scale: Skedaddlers

Skipping, leaping, cooperative games, and dance
Approximate age: 4 years and older

The Senses

Balance

Intuition

Sensory

Reflexes

Language

Power

Coordination

Control

Motor

Move-to-Learn Activities Guide

In the following chapters, we'll explain in detail how to use the Kinetic Scale to help you plan movement activities. But for a snapshot of how the Kinetic Scale translates into real-life play, take a peek at the Move-to-Learn Activities Guide.

Note how these classic play patterns all have a role in developing the full range of physicalities. Of course, many of these play activities serve multiple

The Kinetic Scale: Move-to-Learn Activities Guide

The Senses
Sight
Hearing
Smell
Taste
Touch

Sights
Sounds
Smells
Tastes
Textures
Massage
Eye fitness
Object permanence
Sorting
Sequencing
Patterning

Music and movement

**Balance
(Vestibular)**
Posture
Balance
Alertness
Concentration
Stillness

Rolling
Spinning
Swinging
Rocking
Balancing
Turning upside down

**Intuition
(Proprioception)**
Body and spatial awareness
Body subconscious
Strength management

Tunneling
Inclines
Body awareness
Pushing and pulling
Lifting and carrying

developmental purposes. A great example is movement and music, which serves all six physicalities.

Of note: When planning movement activities for young children, be sure to first understand and respect their current can-dos. Always start there. Then gently encourage them to take the next step. In other words, approach movement the way kids do, *one step at a time.* And remember, always follow the child's lead.

Power
Strength
Stamina
Flexibility
Agility

Crawling
Walking
Running
Jumping
Hopping
Skipping
Climbing
Tumbling
Stretching
Wheels play

Coordination
Midlines
Dominance
Body rhythm
Temporal awareness

Crawling
Hopping
Climbing
Marching
Skipping
Bicycling
Ball play
Stepping-stones

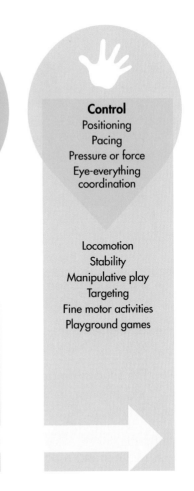

Control
Positioning
Pacing
Pressure or force
Eye-everything
coordination

Locomotion
Stability
Manipulative play
Targeting
Fine motor activities
Playground games

Chapter Summary

- **Well-balanced physical diet:** Just as children need a well-balanced diet of food, they also need a well-balanced physical diet for whole-body and whole-brain development.

- **Tilting the scale:** Children's physical movement needs change as they grow. For young children, the scale tilts toward sensory stimulation. As they grow, the scale tilts toward motor development. But all children, at all stages, need experiences on both sides of the scale.

- **Individualization:** No two children develop in the same way or on the same timetable.

- **Assessment:** The best way to assess a child's physical development is looking at what she can do.

- **The six can-do developmental stages** are snugglers (birth to rolling over), squigglers (rocking, crawling, and sitting up), scampers (pulling up to walking), stompers (running and jumping), scooters (hopping and climbing), and skedaddlers (skipping, leaping, cooperative games, and dance).

- **Move-to-learn activities:** The things kids love to do benefit them developmentally, so by all means, go play!

CHAPTER 18

Creating a Kinetic Classroom

//

When we embrace nature's move-to-learn plan, leaning into the wiggles and giggles rather than trying to contain them, we open up more opportunities for deep, meaningful, and lasting learning. This doesn't mean radically changing the lesson plan. But it does mean teaching to the "kinetic grain" of young children. Because for kids, learning never sits still.

Building the Lesson Plan: The Six Physicalities of Learning

Using the Kinetic Scale as our guide, we can integrate movement and learning to create a more holistic learning environment for young children. To do that, let's examine teaching practices against the landscape of the six physicalities.

The senses help children understand concepts more deeply. Information drawn from many sources provides a more vibrant and meaningful picture. Make all learning multisensory. After all, lime green looks green against a field of yellow. But lime green looks yellow against a field of green.

Balance teaches children to take nothing at face value. How people see things depends on their angle—physical, emotional, or otherwise. Make all learning multiperspective. A green leaf looks different from the ground than from up in the tree.

Intuition respects the individuality of the child. A child is the center of his own universe, and all learning begins within him. Make all learning

> Learning never sits still.

> Make all learning multisensory. Make all learning multiperspective. Make all learning personal. Make all learning nonjudgmental. Make all learning challenging. Make all learning boundless.

personal. Start with the known and work toward the unknown—from red apples to green apples.

Power values effort. All effort yields advancement in learning, even if a child doesn't achieve a goal in the allotted time or using a conventional method. Make all learning nonjudgmental. Celebrate pink frogs.

Coordination unlocks wonder. Start with one piece of the puzzle, then add another and another to create bigger and bigger ideas. Make all learning challenging. Build complexity. Yellow is yellow. Blue is blue. But together they make green.

Control puts the learner in charge of the learning. The freedom to adapt ideas is the basis of all inspiration. Make all learning boundless—from green grass to grass stains.

That said, anyone responsible for young children will tell you, it's not quite as easy as laying out a lesson plan and having everything go according to schedule. Little ones can trip over the simplest of tasks sometimes, leaving adults scratching their heads. And that's where understanding the relationship between movement and learning can help. In so many ways, movement is the language children speak most fluently, so learning to "read the moves" gets the grown-ups and the children on the same wavelength.

Reading the Moves

Have you ever had any of these children in your classroom (or living under your own roof)?

The Eye Rubber might not be ready to read on his own. Eye muscles need strength and fitness for the highly refined movements of reading. A child who rubs his eyes, blinks a lot, looks away from the page, or avoids reading altogether may need more time to develop his eye fitness before tackling independent reading. (See Chapter 7.)

The Ear Muffer covers his ears when the room is noisy. He may be struggling to make sense of the sounds, and when he can't, he tries to block them all out. He may need more quiet space in order to concentrate and more participation in activities that develop his auditory figure ground. (See Chapter 7.)

The Clean Freak avoids messy play. You can see "Yuck!" written all over his face. Patient, gentle exposure to a variety of tactile stimulation is in order. (See Chapter 7.) But always follow the child's lead.

The Fidgeter can't sit still. He's moving and wiggling all the time. You often find him at the back of the pack, where there's more room to move. Fidgeting isn't necessarily a sign of disinterest. In fact, it may well be a sign he's trying to concentrate (or he might just need to go to the bathroom!). (See Chapter 8.)

The Spinner loves to make himself dizzy by spinning around on his own, on the swing set, or any other way that lets him whirl around. This is not necessarily a sign of hyperactivity, but instead, an indication his brain craves vestibular stimulation. Slowing down the spinning will likely satisfy that craving. (See Chapter 8.)

The Chair Tipper, despite a hundred admonitions to be careful, may not be the daredevil he seems. Instead, he probably just needs the sensation of rocking. Vestibular stimulation is in order. (See Chapter 8.)

The Kid Who Goes Bump into the furniture and his friends isn't necessarily clumsy or unobservant. He just may not understand where his body begins and ends. Body awareness activities are probably a good idea. (See Chapter 9.)

The Toucher touches everything— absolutely everyone and everything. He's up close and leaning right into you. But that doesn't necessarily mean he's grabby or needy. More likely, he feels adrift without grounding himself through physical closeness or contact. He probably needs to develop more spatial awareness through fitting into things in his environment. (See Chapter 9.)

The Pencil Breaker breaks the lead in his pencil all the time. He may also be the kid who pushes or pulls too hard on the playground. This child seems aggressive, but he simply may not know his own strength. He might need experience with delicate tasks that require adapting and controlling his muscles, such as pouring water without spilling it. (See Chapters 9 and 13.)

The Clumper runs all his words and letters together when he's first learning to write. This is partly due to inexperience, of course, but it's also a sign that he needs more physical experiences moving his body in, out, over, under, through, and around different kinds of space. (See Chapter 9.)

The Slumper struggles to sit up straight for long periods of time. He looks bored, but he may just be tired. Good posture depends on core muscle strength. More whole-body movement—especially games and activities that challenge the core muscles—is probably a good idea. (See Chapter 11.)

The Jumper flits from activity to activity. It might look like he can't focus or lacks determination. But in early childhood, it's more likely that he switches gears a lot because his muscles lack stamina. (See Chapter 11.)

The Quitter asks if it's time to go home at 10:00 a.m. When this happens regularly, there's probably a physical reason for it. Chances are he's tired—not necessarily from lack of sleep, but from lack of physical readiness. (See Chapter 11.)

The Hand Swapper changes hands when he's drawing or writing across a page. He's not doing this for fun, necessarily (although it is fun to try). Likely he's doing it because he has to. This is a

© JOSE MANUEL GELPI DIAZ | DREAMSTIME.COM

classic signal his midlines still need work which means his hand dominance isn't fully in place yet. Some time doing cross-patterning activities will do him good. (See Chapter 12.)

The Letter Reverser writes his letters backward sometimes. This common mistake is probably not a matter of misunderstanding the letterforms. It may simply be a matter of immature midlines which can result in misinterpreting the direction and order of the shapes that make up the letters. (See Chapter 12.)

The Pretzel contorts his body to do simple tasks like writing his name. When children strike unnatural positions, they're likely working around or avoiding the midlines. Homolateral activities may help straighten out those pretzels. (See Chapter 12.)

The Fist struggles with proper pencil grip. His hand, arm, and shoulder muscles likely aren't strong enough, and he's adjusting his hand to the most comfortable position he can find. Chances are, he needs more time on the monkey bars and doing other activities that build strength in the upper body, hands, and fingers. (See Chapter 13.)

The Speed Demon has only one speed: fast. When asked to slow down, he can't. Chances are, he's struggling with modifying movements and hasn't yet mastered full control of his muscles. Challenge the speed demon to do things slowly. Try staging an entire "slow day" and see how long everyone lasts! (See Chapter 13.)

The Last Kid Picked for the Team is usually the one his peers see as the worst player in the group. Most team sports (soccer, T-ball, basketball, and so on) require manipulative skills. If a child struggles in this area, use bubbles, feathers, and other objects that move slowly so his eyes, hands, and feet have more time to work together. (See Chapter 13.)

Learning to read children's moves makes it easier to use those moves for learning. But how do you create an environment conducive to learning when children are so full of fidgeting, slumping, bumping, and the like?

Creating a Move-to-Learn Space

To launch themselves into learning and life, little ones need an environment with a physical design and emotional energy that makes the most of their move-to-learn nature. Let's explore principles we can apply in childcare facilities, in classrooms, in outdoor play spaces, at home, or anywhere else little ones are moving and learning. For this discussion, we'll use an imaginary preschool classroom called the Can-Do Room as our example.

The Magic Door

First impressions last, so they'd better be good—even magical. That's why the Can-Do Room begins at the Magic Door. The Magic Door is a transformative experience not from the hallway into the classroom but from an ordinary day into an extraordinary adventure. It's a kid-logical, giggle-inducing, wow-producing field trip across the threshold into a place where the imagination and learning will fly!

A welcome that says "This is a special place just for you" makes children feel at home, part of the community, and ready for whatever may unfold. And all it takes to create a Magic Door is knowing what kids already love and greeting them at the door with exactly that: movement!

Motorvator

The Magic Door: Make a Magical Entrance Every Day

Making a Magic Door doesn't take much time, material, or effort. Here are 50 Kinetic Scale–based ideas to help you create a magical start to each day at school, at home, or any other place you want to make inviting for children. And of course, if it suits your environment, you can use the Magic Door for end-of-day rituals, too.

Sensational Beginnings

- Ring a bell or honk a horn as you enter.

- Sing a song as you step in.

- Use bubble wrap as a welcome mat.

- Shout at the door, "Yahoo, it's time for school!"

- Give each child a musical instrument as he enters. Whenever another child enters, have the whole band play a welcome song.

- Have the kids line up and high-five the others as they come in.

- Hang crepe paper streamers in the doorway.

- String twinkle lights around the door frame.

- Tape festive balloons around the door.

- Cover the door with plastic wrap or bubble wrap. Cut a slit and have the children wiggle through it.

- Make paper plate masks one day. Have the children enter the next day wearing their masks. Challenge the children to guess the identity of each new arrival.

- Play a matching game. Put a series of pictures on the door. Have each child match a pair of pictures before he can enter.

- Offer a fortune cookie. Break it open and find a surprise that leads to the day's learning.

Balancing Acts

- Spin like a top.

- Roll like a pencil.

- Somersault.

- Put a rope on the floor and have the kids jump over it or walk along it.

- Have parents carry the children through the door—upside down!

- Set up a trail of pebbles or paper spots that start outside the door and work their way in and around the classroom.

- Place paper stepping stones along the floor. Mark them with letters, numbers, shapes, or colors and have the children follow the path.

- Set up a Twister-style entrance. Place colored spots on the floor labeled "right foot red," "right hand green," and so on.

- Do the dino stomp! Hide plastic dinosaurs around the classroom. Place paper dinosaur tracks leading from the door and have the kids hunt for dinos.

- Have the kids pretend to be pirates walking the plank through the door.

Intuitive Starts

- Set up a play tunnel to crawl through.

- Set up some climbing blocks to climb over.

- Set up a small plastic slide and have the kids slide into class.

- Shoot a basket from the door into the classroom.

- Make a maze. Have the children construct a maze they can use the next day to crawl through.

Power Plays

- Do the crab walk.

- Wiggle like inchworms.

- Jump like frogs.

- Place a bar across the door and limbo under it.

- Sit down and bum-shuffle into class.

- Have parents lift the children's feet and play wheelbarrows through the door.

- Leapfrog over classmates—or the teacher—to enter.

Coordinated Moves

- March.

- Hop.

- Play hopscotch.

- Dance to music.

- Set up hoops and have the children jump in them.

- Bounce a ball as you cross the threshold.

Control Factors

- Walk on tiptoe.

- Walk backward.

- Walk pigeon-toed.

- Walk heel-to-toe.

- Hang a big piece of paper at the door and have each child sign his name as he comes in.

- At the end of each day, tell the children a special password or door knock to remember to enter the next day.

- Have the kids make a cardboard road barrier. Assign two children to manage the door and lift the gate as the others arrive.

- Cover the door with pictures of different animals. Have each child pick an animal and move through the door as that animal. The others guess which animal he is.

- Make a special play key for the door that the children will use the next day to enter.

And once the kids get the idea, encourage them to discuss and decide as a group what they'd like the Magic Door to be so that they can be magic makers, too! Rocket ship, anyone?

Kid's-Eye View

Once we've crossed the threshold, it's clear the Can-Do Room is not for adults. It's for little ones. And to see it for what it really means to them, we have to get down to kid level. To give you a sense of this, if you can, get down on the floor and look around at the space you're in right now. Ask yourself:

- How much play space do I have? What obstacles are in my path?
- Can I run here? Tumble? Jump? Dance? Wiggle?
- Do I feel safe here? Do I feel happy? Am I excited? Enchanted? Intrigued?
- What's interesting in this space? What's within my reach? What's out of my reach?
- If I could design this space, what would I do differently?

Understanding how a child see things changes our perspective and probably our choices for designing the environment. And of course, the most important thing in the room is room for all those elbows and knees going every which way.

Room to Move

Traditionally, when adults picture a classroom they envision rows of desks and chairs with children sitting still and listening carefully. But of course, that's not how young children learn best. So, here in the Can-Do Room, children move and explore, which necessitates a very different kind of space.

On the first day of school in the Can-Do Room, the space is wide open and ready for anything. The essentials are there, of course: the teacher's desk, a materials cupboard, cubbies for the children's belongings, a writing board on the wall, and a big mat for circle time. There's a shelf for everyone's favorite books, and a toy box to explore. But that's it. No desks, no chairs, no tables. Not yet, anyway.

The Importance of the Floor

A child's natural learning environment is the floor for two simple reasons. It's easy to get to, and you can't fall off.

The floor offers not only room to move but also physical choices that make the learning feel right to a child's body. He can sit cross-legged, lie on his belly, crouch, stand, roll around, or whatever suits him and the topic. Without physical obstacles in his way (like a desk or table and chair) he can simply drop to the floor and dig right into the learning.

Co-Creating the Can-Do Classroom

Open space also presents children with the opportunity to co-create their environment.

During the first few weeks, as the Can-Do Room teacher introduces new learning activities the children can explore them anywhere they want within the room. Sometimes they use the big open space. Sometimes they sit by the window. And sometimes they form small groups in different parts of the room.

As time goes by, an organic flow begins to emerge. And it comes largely from the children themselves. They know which parts of the room are best for different activities and create learning centers all on their own. Each child discovers his own space for time alone or with friends. Furniture may be brought in for certain activities, but the children choose when and whether to use it. And they'll create stations around the periphery as needed. For instance, after several class cleanups of messy play, the children might vote to isolate messy play in one corner of the room.

Indoors, Outdoors, Everywhere

There are some adults who hold preconceived notions that indoors is for learning, and outdoors is for play. But that's not how we see things in the Can-Do Room. The room has walls, just like any classroom, but those walls are never boundaries for moving, playing, and learning.

Easy access to the outdoors is essential for creating the biggest possible learning environment. With even more room to move, learning intensifies outdoors as children challenge their bodies in new and different ways.

And the teacher is right there to monitor and narrate the monkeyshines, encouraging and guiding the movement to enhance the learning. For example, as we discussed in Chapter 16, the playground is an ideal place to explore directional concepts. So today, we're focused on the word *under*. The teacher challenges the children to discover all the ways they can move *under* things. This focuses their physical energy while creating tangible experiences that will one day become transferable abstract concepts.

And of course, when they head back inside, they bring *under* with them— under the tables, under the chairs, under each other, under the teacher—under, under, everywhere!

With so much moving going on in the Can-Do Room, adults naturally worry about safety. So in the next chapter, we'll talk about how to keep children safe as they follow their natural need to move.

Gill's Notebook

Learning on the Move

I often get this question: "I understand how important movement is. But what if it's raining outside?"

Some adults have adopted the notion that movement is an outdoor activity and that "real" learning only happens indoors.

To help parents and teachers get beyond this indoor/outdoor bias, I suggest trying Motorvators. You've already seen these sprinkled throughout the book. They're quick movement "snacks" for use anytime, anywhere throughout the day, and yes, indoors or out. Motorvators are great for transitions or just shaking things up a bit and providing some "motorvation" for kids and grown-ups alike.

Start by introducing one Motorvator at a time and sticking with it for a day or more. Multiple chances to practice give children time to develop confidence with the activity. Once children have mastered it, they often begin to improvise. When that happens, it's probably time to try another Motorvator. Here are 10 quick Motorvators to get you started.

Bunny Hopping

Two-footed jumping is an important prerequisite for more advanced physical skills, such as hopping on one foot or leaping forward. Two-footed jumping develops strong leg muscles and physical confidence. And of course, it's a chance to defy gravity right in the middle of the day!

Caterpillar Creeping

Start by having the children get on all fours. Have them walk their hands out in front of them, leaving their knees in place. Then have them walk their knees toward their hands. This is a terrific activity for building coordination, because it moves one part of the body while the other stays still. It's tricky at first, so give the children time to practice. If you keep at it, by the end of the day most kids should have it down!

Seal Crawling

Have the children lie on their tummies and wriggle their way across the room without using their arms or legs. You want them to use their core muscles—and their funny bones. And don't forget to bark like a seal!

Crab Walking

Start in a sitting position on the floor. Have the children lean back on their hands and lift their bottoms, supporting their bodies on their hands and feet. Have them walk forward (or backward for more advanced play). This is a tough one for children lacking upper-body strength, which is critical for school-day stamina, so watch to see if anyone tires easily. They may need more time building their strength.

Leapfrogging

For this activity, organize the children in groups of two to four and have them leapfrog over one another to get from place to place throughout the day. This activity not only provides a quick high-energy burst, it also requires teamwork. Who goes first is usually the first thing they need to work out. Try not to step in unless negotiations get confused or heated.

Masking Tape Maze

Run masking tape in different directions all over the floor to create different lines and shapes for all kinds of learning activities. As a quick Motorvator, have the children transition from one activity to the next by walking on the lines. When they get good at that, have them try walking heel-to-toe on the lines. For even more challenge, have them try walking backward on the lines.

Spot the Spots

Cut out different-colored spots and tape them around the room—on the floor, the walls, the furniture, and so on. When it's transition time, call out a color and have the children make their way from spot to spot, using that color only, to get where they're going.

Beanbag Balance

Give each child a beanbag and have him balance it on his head during transitions. This will slow the children down a bit and give them great practice in controlled movement and spatial awareness. Once they've mastered walking, have them stoop down and touch the floor without dropping the beanbags.

Under and Over

During each transition, have the children climb under something (a desk, a chair, each other) to get where they're going. On another day, have them climb over something. Reinforce directional language by using the words *under* and *over*.

Choo-Choo!

For each transition, have the children form a line to create a choo-choo train. Appoint a new engineer each time, so everyone gets a chance to decide which way to steer the train.

Chapter Summary

- **Learning never sits still.** Children learn best on the move.

- **Teaching through the six physicalities:** Make learning multisensory, multi-perspective, personal, nonjudgmental, challenging, and discovery-rich.

- **Reading the moves:** Movement is a language children speak fluently. Learning to read the moves makes it easier to use those moves for learning.

- **Creating move-to-learn space** means seeing the space as the children see it and leaving lots of room for flying elbows and knees!

- **The Magic Door** invites children into a world of learning and says "This is a special place just for you."

- **Floor power:** The floor is a child's best, first playground and the most natural learning environment.

- **Co-creating the classroom:** Have the children help design their own learning space.

- **Indoors or outdoors:** Movement and learning can happen anywhere.

- **Motorvators:** Look for opportunities any time of the day to inject a little "motorvation" into a moving child's day.

CHAPTER 19

The Zone of Uncertainty: Managing Safety

A child on the move is constantly pushing at her physical boundaries—and undoubtedly that's going to cause a few tumbles along the way. Let's discuss the important matters of physical safety in guiding a moving child in these early years.

If you are a parent, you know your child better than anyone else. As a teacher or childcare provider, you are trained to understand children's abilities and anticipate their needs. And you are responsible for their safety. So let's be clear: in matters of safety, the final call is always yours—child by child, day by day, situation by situation.

Managing Uncertainty

Most adults see risk on a straight line continuum that looks something like this.

The Risk Continuum

Complete safety
No supervision required

Zone of uncertainty
Supervision required

Extreme danger!
Off limits!

In matters
of safety,
the final
call is always
yours.

Chances are, if you're in charge of active little ones, you spend at least part of your day in the zone of uncertainty—that place where there might be an issue with safety. And while physical safety is your first, most important job as a child's guardian, it's not your only job.

How you handle situations in that gray area between obviously safe and obviously dangerous—the zone of uncertainty—is critical not only for the child's physical safety, but for her intellectual and emotional growth. You see, in that zone lies the richness of life and the essentials of learning she needs and can only get when she goes there. That's because exploration and experimentation mean doing something new, and anything new carries with it the potential for risk.

So how do you strike the right balance between the potential risks and learning rewards of play?

The Balance of Play

Identifying the risk of play without valuing its rewards is like tying one hand behind a moving child's back. Instead, let's look at the whole picture. The Balance of Play diagram on page 208 illustrates what happens when we evaluate both the physical risk *and* the learning rewards of movement.

Note how the field of possibilities for fun and exploration grows and expands when we examine the zone of uncertainty against the axis of stimulation. By and large, the center circle encompasses most of what children do during the course of an ordinary day of play—everything from quiet concentration to broad adventure. And all of this in its many varieties works in their learning favor. But in particular, note how this analysis considers two dynamics completely off limits to young children: (1) activities that pose extreme physical danger, of course, and (2) those that provide little to no active stimulation.

Family Moves

Print the "Play, Safety, and the Zone of Uncertainty" handout from the digital file and share it with parents.

With that, the Balance of Play diagram reveals three essential types of play: moving and learning, big moves and big ideas, and quiet concentration. We'll discuss these play categories in more detail in the next chapters, but for now, remember, the key point is this: All learning takes some measure of risk. And all risk results in some measure of learning. As a teacher, caregiver, or parent, helping a child balance both rests with you. So let's talk about some strategies that may help.

Managing Risk: Pause, Prompt, and Praise

Children learn best by doing—by immersing themselves in whatever interests them, with their whole brain and body. There's just one problem. Young children don't have much experience, which means they have little sense of what is and isn't risky. Which brings us to the age-old, inevitable crossroad: How do I let a child try new things that may be risky while keeping her safe from harm?

You know the children in your care best, and hazard assessment is your call. If you decide to let a child try something risky, take a deep breath, drum up your courage and common sense, and consider this classroom mantra: *pause, prompt, and praise.*

1. **Pause.** Knowing the child as you do, when you see a potential problem that is *not immediately hazardous,* pause for a moment before reacting. For instance, a child may get stuck on a piece of playground equipment. If there's no obvious, immediate danger, give her time to work through the problem herself.

2. **Prompt.** Then, if you feel the need to step in, do so. Try not to do everything for the child. Instead, gently prompt ways to solve the situation. Be the helper, not the leader. For instance, you might say, "I wonder how we can help you get unstuck. What if I hold your arms while you lift your leg?"

3. **Praise.** As the situation resolves, praise the actions the child took to solve her own problem. Be specific. "Good job" doesn't tell her what to do next time. Instead, review the situation verbally so she knows what she did well. For example: "I love the way you lifted your knee up to get unstuck." Chances are, the next time she gets stuck, she'll remember to lift her knee.

The Balance of Play

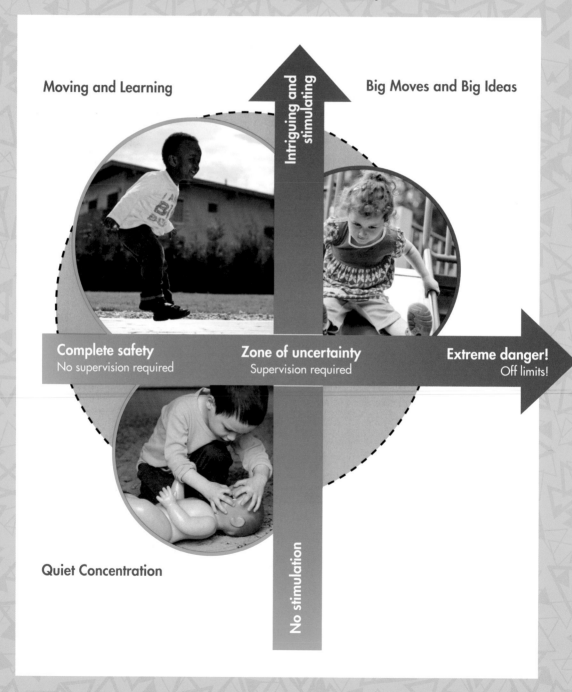

Moving and Learning

Big Moves and Big Ideas

Intriguing and stimulating

No stimulation

Complete safety
No supervision required

Zone of uncertainty
Supervision required

Extreme danger!
Off limits!

Quiet Concentration

Teaching Children to Think About Safety: Take a Safety Safari

As you shepherd children through the zone of uncertainty, you are also teaching them about safety. For instance, explaining why some things are off limits to them is a great way to help them understand why they can't always do what the big kids do.

But what about the times when you aren't there to provide guidance? To manage those situations, help them learn to think through the safety assessment process—the idea of consequences. And that begins with the simple question "What would happen if . . . ?"

Tour your environment together and ask the child what she thinks is safe and unsafe for her to do in various areas. Gently prompt her if necessary, and praise her when she correctly identifies an area for play that is safe or unsafe.

> If you decide to let a child try something risky, take a deep breath, drum up your courage and common sense, and consider this classroom mantra: pause, prompt, and praise.

Offer open-ended questions that help the child imagine consequences. For example:

- "I wonder if chasing games would be a good idea in the kitchen? What do you think would happen if the floor was wet, and you ran on it? Where would be a better place to play chasing games?"

- "Remember the time I dropped the cup, and it broke into lots of sharp pieces? The cup was made of glass. What else is made of glass? What would happen if someone bumped into something made of glass, like the window?"

- "You're really good at doing somersaults. I wonder if this would be a good place to somersault? Why wouldn't this be a good place? I wonder where would be a better place?"

Getting a child to think about safety in this way not only will help her understand what to look out for, but also might lead her to think safety is *her* idea. And when it's her idea, it's bound to be a good one!

Chapter Summary

- **Safety is always your call.** You know the children best, so only you can decide what is and isn't safe for them.

- **The zone of uncertainty.** Risk falls on a linear continuum from complete safety to extreme danger, with a large zone of uncertainty in the middle.

- **Balance of play.** Three essential types of play exist at the intersection of risk and stimulation: moving and learning, big moves and big ideas, and quiet concentration.

- **Pause, prompt, and praise.** Unless there's an immediate physical hazard, apply this mantra to help children learn to work out physical challenges on their own.

- **Take a safety safari.** Help children be safe by learning to think about safety for themselves.

PART 5

Put It in Play

CHAPTER 20

The Balance of Play

//

Knowing how much movement matters in a child's development, the question now becomes how to put it into practice. And again, nature has the answer: play. For little ones, play is nature's movement motivator.

Play: Nature's Movement Motivator

Let's examine how play packs a move-to-learn punch by taking a closer look at our Balance of Play diagram.

Moving and Learning

Moving and learning activities are the classic, indoor-outdoor active play patterns of everyday adventures. They offer kinesthetic, sensory, and whole-body experiences. And chances are, if children have adequate free play time, they're doing lots of this already!

Big Moves and Big Ideas

We recommend that about 80 percent of a young child's day be devoted to moving and learning and big moves and big ideas. The remaining 20 percent should be contemplative or artistic pursuits.

Big moves and big ideas are thrills that develop the confidence to try, try, and try some more, which leads to new concepts of what works and what doesn't for the child. The biggest moments in a child's day are those that challenge him to do things with his body he's never done before. Exciting and exhilarating conquests allow him to reach new heights, new speeds, and new sensations of space. This type of play includes playground play, water play, roughhousing, anything on wheels, and anything else that keeps little ones moving forward.

A Closer Look at the Balance of Play

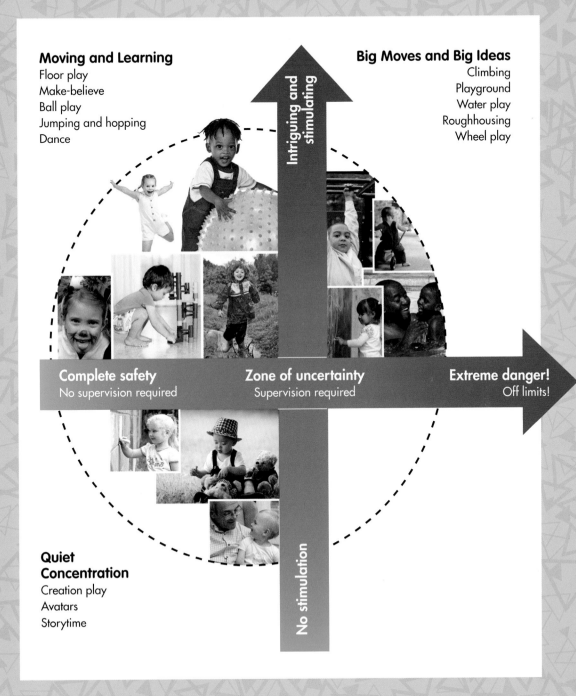

Moving and Learning
Floor play
Make-believe
Ball play
Jumping and hopping
Dance

Big Moves and Big Ideas
Climbing
Playground
Water play
Roughhousing
Wheel play

Intriguing and stimulating

Complete safety
No supervision required

Zone of uncertainty
Supervision required

Extreme danger!
Off limits!

No stimulation

Quiet Concentration
Creation play
Avatars
Storytime

Quiet Concentration

Quiet concentration provides children with the downtime they need to digest all they've done and think things through. It includes a healthy amount of nothing-to-do time, when they can discover what their imagination is really made of. Quiet concentration activities include creating and making (arts, crafts, and construction), playing with avatars (dolls, action figures, vehicles, and animal figures), and storytime.

As we take a closer look at the Balance of Play diagram (page 213), take particular note of the proportions it suggests, emphasizing *active* activity. In fact, we recommend that about 80 percent of a young child's day be devoted to high-energy, physical, sensory-stimulating types of play that fall under the categories of moving and learning and big moves and big ideas. The remaining 20 percent should be contemplative or artistic pursuits.

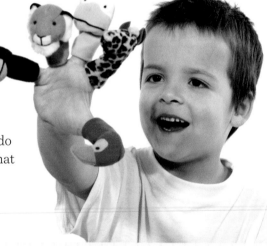

In the next few chapters, we'll look at these types of play more closely, exploring why kids do what they do and what all that "doing" does for them.

Gill's Notebook

Count the Giggles

In today's achievement-obsessed world, kindergarten is the new first grade, preschool or preK is the new kindergarten, and who knows where toddlerhood is headed. More and more children are losing precious free playtime to well-intentioned "enrichment" classes and other structured experiences intended to provide children the best possible start in life.

Now, many adults claim remarkable learning results from these classes. And many say the structure provides other benefits, such as learning to follow directions, socializing with other children, or simply being exposed to new ideas. And that's all well and good, except for one thing: Play does all of these things better.

Play comes from within. It doesn't need anyone else telling the child what to do or how to do it. It only needs the child.

Play is immediate. It meets a child's needs right here and right now, speeding up or slowing down on command. Play has no pickup time.

Family Moves

Parents understand that kids love to play but sometimes don't see the contribution play makes to kids' development and learning. Print "Gill's Notebook: Count the Giggles" from the digital file and share it with parents to inspire families to see the value of unstructured play.

Play respects a child's choices because it knows his needs from the inside out. The rest of us are pretty much just guessing.

Play gives the imagination somewhere to go. Imagination is nature's way of helping a child interpret and experiment with life. It shapes his world vision and defines his point of view. At play, a child is in control of what's real and what's important.

Play is flow. At play, a child is free to set, change, and achieve his own goals without judgment. Self-satisfaction is his report card.

There's just one problem. The immeasurable benefits of play are not measurable. You can't take its temperature to see if it's working. It doesn't provide progress reports, and you can't compare it to the kid next door. And for some, that's just not good enough. So for those who need data points, here's what you can measure:

- Count the giggles. How many times a day does he laugh out loud?
- Count the quiet moments when he's so engrossed, he forgets to go to the bathroom.
- Count how many stories he tells about space aliens, pirates, princes and princesses, elves and fairies, robots, puppies and kitties, and a big hairy monster named Lou who hangs out in his closet.

And when you've finished counting, consider this: Play produces children capable of pure joy, deep reasoning, and ideas nobody's ever thought of.

And by any measure, that's a start in life worthy of our children.

Chapter Summary

- **Moving and learning** activities are the classic, everyday indoor-outdoor active play patterns. They offer kinesthetic, sensory, and whole-body experiences.

- **Big moves and big ideas** are thrills that develop the confidence to try, try, and try some more. This type of play includes playground play, water play, roughhousing, and anything on wheels.

- **Quiet concentration** provides children with the downtime they need to digest all they've done and think things through. Quiet concentration activities include creating and making things; playing with dolls, action figures, vehicles, and animal figures; and storytime.

- **80-20 guideline:** About 80 percent of a young child's day should be devoted to the types of play that fall under the categories of moving and learning and big moves and big ideas. The remaining 20 percent should be quiet time.

- **Play motivates movement.** It is immediate, child-driven, and activates the imagination. It is essential and its value is immeasurable.

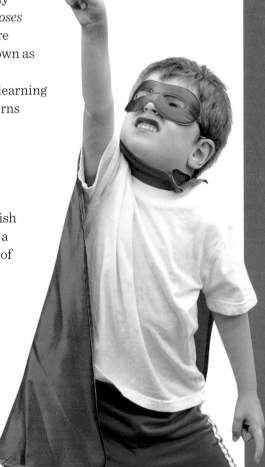

CHAPTER 21

Moving and Learning Play

///

The ancient Greek philosopher Sophocles said, "One learns by doing a thing; for though you think you know it, you have no certainty until you try." Moving and learning play is all about doing, and for little ones, it hardly matters what the "doing" is. As long as the child *chooses* it and is *physically* involved in it, fun and learning are bound to follow. This is the very basis of what is known as play-based learning.

Almost all play is a combination of moving and learning for young children. But here are a few key play patterns to note.

Role Play: Who Am I?

Why Kids Play This Way

When you watch a stick turn into a magic wand, a dish towel into a cape, a hairbrush into a microphone, or a table into a cave, you are witnessing the emergence of representational thinking and metaphor. Role play helps the brain transform "what is" to "what if" and open the gates to make-believe.

Moving Through Play

Through role play, a child uses the transformative power of storytelling. When a child borrows a character's physical characteristics—size, strength, speed, bravery, agility, grace, silliness—it requires her to move her body in new ways. And she may surprise herself (and you) with abilities she didn't know she had.

For instance, a child might stop and think before jumping over a log. But Batman would never hesitate. With the awareness that "I can do what Batman does" comes the confidence and motivation to push herself even further.

Developmental Benefits

- Kids master new physical challenges by mirroring the actions of others. In addition to expanding her physical horizons, role play lets a child safely examine the edges of her emotional spectrum.

- In role play, strategic planning and creative problem solving are happening moment to moment, which helps develop children's independent decision making and the ability to think on their feet.

- When children role-play in a group, sophisticated social dynamics emerge, including responsibilities, teamwork, competition, victory, and defeat. And as the storytelling unfolds, language and communication skills evolve.

- Representational thinking sows the seeds for letter and number recognition and, eventually, reading and math.

- And of course, a child's imagination fuels every escapade, making role play one of the most personally satisfying kinds of play.

What You Can Do

Respect the realness. Just because it's make-believe doesn't mean it's not real. A child's imaginative journey into worlds she couldn't otherwise know is her natural way of learning and essential for her well-being.

> Role play helps the brain transform "what is" to "what if" and open the gates to make-believe.

Play your part sincerely. When a child invites you to role-play with her, accept your assignment and follow her lead. Stay in the moment and in character unless a safety issue crops up.

Let the child play her way. In role play, there's no room for logic or correction (unless safety is at stake). If you're unsure what the child is driving at, keep it to yourself. Try not to put ideas in her head. That can interrupt the flow and undermine her ability to come up with her own solutions. Instead, ask questions that help her describe her ideas so you can play along with the direction she sets.

Ball Play: Managing Unpredictability

Why Kids Play This Way

A rolling, bouncing, spinning, soaring ball is an apt metaphor for a child at play. A ball moves in much the same way a young child does—tirelessly rolling from one thing to another with just a simple nudge in any direction.

And just like a little kid, a ball reacts to that nudge in endlessly unpredictable ways. Which way will it roll this time? How far and fast will it go? How high will it bounce? Where will it go after that? And who's going to be there to catch it?

Moving Through Play

The objective of pretty much every ball game is to move the ball. How, where, and when you move it depends on the game you choose, but by and large, ball play is high-energy play. It involves whole-body movements like throwing, rolling, kicking, bouncing, and batting which all require sophisticated sensory and motor development.

Ball play helps a child learn how hard to throw, roll, or kick a ball to send it where she wants it to go. That requires body awareness and strength management. (See Chapter 9.)

In order to catch a ball, you have to be in the right

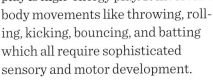

place at the right time, and that takes both spatial and temporal awareness. Anticipating the distance and speed of the ball unlocks important thinking tools such as estimation and prediction. (See Chapter 9.)

Catching a ball also requires directional reasoning. A child must know where she is in relation to the ball in order to move her body to meet it. (See Chapter 16.)

Ball play is an especially powerful tool for helping little ones develop dynamic equilibrium (staying in balance while on the move). Kicking a ball with one foot appears simple, but it requires sophisticated, whole-body balance and homolateral midline maturity. (See Chapter 8.)

And the perpetual motion of the ball is a great way to refine eye-hand and eye-foot coordination. (See Chapter 13.)

Developmental Benefits

- Chasing a ball around creates a playful environment for learning important social, emotional, and cognitive lessons, too.

- The object of most ball games has something to do with passing the ball back and forth. Learning how to get along with others is much like the unspoken agreement underlying a game of catch—throw the ball to your playmate and she will throw it back. That's called sharing.

- As we've said, the enigmatic nature of a rolling ball is a great lesson in managing the unexpected. And this lesson goes well beyond the playground, backyard, or ball field. Life is full of ups and downs, and learning to roll with them is an important part of growing up. A child who learns to manage her reactions to changing situations is much more likely to have the confidence and resilience necessary for situations far more important than a "bad bounce."

- By virtue of its unstructured nature, a ball is a cooperative playmate for any game kids want to play, including anything they can think up!

What You Can Do

Start early. Even before a child is independently mobile, you can play ball with her. Roll the ball back and forth in front of her or toward her. This develops eye tracking while gently introducing the idea of ball play.

Play indoors and out. Ball play is not just for outdoors. Soft, lightweight foam balls let the fun come inside.

Encourage boys and girls to enjoy ball play. Ball play is often associated with sports, which are sometimes associated more with boys than with girls.

Keep in mind that the benefits of playtime with balls are vast and important for girls and boys alike.

Remember it's not a training camp. The association of balls with sports often leads adults to overemphasize precision and skill rather than keeping the play open to exploration and experimentation. If a child throws underhand, that's because it feels natural to her. Trying to correct technique is a waste of time and may interfere with the development you want to encourage. In time, a child will want to throw like the big kids, and she'll let you know when that is.

Variety! Variety! Variety! There are *so* many games you can play with a ball, making it the perfect companion for developing a broad range of capabilities. Try lots of different activities and encourage the child to make up her own games. When she does, remember: she's the rule maker—even if the rules change with every turn.

Jumping, Hopping, Leaping, and Skipping: Self-Regulation

Why Kids Play This Way

Adults often think of "jumping for joy" metaphorically. But think about the last time you were truly excited—for example, when your hometown team won a big game. Chances are you actually did jump (or at least wiggle or dance around) for joy.

It's natural to move our bodies in accordance with our emotions. When we're sad, we curl up and make ourselves small. When we're happy, we defy gravity to make ourselves bigger.

Kids jump when they're feeling good—and because jumping feels good. The bigger the leap, the bigger the feeling. We might interpret this as an outburst of uncontrolled emotion. But in fact, jumping, hopping, leaping, skipping, and other gravity-defying movements are actually powerful demonstrations of physical control and emotional self-regulation.

Moving Through Play

Humans aren't meant to fly like birds, but that doesn't stop kids from trying. When they do, they use whole-body effort and coordinated control, particularly in the following areas:

- Jumping is a whole-body movement. While the legs provide the power, the arms play a key role in upward momentum.

- Jumping requires balance. Anytime one or both feet leave the ground, they challenge the vestibular system to maintain balance. (See Chapter 8.)

- Jumping develops the midlines. One- or two-footed jumping, hopping, and leaping all require refined midlines. That means a child must be able to do things bilaterally (move both sides of the body in mirrored fashion) or homolaterally (move one side while keeping the other still). Skipping takes it a step further, requiring a lateral movement pattern (moving both sides in opposite ways). In fact, skipping is one of the most complex midline movements and a sign that physical coordination is reaching maturity. (See Chapter 12.)

- Hopping and skipping require body rhythm and timing because of their repetitive nature. Body rhythm creates a regular pattern of hops or jumps, which helps balance and control the body and develop timing. (See Chapter 12.)

Developmental Benefits

- Jumping, hopping, leaping, and skipping—whether outdoors, indoors, or even in the water—provide great aerobic fitness training for anyone at any age. But they're particularly helpful for strengthening young bones and muscles. (See Chapter 11.)

- There's something contagious about jumping. When one kid starts, the others jump in, too, and before you know it, they're jumping in unison. When kids mirror one another's movements like this, they are making unspoken emotional connections and forming the bonds of community.

- Jumping helps kids live large. A child who jumps with excitement is a child who feels deeply. When a child feels safe to *express* her emotions— happy, sad, or mad—she is more likely to develop the ability to *manage* her emotions. Being reassured that her emotions are true and legitimate is the first step toward self-regulation.

- Brain development is greatly enhanced by the whole-body activity of these kinds of movements. When the body works both sides, the brain does, too, integrating and speeding up the processing between the left and right hemispheres. (See Chapter 12.)

> Jumping, hopping, leaping, skipping, and other gravity-defying movements are powerful demonstrations of physical control and emotional self-regulation.

What You Can Do

Let 'em jump. The first rule of jumping is to let it happen. Often adults worry that a child will get too worked up or get hurt while jumping around. Instead, this kind of physical energy releases emotions that *need* to be freely expressed.

Encourage jumping games. Challenge children to use their jumping energy to push themselves to new heights and distances. Don't set this up as a competition against one another, but rather challenge each child to beat her own best effort if she can.

Add rhymes. Encourage repetitive jumping by adding rhymes or songs. Jumping to the beat of a rhyme or song sustains the play while helping a child refine her body rhythm and temporal awareness. (See Chapter 12.)

Jump rope. Introduce the idea of jumping over a rope by laying one on the ground and challenging her to jump over it. When she's ready, lift the rope a couple of inches off the ground so she has to jump higher. She might trip once or twice, but she'll learn to jump higher eventually. As her skills and coordination develop, introduce the idea of skipping rope.

Introduce jumping toys. Hopping balls, pogo sticks, and other jumping toys offer great bouncing fun as children refine their balance.

A Word About Bouncing on Furniture, Trampolines, and the Like

Safety must be your first concern here. Young children should never jump on a bouncy surface without holding onto steady support, such as an adult's hands, a railing, a handle, or some other safety device.

Beyond safety, the unpredictable trajectory a child gets from a bouncy surface does not provide the consistent experience she needs to practice, refine, and master her jumping skills, develop balance and intuition, and strengthen her muscles. When the surface boosts the bounce, the muscles actually do less work. It may give a child more air, but it doesn't do more for her development.

Dance: Let Me Show You!

Why Kids Play This Way

Dance is a party for your body! For our purposes, we define dance as any form of physical movement—with or without music—that expresses an idea, a story, or an emotion. And by that definition, we—and especially kids—are dancing all the time. Dance is an essential form of body language, telling the story of who we are, often revealing our innermost feelings.

Expressing our emotions and ideas with our bodies promotes positive self-esteem and social demeanor as well as an optimistic, open outlook on life. Dancing—and dancing often—is great for little ones who are still getting used to the skin they're in. As a child dances, she feels her body and stimulates her brain in new and different ways. And when she's dancing with others, she's learning how to be part of a group.

Music is not mandatory for dance of course, but it *is* its perfect, mirrored partner. You see, music comes from the outside in. Dance comes from the inside out. And anything that begins from within is bound to have deep and lasting benefits.

Moving Through Play

Dancing is easy, intuitive, and visceral for young children, which is probably why it's so much fun.

Dance requires balance. The quick movement changes in dance challenge the brain to manage balance in whole new ways. (See Chapter 8.)

Dance develops body rhythm, refining the brain's internal sense of timing. This timing is essential not only for highly coordinated movement, but also for cognitive and social development. (See Chapter 12.)

Dance develops fitness. The nonstop motion of dance oxygenates the blood while building muscles and increasing coordination, flexibility, and agility. (See Chapter 11.)

© JIRI HERA | DREAMSTIME.COM

Developmental Benefits

- Free-form dancing lets a child experiment with her body in an open, uninhibited way. This fosters a healthy, natural sense of self, which in turn builds self-esteem, confidence, and emotional self-regulation.

- Structured dancing requires following instructions while sequencing and patterning movements. Here a child is learning how to get and stay in step with others, which is foundational to forming relationships. The physical and cognitive demands of following movement patterns help her learn the importance of paying attention to details. And of course, dance is one of the great human connectors. Dance creates an invisible energy that draws people together.

- As we noted in Chapter 15, when children put multiple languages together—music, lyrics, and movement—the combination strengthens neural pathways.

- Dance helps a child develop an easy relationship with her body. Among other benefits, this helps a child better communicate with others using body language, gestures, and expressions to emphasize important emotional messages. (See Chapter 14.)

- And, dance may well be a child's first experience with symbolic representation. For instance, when a child acts out "The Itsy Bitsy Spider," the finger play physicalizes the spider's crawl, the falling rain, and the reappearing sun. In creating pictures with her body, she is not only expressing simple ideas, but learning to think symbolically, which will naturally lead to literacy and numeracy down the road.

What You Can Do

Turn up the music and go for it! Use a variety of musical genres to set different moods. And there's no choreography required. Instead, encourage children to create their own steps, then follow their lead so they can feel the connection between you.

Family Moves

Print the diagram "A Closer Look at the Balance of Play" from the digital file and share it with parents to broaden their understanding of healthy play for their children.

Dance along. If you don't like to dance, get over it. You're entitled to your feelings of course, but try not to pass them on. If a child senses your inhibition, she might pick up on that. And if she begins to feel inhibited in expressing herself—especially with her body—what else might she hold back on? Besides, dancing with children is a blast! So take your two left feet out for a spin.

Provide props. Costumes and accessories change the way we behave and move. Add capes, scarves, hats, shoes, and noisemakers to the mix. If you really want to make some noise, add taps to the bottom of the child's shoes. Glue coins to the soles of an old pair of sneakers and have at it!

Exaggerate emotions. Dance is language that expresses emotion. This makes it a perfect choice for exploring feelings like happy, sad, mad, and silly. Lead by example. Show children how to express their feelings through their movements.

No music? Dance anyway! Dance doesn't need music to be dance. Create a secret handshake or hand signal. Play clapping games or charades. These are forms of dance you can do anytime, anywhere.

Dance classes. Early childhood dance classes can be fun, but only if the child wants to, and only if the class is structured to focus more on freedom of movement than precision skill building. The years ahead offer plenty of time to learn how to plié properly.

Chapter Summary

- **Moving and learning play:** Experience is the best teacher. As long as young children are physically engaged in play, they're learning.

- **Role play:** Pretending to be something they're not—bigger, stronger, faster, braver, and so on—requires children to move their bodies in new ways.

- **Ball play** teaches children the fine art of managing unpredictability because it requires quick thinking and quick moving.

- **Jumping, hopping, leaping, and skipping** defy gravity while developing children's fitness, balance, and control.

- **Dance** is an essential form of body language, emotional expression, and socialization.

CHAPTER 22

Big Moves and Big Ideas

Double-dog dares are as old as childhood and as vitally important today as they've ever been (if not more so).

Children challenging themselves to accomplish things on their own requires big moves—stretching beyond hitherto unknown capacities into the great, big, juicy world of, "Gee, I didn't know I could do that!" And from those moments of personal triumph comes the biggest idea of all: "I can!"

And it remains true. A lifetime of visionary optimism, self-startership, and courageous undertakings begins with a child's first, breathtaking *"Wheeeeeeee!"*

Gill's Notebook

Big Moves, Big Ideas

I've spent a lifetime studying the impact movement makes in early childhood development and learning. And here's what I've learned: every move counts—big and small. So in this chapter, I'll share my thoughts on some of the biggest moves of all—the kinds of play that challenge the whole body while building confidence and character.

Huff-and-Puff Play: "Learning Off" Energy

Parents and teachers often tell me, "I like to let children run around and burn off energy." Well intended though that sentiment may be, it's actually a pet peeve of mine. Here's why.

The dictionary definition of *burn off* is "to exhaust, deplete, waste." For little ones, that usually means getting those ants out of their pants. Now, in my line of work I understand antsy kids, and appreciate any adult wise enough to spot the signs and let kids loose. But the implication of "wasting" time and energy is what's so troubling when, in fact, all that running around and general silliness is the most essential fuel of early childhood development and learning. And not because I say so. Because nature says so. Maybe that's why all those ants come so effortlessly to children.

I call this huff-and-puff play. Let's examine its benefits a little more closely.

Body freedom. Moving his body with abandon is a child's chance to experience every inch of himself without order, structure, or limits. In so many ways, this is how he's getting to know himself, physically and emotionally. And while it may look out of control to us, this self-exploration is actually helping the child learn self-control.

Learning limits. Running until you can't run anymore is one of nature's clever ways of helping a child understand that there is such a thing as going too far. You see, if it feels good, he's naturally going to want more of it, whether it's running at top speed, roughhousing with his sister, or scarfing down more ice cream. And while the grown-ups in his life provide the important boundaries he needs, not until he experiences his own physical limitations will the *idea* of going too far become real, tangible, and concretely understood.

Emotional practice. Life doesn't happen at one speed, nor do emotions. Free play—with as few restrictions as safely possible—gives children a place to practice their emotional range and push beyond what they've felt before. For instance, climbing on the monkey bars is usually a process that involves repeated attempts. Few kids race to the top on the first try. But over time, they will challenge themselves to climb up another level and see how it feels—expanding their own comfort zone in their own way and time.

Being in the moment. When fully engaged in physical activity, the body and brain are harmonized. Endorphins start the party and before you know it, you've lost all track of what's past or what's next, content to be in the moment and with the movement. It's that sense of being in the moment that young minds and fertile imaginations need in order to interpret and absorb all the new sights, sounds, sensations, experiences, and ideas they encounter each day.

So, the next time you see children running, jumping, or just plain letting loose, try to see it the way nature does and say to yourself, "I like to let them run around and *learn off* energy!" Because that's energy we can't afford to burn.

Barefootin'

In a world seemingly obsessed with carefulness these days, one of the things I fear being lost is the joy of going barefoot, and along with it all the benefits. Here are five great reasons for bare feet:

Body mapping. Little ones who have their feet stuffed into footed onesies, slippers, socks, or shoes all day and night run the risk of never truly getting to know their toes.

Strength. Feet have a big job every day holding our weight. Wearing shoes and socks provides support but also takes some of the responsibility off the muscles in the feet. Going barefoot is the most natural way to keep feet in tip-top shape!

Motorvator

10 Great Things to Do Barefootin'

1. **Foot massage.** Massage feels good at any age, but is particularly great for babies just learning about their bodies.

2. **Cold feet!** For older kids, rub an ice cube over the child's feet for a great, shivery, sensory experience! Of course, be guided by the child. If it's too cold, it won't be fun.

3. **Texture track.** Scavenge around for different textures to walk or crawl on, including bubble wrap, sandpaper, tinfoil, and just for the fun of it, sticky tape!

4. **Barefoot soccer.** Outdoors in the grass, practice dribbling a soccer ball in bare feet. Indoors, set up a game of soccer on the floor using a beanbag as the ball!

5. **Piggie painting.** Outdoors, lay out a large sheet of paper and fill two foil pie plates with different colors of paint. Have kids step into the paint, then onto the paper, and see just how creative their feet can be!

6. **Toe tickles.** Put a feather between the child's toes and challenge him to tickle his own nose, ears, elbows, and so forth.

7. **Foot fishing.** Scatter some small blocks or toys on the floor and have the child pick them up with his toes and put them in a bucket or tray.

8. **Toe to toe.** Have children sit facing each other and press their feet together. Lift the feet and "dance" in midair to some high-energy music.

9. **Footraces.** Set up a race course and have children run different "footraces" on different parts of their feet—their toes, heels, and the inside or outside edges of the feet. Once they get the hang of it, have them try racing sideways or backward.

10. **Ten tall tootsie tales.** Invite the child to paint faces on his toes. Talk about the different toes and make up different personalities for them. Then walk, run, and jump through the day, telling tall tootsie tales!

Adaptability. When I was a kid, I couldn't wait for summer so I could run barefoot outdoors. But those first days were always a little hard on the feet. Softened up by the padding of socks, shoes, and indoor carpeting all winter, my feet had to toughen up. It hurt a little, but it was worth it! Not only does going barefoot give kids a great sense of personal freedom, it teaches them a fundamental principle of independence—how to adapt to different situations—even the rocky ones. Of course, city kids have it different I realize, so find a park if you can. In your early childhood setting, work toward making your playground a shoe-free zone, weather permitting. And remember, going barefoot indoors has many of the same benefits.

Confidence. When children feel their steps directly, they are much better able to understand the intricacies of even the trickiest terrain and navigate it more adeptly. This is true for flat surfaces as well as inclines. Indeed, shoes tend to slip when children climb on playground equipment, while feet are naturally designed to provide sensitive traction, and the toes flex to give better grip.

Connectedness. Feet are our connection to the earth. They are where we meet gravity. Which makes me wonder: Could our modern, "head first" image of ourselves be upside down? What would the world be like if we believed we begin in our feet and end in our minds?

Outdoor Play: You Can't Run Uphill Indoors

Most articles advocating outdoor play rightly argue that children need fresh air and sunshine for good health and an appreciation of nature for their overall well-being. Adults know this intellectually. Kids know it intuitively. Researchers back it up. And I wholeheartedly agree. But I'd like to add a few more reasons.

Kids Need to Move a Lot

Kids need to move their bodies every day in lots of ways. They need as much freedom of choice as is safe and practical in order to develop both their bodies and their brains. To that end, keep this in mind:

More movement is possible outdoors than in. It just is.

"Don't run inside. Don't make a mess indoors. Don't roughhouse in the house." Sound familiar? They're all reasonable restrictions on indoor play. Years ago, the solution was simple: shoo the kids outside. But that's not always the case today. At school, recess is being cut. And in some cases, childcare providers don't always have the time kids need for outdoor exploration throughout the day.

Today, adults sometimes seem afraid to let children go outdoors. They have a variety of reasons for this, from stranger danger to busy streets to the thinning ozone layer—and everything in-between. Now, I'm not going to tell any parent, caregiver, or teacher what's right or wrong about their choices for children. But I do want to plead the case for a child's need to move *a lot*, which requires the kind of large, open, and varied space that only the outdoors can accommodate.

> Children need to build up their knowledge and familiarity with nature in order to develop respect for it.

For instance, a child can't run as fast as his legs will go indoors. Nor can he run uphill or downhill, through tall grass or sand or a puddle, or over an icy slope. But children need these diverse conditions to challenge their abilities. If a child can't get outside to play as often as he needs and wants to, it's unlikely he'll stretch himself to his full potential.

Growing Environmentalists

Some futurists predict the single greatest challenge today's children will face is environmental degradation. They'll struggle with climate change, energy sources, clean air and water, fresh food supplies . . . the list goes on.

Given that, it's hard to imagine how this next generation is going to save the environment if they haven't actually spent much time in it. Children need to build up their knowledge and familiarity with nature in order to develop respect for it. So I say, it's best to start early.

Discovery

Once children do get outside, the discovery never ends. Nature is a boundless treasure trove of things large and small that fascinate the curious, inspire the imaginative, and humble us all. Like a small child, nature never stops growing and changing. And like a great teacher, nature always has something new to share.

Nature Has No Substitute

Arguably, the biggest competitor nature has for children's time and attention is technology. And as compelling as the images, sounds, and "interactive" elements are, the flat confines of a screen are no substitute for the sensory impact of being in nature—seeing it, hearing it, touching it, smelling it, tasting it, running through it, and getting dirty in it.

Nature Is Us

If you're reading the print version of this book, you're holding a tree in your hands. If you're reading this book on a screen, you're holding a dinosaur bone known today as plastic.

Everything comes from nature—including us. And we'd all do well to step outside and remember that.

Playgrounding: Top 10 Things to Look for in a Great Playground

I've spent a lot of time on playgrounds in my work. And knowing how important it is for kids to get a well-balanced, daily diet of movement, I've developed a view to what constitutes a great playground. And it starts with the ground itself!

> *Important Note:* Local playground safety standards and legislation vary from state to state, province to province, and country to country. Please consult with your local authorities before making any enhancements to your playground.

1. **Hill.** Many playgrounds are flat as a pancake, no doubt carefully leveled to ensure safe installation of large-scale equipment. And that's all fine, but for kids, there's something irresistible about scampering to the top of just about anything. Maybe it makes them feel bigger, or maybe it's the "because it's there" nature of things meant to be climbed. Whatever the reason, I've never seen a playground hill fail to become the center of attention while helping kids develop their balance, intuition, and midlines.

2. **Tree.** Playing in nature is always the best option for developing a healthy movement curriculum. Trees are nature's monkey bars, and if you've got a good climbing tree, take advantage of it. For little ones, hang a swing and let them have fun. For older kids, supervised climbing will build physical strength and self-confidence.

3. **Modular elements.** Modular play elements are great for presenting kids with new challenges every day. Introduce simple objects such as hoops, cones, blocks, and beams. And add some A-frames so the kids can make their own bridges and tunnels.

4. **Monkey bars.** Monkey bars are the king of the playground in my opinion. Climbing, hanging (right side up or upside down), and swinging build upper-body strength, balance, spatial awareness, and midline development as children challenge themselves to move in new and creative ways.

Get a Grip

The monkey bars are great for preparing little hands for a proper pencil grip. When children are climbing or just hanging around, encourage them to use the cortical position or a locked grip (with the thumb under the bar). This is a safer grip for big climbs and strengthens the finger and thumb muscles.

5. **Swings.** Swings let kids feel what it's like to fly! Swinging independently requires children to shift their weight in order to propel themselves. This is a complex yet subtle movement that refines balance, coordination, and control. And, of course, the pendulum-like movement reinforces children's internal sense of rhythm and timing.

6. **Merry-go-round.** Controlled spinning is critical to children's balance, so a merry-go-round or any other type of spinning apparatus is a must-have on every playground.

7. **Planks and beams.** A simple, sturdy board can be the source of hours of innovative movement activities. Be sure to design it to be modular so it can be raised or lowered for children at different skill levels.

8. **Tunnels.** Just about every kid loves tunnels. Small spaces fit them just so—and perhaps deep down make them feel big. But more, tunnels help them develop a sense of how they fit both literally and figuratively into our world. (See Chapter 9.)

9. **See-saw.** Balance is the name of the game on the see-saw. And since it requires two people, it's a great training ground for the give-and-take of social relationships. When the balance is right, the ride is great for both players!

10. **Slide.** Slides are all about speed. On the short ride from top to bottom, little ones feel the thrill of being out of control. Understanding that some things in life *are* out of our control (including gravity) helps young children develop the confidence, courage, and positive outlook that will see them through challenges and obstacles, which are often defined by our inability to control events. In other words, learning to let go is part of learning how to get and stay in control.

While those are my top 10, there are dozens of other great elements that can round out your playground, including stepping stones, spinning bars, sandboxes, water play areas, rope ladders, bridges, cargo nets, cubby spaces, sensory pathways, and so much more.

And whether your playground is in the middle of a city or out in the countryside, be sure to introduce as much nature as you can for the most natural time of every day: playtime!

Climbing: "I Get Up!"

One Sunday when my granddaughter was sleeping over at my house, I was preparing dinner. I felt a tug on my trouser leg. A voice from somewhere around my knees called out, "I help you, Granny. I get up!"

The next thing I knew, she'd pulled up a stool and scrambled up to sit on the counter. Shoulder to shoulder, we cooked up our meal, mashing and mixing and stirring and tasting. I realized she'd made herself my size all on her own. And that got me thinking about what it must be like to be a kid at kneecap level, where everything's over your head. No wonder climbing comes so naturally to kids.

Climbing provides enormous benefits across the full spectrum of developmental needs.

Children's bodies crave challenge. Their little bones and muscles are eager to grow strong. Their brains are hungry to monitor and record the sensations of climbing for future use.

Climbing gives children the power to change their perspective, which fosters curiosity, discernment, critical thinking, and creative problem solving. But don't get me wrong. I'm not talking about Mount Everest here. When you're only three feet tall, the height of the couch is more than enough to see the world in a whole new way.

And of course, there is no better feeling than reaching the top of any climb for the first time. Summiting builds confidence through hard-fought, whole-body, whole-brain achievement. And just look what you can see now!

Water Play

Important Note: Anytime a young child is near water, safety must be your number one priority. **Never allow a young child near water without supervision at all times.**

With water play, safety comes first. But water safety is more than lifeguarding the experience. It must include helping children feel comfortable, capable, and confident in and around water. And that starts long before the first trip to the swimming pool or beach.

Whether it's the bathtub, sprinkler, wading pool, puddle, babbling brook, or the deep blue sea, water is a natural magnet for kids and a whole new world to explore with their bodies. The benefits are many:

Sensory development. When children are immersed in water, it provides physical stimulation like no dry experience can. The skin feels every nuance of every movement.

New kinds of movement. When children enter water, gravity takes a holiday. They can explore body movements that are hard or even impossible on land. Spinning, turning, tumbling, floating, and bobbing are effortless. Whole-body coordination, sensory invigoration, body awareness, and midline development light up in water, giving the brain new understandings of the body and the environment.

> When children are immersed in water, it provides physical stimulation like no dry experience can.

Effecting change. Playing with water gives a child a willing partner in the process of effecting change. For instance, with the magical transformation of dirt to mud a child demonstrates to himself his own power to control circumstances—even something as uncontrollable as water itself.

Roughhousing

Roughhousing isn't what it seems. It's rough, sure. But it's not out of control. It's physical, definitely. But it's not about power. It's loud, of course. But it's about unspoken communication. And yes, it's aggressive. But it's all about trust.

Roughhousing *isn't* at all what it seems.

The Benefits of Roughhousing

Adults often discourage roughhousing because they're worried it will end in tears. And sometimes it does. But that's what happens when you're pushing at new social and emotional boundaries while you're still figuring out your own physical strength. You see, the very point of roughhousing is to come right up to the edge but *not* cross over it. And that level of physical, emotional, and social finesse takes a lot of experience, and yes, that sometimes means flirting with the edge. How does roughhousing benefit kids?

> **Family Moves**
>
> Print the "10 Great Things to Do Barefootin'" Motorvator and the "Roughhousing" and "Cycle of Wheels" handouts from the digital file and share them with parents.

Body control and intuition. Roughhousing helps kids understand their own strength and learn to modify and adapt their movements (intuition) to meet the situation. And because roughhousing is usually a highly charged, fast-moving experience, the body-brain communication is challenged in fast and fun ways.

Thinking on their feet. Roughhousing is an adrenalin rush and physical outlet (especially for containerized kids). But that doesn't mean it's a great big "no-thinking" zone. In fact, the improvisational nature of the play demands quick thinking and strategizing.

Emotional development. Learning to control your emotions sometimes requires pushing them to the edges to see what they feel like. Roughhousing is a kid-sized taste of big emotions.

Self-respect. Contrary to what it appears, roughhousing actually teaches kids to control their aggression while learning to be assertive. The play physicalizes two concepts that impact social interactions at all levels: self-respect and respect for others. First, kids must learn what does and does not feel right to them. This means deciding for themselves their own personal boundaries.

Respect for others. By recognizing their own personal boundaries, children can then begin to understand, accept, and respect other people's boundaries, including when someone doesn't want to play or wants the play to stop. And just that simple act of stopping is often where friendship begins.

In short, roughhousing helps a child learn to control his emotions *and* his actions.

Be Ready for Roughhousing

Set ground rules. By its very nature, you can't schedule roughhousing, but you can be ready for it with a few simple ground rules:

- Together with the children, identify safe spaces for roughhousing and agree to limit it to those areas. Make sure children know what's out of bounds (hard surfaces, sharp corners, crowded spaces, and so on) and why.

- Together, create a cue word that means "I want to stop." Be sure everyone—including adults—understands and honors that cue with no teasing.

- Adults get the final say. When they say stop, kids must comply. But don't intervene too soon. That takes the fun (and learning) out of it.

Be an instigator. Start a roughhousing session with a well-timed tickle or two!

Share the lead. Often we advise that when adults play with children, it's best to let the child lead. But the point of roughhousing is shared respect, which means being equals in the play.

Embody safety and trust. Use open, playful body language to help the child feel safe enough to let loose and have fun roughhousing with you.

Suppress your inner referee. Roughhousing can and often will go too far, and one party will feel aggrieved. But that's part of the play. Real life doesn't come with a referee. Unless you feel serious safety issues arise, curb your instinct to intervene. Children must feel what it's like to go too far—whether they are the aggressor or the aggrieved—in order to learn how to stop themselves or respond when someone else has crossed the line.

Roughhousing's rough, physical, loud, and aggressive nature yields self-control and emotional regulation, the give-and-take of healthy relationships, and a true sense of belonging and safety.

Wheels: Charting Their Own Course

For today's stroller-strapped kids, wheel play gives them the tools they need to steer past old boundaries to new and exciting places.

Wheel play offers a child new ways to challenge his body while building power (strength and stamina), balance, intuition, and control. And mastering a machine as big as or bigger than himself gives him a sense of independence, power, and excitement he's never had before—plus one more thing: speed!

Ironically, the thrill of speed and the uncertainty of just how far to push himself actually increases the child's need for focus and concentration. That is, the more a child pushes himself toward being out of control, the more control he needs to employ—physically, cognitively, and emotionally. For instance, steering takes tiny, precise, and subtle movements, all while going at speeds he's never felt before.

And once he's on a roll, seeing the world at a different speed gives him new perspectives on old terrain and opens his eyes to things he may never have noticed before, like that bump in the sidewalk.

As milestones go, learning to ride a two-wheeler is right up there with the first tooth, the first word, and the first step. It's a "ride of passage" toward independence that will give him the foundations he needs to go a little faster and a little farther—whether he's on wheels or not. But a lot has to happen before a child is steady on his wheels.

The Cycle of Wheels

Ride-Ons

When a child becomes steady on his feet, it's time to introduce a ride-on. This is a great start on the road to wheeled proficiency. A ride-on provides stability for his uncertain balance and encourages his emerging midlines by allowing him to move his legs together (bilaterally) and, later, in opposition (laterally).

Three-Wheeled Scooters

Adults often move children straight from a ride-on to a tricycle, but I recommend a three-wheeled scooter first (or around the same time). Scooters develop homolateral movements and balance while refining intuition through steering. Neither ride-ons nor tricycles challenge these skills the way a three-wheeled scooter can. And as a bonus, scooters help develop body rhythm and temporal awareness.

Tricycles

Tricycles introduce pedaling for the first time, which develops lateral movements. Meanwhile, a trike provides a steady base so the child doesn't have to concentrate on balancing while pedaling. Pedaling combined with stability lets him try out speed! Learning to manage how fast he's going is an essential step before braving two-wheelers, and it challenges him to concentrate on his body control (and his emotional control, too).

Gliders

There's nothing quite like the sensation of two wheels and the open road! A glider bike gives a child the feel of a big-kid bike while working on his balance without worrying about pedals just yet.

Bicycles

Finally, the big day arrives! The child is ready for a real two-wheeler that demands he put all his wheel skills together: coordination (lateral midline) for pedaling + balance for control + intuition for steering = two-wheel control!

And note: If he has slowly and gradually built up these skills, there's a pretty good chance he won't need training wheels.

Two-Wheeled Scooters

Two-wheeled scooters challenge a child's homolateral development while adding the complexity of balance.

Skateboards

Skateboards truly are big-kid stuff. They combine homolateral movement with highly refined, look-mom-no-hands balance.

Roller Skates or Inline Skates

Finally, roller skates and inline skates present the ultimate testing ground for a child's suite of motor tools.

Chapter Summary

- **Big moves and big ideas** are play activities that challenge children to stretch themselves physically and mentally, yielding the biggest idea of all: "I can!"

- **Climbing** gives a child the thrill of conquering something bigger than himself and rewards the effort with new perspectives.

- **Speed** is exhilarating. It gives children a taste of being out of control so they can better understand what control feels like.

- **Play outdoors!** Playing outdoors gives children the wide-open spaces they need to fully challenge their physical selves.

- **Water play** allows physical feats and provides sensations not possible on dry land. The first steps toward safe and positive water play is to ensure that a child is supervised and feels comfortable and confident in the water.

- **Roughhousing** gives physical form to the subtle social signals we all need to learn in order to get along well with others. It helps kids understand their own physical strength, teaches them to control their aggression while learning to be self-assertive, and physicalizes respect for themselves and others.

- **Wheels** challenge children to test their own power and control—and to do so on the fly!

CHAPTER 23

Quiet Concentration

///

We all need time to reflect. That's when we find out who we really are.

Creation Play: "What Am I Made Of?"

Why Kids Play This Way

All play reflects who we are and how we feel. But through the act of creation play—arts, crafts, and construction—a child produces a statement of her identity for all the world to see. And with that comes her first taste of authorship, accomplishment, and pride.

Creation play challenges a child to find her own way of expressing what she sees around her or in the mind's eye of her own imagination. As such, this is the quiet time she needs to discover what she *doesn't* yet know. And for little ones, knowing what they don't know unlocks a great big learning idea: "What else is there to know?"

This awakening sometimes results in frustration. But just as often, it yields inventiveness, driven by the child's essential human impulse to express herself, understand herself, and feel understood by others.

Moving Through Play

Even when young children seem still and quiet, their whole minds and whole bodies are actively engaged in the creative process. Traditionally, of course, creation play requires manipulation skills to control tools and materials. Beyond that, detailed work

243

builds coordination and strength in the muscles, ligaments, and tendons of the hands and any other parts of the body involved in the play.

Creation play begins with what a child envisions and is realized through the delicate orchestration of her eyes and her body. But it takes more than finding the paper with your crayon. Controlling a paintbrush or crayon with subtlety and flair takes a refined sense of intuition.

Developmental Benefits

- Creation play boosts concentration. With a laser focus on detail, creation play sows the seeds of persistence and problem solving.

- That level of intense concentration is possible only when the whole body and whole brain are engaged, woven together by the child's active imagination.

- When a creation doesn't go according to plan, the artist or builder has two choices: throw it out or work with it and see what happens. The choice is always the child's. After all, this is *her* masterpiece. In making that choice, she's learning how to adapt her plans to changing circumstances.

- The free-form, adaptive nature of creation play unlocks a child's courage to experiment and try new things.

- And of course, there is joy and satisfaction when she's decided she's done. Creating something truly original that she feels strongly about helps her learn to express herself, resolve feelings, and take pride in her abilities.

Through the act of creation play—arts, crafts, and construction—a child produces a statement of her identity for all the world to see.

What You Can Do

Make creation play accessible. Indoors, keep a cubby or container of arts-and-crafts supplies, blocks, and other construction materials accessible to children. Together, choose a space where it's always okay to create, with or without an adult.

Encourage natural creations. Outside, spend time with the child building and creating with natural materials like sticks, stones, grasses, seeds, pinecones, and so on. Hunt for materials that might be fun to create with. Store them in a basket or bin where they'll be available whenever inspiration calls.

Don't save it for rainy days. Encourage creation play often—not just on days when there's nothing else to do. And don't restrict it to indoors, either.

Introduce, then step away. Once a child understands how to work with the materials, let the process be her guide.

Try not to ask, "What is it?" Adults have a tendency to want to make everything logical. Kids don't work that way. When a child proudly presents you with her work, ask her to tell you about it. Don't assume you know what it is, and don't make it something it might not be.

Be encouraging. No matter what the process looks like, and no matter what the end result winds up being, be the child's biggest fan! Remember that creation is very personal.

Keep it open-ended. Building-block sets and modeling kits often offer instruction sheets for prescribed outcomes. This can be fun and can help develop attention to detail, respect for rules, and manipulative skills. But open-ended creation offers those benefits and a whole lot more! Buy blocks in bulk and throw away the instruction sheets.

Don't mind the mess. Creation play can get really messy. As we discussed in Chapter 7, messy play is full of important developmental nutrients. It encourages sensory exploration through elbow-deep experiences. Just remember, it's worth the mop time.

Avatar Play: Dolls, Action Figures, and Learning to Be in Charge

Avatars (dolls, action figures, toy vehicles, miniature animals, dinosaurs, aliens, and the like) have been around for millennia, and for good reason. By shrinking the world to fit in the palms of their hands, children can work out complex emotional concepts in a manageable way.

Gill's Notebook

My Little Hero—How Kids Learn Responsibility

Taking Charge

Little ones often think size means power. After all, grown-ups are big, and they seem to think they can tell children what to do.

When a child plays with avatars, suddenly she's the biggest being in that world. She finds out how it feels to be in charge. And she discovers that, as Spider-Man says, "With great power comes great responsibility."

Avatars put children in the role of fixing and tending to things, just as they see parents, caregivers, and teachers do. Children aspire to become the heroes they see in us every day—the ones who respond to need. The central theme of most avatar play is caregiving—from feeding baby dolls to gassing up toy trucks, from defeating bad guys to kissing frog princes. In short, avatars let children figure out how to make everything right with the world.

Boys and Girls

Around the time children begin avatar play, you may start seeing what looks like gender-based choices. And it seems to come out of nowhere. I've had many parents swear to me that they provide a balanced, nongendered selection of toys and don't allow television or computer time.

Still, their sons choose trucks and army guys, and their daughters gravitate to dolls and tea sets.

Not all children gravitate to what looks like gender-based play, but many do. Are these choices hardwired or environmental? I wish I could tell you I know the answer but I don't. Instead, here's what I believe.

In the early years, a child's play choices have little—maybe nothing—to do with gender and everything to do with social and emotional needs. Because avatars give all the power to children, they are ideal for this kind of exploration of self. Any meaning adults may ascribe to a child's choice of doll or action figure, magic wand or light saber, princess carriage or Batmobile misses the point. Avatar play is all the same play: to tend, fix, care for, nourish, rescue, solve, defend. In short, to make better the lives of others.

And in my view, when children are reaching for these values this early in life, something really right is going on, no matter what they pick out of the toybox.

> By shrinking the world to fit in the palms of their hands, children can work out complex emotional concepts in a manageable way. When a child plays with avatars, suddenly she's the biggest being in that world. She finds out how it feels to be in charge.

Nourishing and Caretaking

"It's time for my baby's bottle."
—Suki, 2½ years old

"Gas 'er up and check the tires."
—Jack, 2 years old

Rescuing and Healing

"Here, have some medicine. It will make you feel better."
—Jacob, 3½ years old, to his teddy bear Pancake

"There's a fire on East Street. Don't worry! Fireman Milly is on the way!"
—Milly, 3½ years old

Defending and Restoring Order

"The wicked witch couldn't hurt anyone anymore, and they all lived happily ever after."
—Becky, 4 years old

"Pow! Zam! Ooomph! Take that, Riddler. That'll teach you to rob little old ladies!"
—Marco, 4 years old

Storytime: "I See"

Why Kids Play This Way

Tell a child not to lie, and your words go in one ear and out the other. Tell her the story of "The Boy Who Cried Wolf," and she'll see for herself the con-sequences of lying. By showing a character's journey, a story lets the audience slip into the skin of that character and play out the story for themselves. When a child's vivid imagination works within a well-told story, the story leaves a lasting impression.

> ### Family Moves
>
> Print "Gill's Notebook: My Little Hero—How Kids Learn Responsibility" from the digital file and share it with parents.

Moving Through Play

Often we think of storytime as quiet, passive time. And certainly, it is sub-dued compared to many other play patterns. But movement plays a key role in storytime.

Storytelling is about moving people emotionally. And to do that, a good storyteller must skillfully use facial expressions, gestures, body language, rhythm, and timing. In fact, without these dynamics, the very meaning of the story could be lost. (See Chapter 14.)

As you select and tell stories to children, remember: this is your chance to captivate them and help them learn to captivate others. Throw yourself into the story emotionally and physically, and you'll be helping them tell their own stories someday.

Developmental Benefits

- Storytime helps a child picture ideas in her mind. And the better the story is told, the more immersed in the visualization she'll be. When that happens, she doesn't need pictures in a book or images on a screen to tell her what a particular idea looks like. She knows for herself.

- A good story keeps the plot moving forward. With more and more experience, children sense this forward progression and start anticipating and predicting what might happen next. This helps them understand the continuum of time—past, present, and future. (See Chapter 12.)

- Every story needs a teller and a listener. Storytelling *is* human communication.

- Children learn about appropriate social behavior and the nuances of interacting with others through the stories they hear and tell.

- Good storytelling lets the audience safely experience the full range of human emotions.

- Storytelling teaches concepts of print. Reading to children builds essential foundations for independent reading by providing cues such as where to start reading on the page.

- Sharing a story is like sharing a secret. It belongs to both the teller and the listener.

What You Can Do

Be a chatterbox. Narrate everything you do and everything a child does. Talk, talk, talk. This will advance her use and understanding of language.

Be a storyteller. Storytelling isn't just for circle time or bedtime. Tell a story while you're out for a walk, on the playground, as a transition between activities, and so on.

Read, read, read! Read with children as often as you can. Make it part of your daily routine.

Be a bookaholic. Go to the library often. Join a children's book club. Create a book swap. Always have lots of books on hand—old favorites and intriguing new titles.

Be enthusiastic. Show children your love of story reading and storytelling. When you're the teller, ham it up! It might feel a little goofy at first, but children need to understand broad expressions in order to begin to detect subtler emotional cues.

Make up stories. Improvisation gives everyone involved an opportunity to create stories that are theirs, and theirs alone, forever. But more, making up stories and telling them over and over, each time in a slightly different way, showcases a broader use of vocabulary. In other words, you don't have to stick to a script.

Encourage improvisation. Let children make up their own stories and decide how to tell them. Perhaps they prefer to verbalize their stories, act them out, draw them, or write them down.

Sing! Telling stories through or with music multiplies the communication impact.

Use sound effects. Include lots of silly sounds in your storytelling, and encourage children to make their own to build auditory discrimination. (See Chapter 7.)

Put on shows. Dramatic storytelling helps children practice their communication skills.

Cuddle. Cuddle up while you read together. Feeling safe and together in the moment cements attachment, but may also lead to a lifetime love of reading.

Chapter Summary

- **Quiet time** is something we all need to reflect and absorb the day.
- **Creation play** helps children explore what they don't know yet. This exploration produces the drive to make new discoveries and invent new ways of doing things.
- **Avatar play** puts children in a position of power, where they can explore grown-up concepts such as taking responsibility for others.
- **Storytime** stimulates new ideas, reinforces positive values, and fosters communication skills.

© VADIM YEROFEYEV | DREAMSTIME.COM

CHAPTER 24

Effective Playmating

//

With a better understanding of the catalytic power of play, it's incumbent upon us to consider when, where, and how we as adults can be effective playmates with children. In the previous chapters, we outlined some things you can do to facilitate specific play patterns. Now let's talk about putting it all together to create a move-play-learn strategy.

Play looks different at different stages of development. So let's break this out, starting with newborns and infants.

Infant Play: Providing Stimulation

Infants' needs are simple. They need lots of contact; a warm, loving, calm environment; nutrition on demand; plenty of rest; clean diapers; and play.

Play seems too big a word for such a small child. Still, you'll likely find it comes naturally to both of you. Here are a few things to keep in mind.

> Creating an effective move-play-learn strategy means becoming a better playmate yourself.

Get Close

Babies can't see at a distance, so stay close, make eye contact, and smile. Even at this tender age, babies can sense emotions, and they look to adults for guidance.

Time Alone

Too much of a good thing isn't good—even if that good thing is you. A baby needs his space, just like everyone else. When he's content, leave him that way for a while. Let him get acquainted with himself. Watch from a distance to see what he does. When he needs you, he'll let you know.

Open Spaces

As we discussed in Chapter 5, babies need to sense the space around them and move at will—even if they aren't going anywhere yet. Even the smallest movements stimulate the senses. Lay baby on a blanket on the floor. Lie next to him and talk to him as he gets a feel for this new place. If you like, and the room is warm enough, take off his clothes. The skin contains millions of sensory receptors, so put them to good use.[40]

Get on Baby's Level

When you play with a baby, you should be close and at his level. Until he's ready to get up on his own, play lying down. And never prop him in a position he can't get himself into or out of.

Provide Sensory Experiences

As you play, consider all the sensory tools. (These are discussed in Chapters 6–9.) Gently introduce sensory stimulation such as colors, textures, and sounds. If baby appears to spark to something, let him play with it as long as he likes.

Baby Massage and Gentle Stretching

Help the infant learn more about his body through gentle massage and stretching. Lay baby down and gently massage him from top to toe, talking and singing about all the different parts that make up his little body. We'll show you a few of our favorite touch and massage activities in Part 6.

Eye Tracking

Use objects baby is attracted to in order to engage his focus. Slowly move the object across his field of vision to encourage eye movement.

Talking and Singing

Talk to baby all the time. Narrate what you're doing. He won't understand the words, but he'll love hearing the sound of your voice. And sing, too! Music has a powerful influence on early learning. (See Chapter 15.)

Get Outside Often

When the weather cooperates, take baby outdoors. Fresh air, sunshine, and a change of scenery are good for both of you.

Play with Other Children

Babies don't play *with* one another yet, but playing *near* one another is a first step toward learning to initiate relationships. Give them space to get to know each other without hovering.

Cuddling and Rocking

Devote time to cuddling and rocking baby when it's *not* feeding time. Use this time to gently change his orientation and perspective. Sit in different rooms or chairs. Lift him very slowly up and down. Gently tip him so that his feet are above his head for a few moments. Do these movements slowly and gently, while fully supporting him at all times. And be sure to tell him what you're going to do. Not only does this show respect for him, but the sound of your voice will also cue him that these movements are safe and avoid startling him.

Play Games

Play peekaboo and tell stories and rhymes. These activities will give the infant new sensations while associating you with feelings of love, comfort, security, and playfulness.

Toddler and Preschooler Play: Providing Freedom

Once a child can move independently, he's on the road to richer and more varied play, including free play, directed free play, and structured play.

Recommended Play Diet
For Mobile Children (Crawling+)

15%

25%

60%

● Free play

● Directed free play

● Structured play

Free Play

Free play is uninhibited, unfettered playtime. It happens alone or with peers. It's exploring, discovering, and imagining at will (with adequate supervision for safety always nearby). During free play, children should feel independent, even if you are just steps away.

Free play is by far the most important type of play. Here children set their own parameters and play out scenarios as they see fit. Free play creates a natural, kid-size environment for creative problem solving, independent decision making, and growing self-sufficiency.

Whether a child is alone or with other children, running with abandon or lying on the grass counting clouds, what's important is that he's in charge. Your role is to stay well out of the experience unless safety becomes an issue or the child invites you in.

Directed Free Play

Directed free play is play with gentle, unobtrusive guidance from an adult or another child who steers the play but not the outcome.

Some children love certain types of play and stick to what they love. But all children need variety in play and movement to ensure well-balanced development. Gently prompting different kinds of play helps them expand beyond what they like into new experiences they may like even better.

Structured Play

Structured play is a prescribed activity with a set outcome, directed by an adult or other authority (such as game rules). Structured activities introduce young children to social concepts such as interpersonal and group dynamics, sharing, teamwork, leadership, respect for others, and respect for rules. That said, be careful not to expose children to competition too early.

Early School Years: Balancing Play and Learning

Paradoxically, as a child develops more independent capabilities, his world becomes more structured. At home, there are schedules to keep. At school, there are lessons to learn. And other group activities and classes occupy what would otherwise be free playtime. Add to that the modern trend toward "academic creep," which favors academic pursuits at an earlier and earlier age, and it seems we've lost sight of the timeless truth that for kids, *everything is educational*—including, and especially, play.

Education vs. Academics

To be clear, learning letters and numbers is educational. But so is learning how to tie your shoes, when to say please, how to take turns, what it takes to get to the top of the monkey bars, and how not to get caught with your hand in the cookie jar. These life lessons and thousands more just like them learned through playful experimentation often go unheralded, yet create the foundations for the transition to formal learning. As kindergarten teachers know so well, a child is ready for school when he:

- understands everyday language
- dresses himself
- knows and can use good manners
- shares
- has stamina, coordination, and persistence
- understands there are rules he is expected to follow and consequences when he doesn't—along with a host of other move-to-learn "tasks" that develop from play and exploration

Family Moves

Print the "Infant Play: Providing Stimulation" handout, the "Toddler and Preschooler Play: Providing Freedom" handout, and Gill's Notebook entries "When the Score Doesn't Matter" and "Happy Endings" from the digital file and share them with parents.

It's all educational. It's just not academic. And at this critical, transitional stage, we need to make room for *both*.

Play-based learning does not end at the doorstep of kindergarten or the early grades for that matter. Just as we've outlined in Chapter 18, as much of a child's time as possible—in and out of school— should be free for his own personal, follow-your-nose journey of play and exploration with no agenda other than what's fun and fascinating right now. That's nature's educational plan. The progression from mud pies and monkey bars to textbooks and test scores is a gradual one. Respecting that transition means valuing play as a learning tool in the child's arsenal, even (and especially) when it *feels* like play.

Gill's Notebook

When the Score Doesn't Matter

Today there are so many wonderful programs to introduce young children to sports. From itty-bitty soccer teams to gymnastics, swimming, tennis, and so much more, children are being exposed to sports and sport techniques at a very young age. And in my view, that's all great so long as three things are firmly in place:

1. The child is having *fun*.

2. The child is getting a *variety* of physical experiences.

3. Any notion of judgment or competition (winning/losing, succeeding/failing) is kept *off* the playing field.

The Fun Imperative

Now, the good news is that many programs recognize, honor, and respect what I call "the fun imperative." These programs put the emphasis where it needs to be: on participation, exploration, experimentation, effort, and joy. However, from time to time I run into a grown-up who seems to have something else in mind (or simply forgets what fun looks like).

For instance, a while back I was with my granddaughter at her "'nastics" class. At three, she is bright, loving, smart as a whip, and fully uncoordinated.

As I was sitting and watching her bumble off the 3-inch balance beam four times in five steps, I overheard a mom nearby telling a friend that she wasn't going to sign up her son for another term. "He's not very good at this," she admitted. I looked across the gym and spotted her little boy who was bumbling around the gym, too. But, like my granddaughter, the look of determination on his little face spoke volumes. Sure, by adult standards, he wasn't very good. But then you've got to ask yourself, who needs standards when you're that little and trying that hard? (Besides, who needs the lessons more, the kid who's good at it, or the kid who isn't?)

Variety Matters

Sometimes sports are all a child wants to do. And while I respect and encourage that kind of enthusiasm, research shows that children with a well-rounded background in physical movement are better prepared to specialize later on.

And then there's the burnout factor. Young children who push themselves (or are pushed) into competitive sports too early may well be the ones who burn out early, too.

The Competition No-No

For little ones, being measured or compared on their physical performance can have lasting, negative effects. Beyond demoralizing the child with a premature concept of failure, or pinching his pride, introducing competition too early (especially physical competition) might serve to inhibit what *needs* to be the free and freeing use of his body for his overall development. And I'm not just talking about his physical development. You see, little ones are tangible learners. Any dent in the child's confidence to use his body in ways that feel natural to him may impact his view of his abilities in other areas as well, including how he approaches learning.

Being a Good Playmate

So, for the times when you're guiding or structuring the play, what should you aim for in your own play behavior? Let's take a look.

Sometimes adults struggle with child's play. This likely happens because play is so different from every other part of adult life where we're expected to be strong, mature, and in control. We're supposed to be responsible, efficient, effective, and productive. Yet, it's these very qualities that often make us ineffective playmates. So shake off that grown-up idea of *you* with these playful rules of thumb:

- **Do you know the secret password?** Just like any other playmate, you must wait for a child's invitation to play. Nobody likes a pushy playmate. (Remember, though: safety always trumps etiquette.)

- **Let children take the lead.** When it comes to play, children are better at it than you are. Know your place and follow their lead. With a new activity, you may need to show them the ropes, but aim to relinquish leadership to the children as soon as you can (and again, as long as safety is not an issue).

- **Get shorter.** Whenever you can, bring yourself down to kid level (both physically and emotionally). This is your time to see the world through their eyes.

- **Keep it pointless.** True play has no agenda and no rules. Whatever happens, happens. Keeping playtime open and free encourages children's imagination and helps them learn naturally.

Stimulating New Ideas: Introducing New Things

First impressions are lasting impressions, so paying attention to how new things are introduced is important.

- **Follow, don't lead.** Whatever interests the child is what you should spend time exploring.

- **"Stream of playfulness."** Children don't think the way we do. Their imaginations take them off on tangents we don't see coming. Give a child's "stream of playfulness" space to wander. Importantly, don't insist on things being "correct." *Correct* is a relative term—dependent on context— and in free-form play, only the child knows where he's headed.

- **Wonder aloud.** When you wonder aloud ("I wonder what that flower feels like?"), kids take up the idea and run with it. This is a great way to draw kids in and help them arrive at their own conclusions.

- **Recognize the positive behavior you want, not the negative behavior you don't want.** With new things, children won't necessarily know how to behave at first. For instance, a child might not know the difference between petting a dog and pulling its tail. Focusing on positive behavior is a great way to give him the guidance he needs. For instance, "I like how gentle you are being with the dog. Look. He likes when you're gentle, too."

- **Use *your* imagination.** When you introduce something new, try to imagine what it's like to never have seen it before. Find new ways to explore it so you and the child are each seeing things for the first time. This will make the experience more meaningful and memorable for both of you. And it will show the child that he can look at things in more than one way.

- **Physicalize new ideas.** Help him grasp new ideas by encouraging him to put his whole body into the learning. For instance, if you see a butterfly, wonder aloud what that must feel like to fly. Then watch his imagination take flight!

Gill's Notebook

Happy Endings

My granddaughter Caitlin and I were playing together one afternoon. I had to take a conference call, so I stepped away for a few minutes, leaving her happily playing princess in the living room.

When I returned, I asked her what had happened while I was gone. She didn't answer me. I asked again. Still no answer.

Then I realized she wasn't in my living room anymore. She'd transported herself to an imaginary world.

Deep in Play Means Deep in Learning

Play is the most important thing a child can do to expand her mind, body, and sense of self. Play gets the body up and moving and the imagination out and exploring.

When a child enters into a deep state of play, she's in charge of what's real and what's important. Time stands still as she makes her own discoveries and draws her own conclusions. In those moments of creation and decision making, she lays down the foundations for future learning— she's learning *how* to learn.

For a child deep in play, the "real" world melts away in favor of her own, far more vibrant and, yes, *real* reality. Anything that tries to interrupt (like nosy grannies) gets filtered out.

Interrupting Play

In my view, we should strive to give children opportunities for deep play as often and for as long as possible. But sometimes we must interrupt the play, and that can be tricky. The more deeply engrossed a child is in what she's doing, the bigger the fuss will be.

In hopes of helping you navigate the tantrum-filled waters of "It's time to stop," here are some of my favorite strategies for creating happy endings.

Distraction. A few minutes of distraction are often all you need for a smooth transition. For instance, if she loves fairies, be sure to have a magic wand in the closet in case you need to create an instant fairy moment. In short, always have something fun up your sleeve.

Preparedness. When playing a game, establish ground rules for stopping play *before* you begin. For younger children, set a timer. When it sounds, the game is done. For older children, establish the number of turns each child gets and have them count the turns.

Near the end of the game, advise the kids that the end is approaching. "Time's up soon" or "Two more turns each" is often enough to forego the fuss.

What next? When you can, offer choices for the next activity. For little ones, it's best to offer just a couple of options: "When we finish our game, you can have a snack, or we can read a story. Which would you like to do?" Be sure to honor the child's choice.

For older children, it's a good idea to get them to think stopping is their idea. You could say, "I wonder what we'll do after we finish this game?" Discuss the options and make sure it's a real conversation and collaboration.

The big finish. Play should always end on a high note. But once in a while, an activity will drag on too long. If you sense this, create a big finish.

Kids will follow your emotional lead, so ramp up the energy with your voice and actions. Add intensity to the last minutes of the game. Speed it up. Add a silly twist. Create a big finish! "Ta-da! Hooray! You did it!"

Celebration. Be sure to celebrate the play afterward. Encourage the child to retell the tales of her play. Listen intently. Ask questions. Explore it fully. Have her reenact it for you or draw a picture of it.

Post-play celebrations reinforce the concepts explored during play, and your interest will encourage her to play and explore even more. And that's what I call a happy ending!

Chapter Summary

- **Move-play-learn:** Creating an effective move-play-learn strategy means becoming a better playmate yourself.

- **Infant play:** Focus on providing the right amount of stimulation to engage the child but not tax him.

- **Time alone:** Babies need time to themselves in order to understand their own bodies in the environment.

- **Cuddling and rocking:** For infants and babies, cuddle and rock not only for feeding but at other times to foster bonding and balance.

- **Toddler and preschooler play:** This is the time where independent mobility kicks in.

- **Free play rocks!** As much as possible, children should follow their own interests during free playtime. A preschooler's day should feature about 60 percent free play, 25 percent directed free play, and 15 percent structured play.

- **Follow effective playmating guidelines:** Wait for an invitation to play. Let the child lead the play. Get down at the child's level, both physically and emotionally. Let the play unfold according to the child's dictates, unless safety becomes an issue.

- **Introducing new ideas:** How you do this affects how a child learns. Spend time exploring deeply what interests him. Introduce a new idea and let the child's "stream of playfulness" wander. Wonder aloud to help a child consider new ideas. Focus on the positive behavior you want, not the negative behavior you don't want. Use your imagination. Physicalize new ideas.

- **Happy endings:** Put play to an end with a minimum of fuss. Try not to interrupt play, but if you must, make happy endings with distraction, preparedness, introducing what's next, making a big finish, and celebration.

PART 6

Smart Steps

CHAPTER 25

Introducing Smart Steps

//

In this section you'll find some carefully selected move-to-learn activities we call "Smart Steps." Smart Steps is a step-by-step program designed to optimize young children's natural need for movement in order to strengthen their physical, cognitive, social, and emotional foundations for early learning and school readiness. This developmentally based program includes three key elements:

- The Movement Can-Do Guide, an observational assessment tool

- A planned sequence of move-to-learn activities that offer incremental challenge and achievement

- Teacher's notes for providing positive movement experiences that advance and automate children's foundational physical capabilities

Smart Steps is designed for children from birth through seven years, one-on-one or in groups. Let's start by discussing some overall guidelines.

Automation First

Developing high performance physical skills for the playing field is *not* the aim of the Smart Steps program. Nor is what adults normally think of as "fitness." Instead, the primary objective is to help children refine and automate their movements,

which in turn unlocks their brain power for the thinking, reasoning, and creativity needed for formal learning.

So how do you know if a child has fully automated specific movements?

When a child hasn't yet automated a movement, she'll be fully engrossed and concentrating on it. She'll seem lost in thought. She won't speak, make eye contact, or respond to nonphysical stimulation until she's completed the movement.

To gauge automaticity, here's a quick way to check. While she's doing a movement, ask her to answer an easy question unrelated to what she's doing. For instance: "I can't remember. How old are you?" If the child can move and answer at the same time, she has automated that movement. If she can't think of the answer, doesn't answer at all, or stops moving to answer your question, she's showing that she can't move while thinking about something else. In other words, that movement is not automated. (See Chapter 3 for more on automaticity.)

Respect Individuality

As we discussed earlier, one-size-fits-all never fits any child perfectly. So the driving force behind Smart Steps is to make the activity fit the child, not the child fit the activity.[41]

Each child develops at her own pace, and automating movement takes time and repetition. And along the way to building automaticity, we need to be sure we're building confidence as well. Take time to achieve *both*. Rushing through an activity to keep a group of children at the same level may be counterproductive, both for individual children and the entire group.

> Make the activity fit the child, not the child fit the activity.

Small Steps Are Big

In early childhood, all progress is a big achievement no matter how small. It's essential to assess each child's physical development individually—to consider not where she "should" be but where she began and where she is now.

All effort—in any form, on any front—contributes to a child's advancement. Some children reach their goal on the first try, some on the third, some on the 33rd. Repetition is the key to early learning, so trying things again and again *is* the lesson plan.

Try not to get frustrated. If you do, don't let the child see. If there's no obvious progress over a period of time, or the child is not having any fun, try another activity and come back to this one later. Remember, the brain learns as much or more from failure as from success. Understanding and encouraging effort is the easiest, fastest, and most effective way forward.

Participate and Demonstrate

While children are natural-born movers, guidance ensures they get a well-balanced diet of physical experiences while building up confidence and self-esteem. Often it's best if you demonstrate and participate in the activities yourself, so that children can learn by:

- Seeing what the movement looks like
- Hearing the words and ideas associated with the movement
- Doing the movement themselves (with you and on their own)

Gill's Notebook

Supporting a Moving Child

Children learning new movement skills often need our support. Most children need more support at first and less as time passes. How you give support is important both to a child's physical safety and to her confidence. So here are a few ideas to help you help little ones move and learn with confidence.

Balanced Support

If a child needs your help, support her on both sides of her body. Supporting a child on one side, such as holding one hand, gives the child's brain an unbalanced message. It may skew how the child moves.

I Won't Let You Fall

Often children need support when they're nervous or uncertain. Stand in front of the child so she can see you at all times. Make eye contact and talk supportively about her efforts. Fold your arms in front of you, bend down, and offer them to the child as a handrail. Keep your arms steady and walk backward in pace with her forward movement. This provides physical support and a connection between you in an important emotional moment.

Helping Hands
As the child's confidence grows, try the activity holding both of *her* hands. Stay in front of her so she can see you're her partner in the process. But now, she is doing more of the work.

Don't Worry, I've Got You
Once the child is confident in her abilities, it's important she take the lead. Move to her back and support her with your hands on either side of her waist.

I'm Here Just in Case
As the child progresses, she'll need less and less support from you but will likely still need reassurance. Now hold onto the back of her shirt. This gives her freedom to move without help but lets her know you're there. It's also a great way to help her slow down a bit without interrupting her movement.

Soloing
When the child feels confident enough to go solo, stand behind her with your hands near her waist—but not touching. She'll sense that you're there while proving to herself that she can do it!

Smart Steps at Play

Step 1: Assessment
Sequential teaching takes the learner step-by-step from the known to the new. It's widely used in academics, but less so for children's physical development. To help you create effective, move-to-learn experiences, we've divided the six can-do stages of early childhood movement (see Chapter 17) into three levels: On the Move, Watch Me Grow, and In The Know.

Through simple observation and referring to the Movement Can-Do Guide, you should be able to assess a child's current capabilities and select the Smart Steps activities best suited to help her grow and advance. Please remember: this guide is not meant for comparing children of the same age. And don't use it to gauge where a child should be in her development. She is where she is. Start from there.

SARAH ALICE LEE

The Movement Can-Do Guide

On the Move

Play by Play		Moving into new skills and abilities
Snugglers Birth to rolling over Approximate age: 0–6 months		Primitive reflexes in place Head control (first attempts) Enjoys touch, massage, and skin-to-skin care
Squigglers Rocking, crawling, and sitting Approximate age: 6–14 months		Grasping Mouthing (mimicking mouth movements) Commando crawling (beginning to explore the floor)
Scampers Pulling up to walking Approximate age: 9–24 months		Learning navigation (small spaces) Pulling up to standing (aided) Cruising Bobbing up and down (aided)
Stompers Running and jumping Approximate age: 20 months–3½ years		Running Bobbing up and down (independently)
Scooters Hopping and climbing Approximate age: 3–4 years		Early signs of handedness Balancing on one foot (dominant hand and foot awakening)
Skedaddlers Skipping, leaping, cooperative games, and dance Approximate age: 4 years and older		Leaping (from standing) Cross-walking (crossing one foot over the other)

Watch Me Grow

Growing through practice by playing, exploring, and experimenting

In the Know

Automating skills while building confidence to try more

Watch Me Grow	In the Know
Hand and foot recognition starts Hip tips (attempting to roll) Discovery through senses emerging (especially mouth)	Fascinated by faces (studies facial expressions) Rolling independently Pushing up (from tummy) Postural reflexes emerging (primitive reflexes abating)
Up on all fours Rocking Releasing grasp (voluntarily) Changing hands	Crawling Pincer grip Pushing into sitting position
Standing independently Climbing on furniture or stairs	Eye-hand coordination emerging (self-feeding) Toddling and walking
Jumping (on two feet) Upper body strength (beginning to hold own weight)	Jumping (forward or backward) Manipulative skills (using objects to affect other things) Temporal awareness emerging (attempts to catch, bat, or kick moving ball)
Marching Hopping on one foot Coordinated climbing	Galloping Midlines sharpening Dominant hand and foot developing
Leaping (from running) Skipping (no rope)	Automated, coordinated movement such as dance, skipping rope, and playground games

Step 2: Get Moving

Knowing where to start is half the battle. Once you've done a can-do assessment, it's time to get moving. Let's preview how each activity is set up.

Smart Steps Activity Preview

Get Ready!
Preparation needed and introduction for the activity

Watch Me Grow
Sequential level 2 activity

Can-Do Guide
Appropriate developmental stages for this activity

Kinetic Benefits
The developmental benefits (high, medium, or low) for each of the six physicalities in the Kinetic Scale

Underlying Benefits
Specific developmental benefits this activity encourages

Language
Key words and language concepts to introduce and explore throughout the activity

Safeguards
Safety guidelines

Equipment
Equipment list

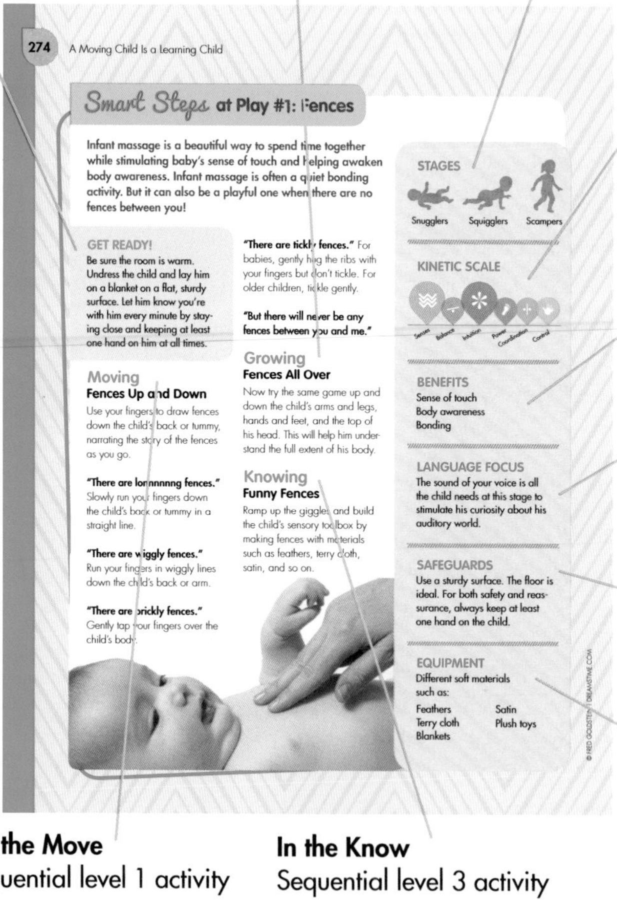
274 A Moving Child Is a Learning Child

Smart Steps at Play #1: Fences

Infant massage is a beautiful way to spend time together while stimulating baby's sense of touch and helping awaken body awareness. Infant massage is often a quiet bonding activity. But it can also be a playful one when there are no fences between you!

GET READY!
Be sure the room is warm. Undress the child and lay him on a blanket on a flat, sturdy surface. Let him know you're with him every minute by staying close and keeping at least one hand on him at all times.

Moving
Fences Up and Down
Use your fingers to draw fences down the child's back or tummy, narrating the story of the fences as you go.

"There are lonnnnnng fences." Slowly run your fingers down the child's back or tummy in a straight line.

"There are wiggly fences." Run your fingers in wiggly lines down the child's back or arm.

"There are prickly fences." Gently tap your fingers over the child's body.

"There are tickly fences." For babies, gently hug the ribs with your fingers but don't tickle. For older children, tickle gently.

"But there will never be any fences between you and me."

Growing
Fences All Over
Now try the same game up and down the child's arms and legs, hands and feet, and the top of his head. This will help him understand the full extent of his body.

Knowing
Funny Fences
Ramp up the giggles and build the child's sensory toolbox by making fences with materials such as feathers, terry cloth, satin, and so on.

STAGES
Snugglers Squigglers Scampers

KINETIC SCALE
Senses Balance Intuition Power Coordination Control

BENEFITS
Sense of touch
Body awareness
Bonding

LANGUAGE FOCUS
The sound of your voice is all the child needs at this stage to stimulate his curiosity about his auditory world.

SAFEGUARDS
Use a sturdy surface. The floor is ideal. For both safety and reassurance, always keep at least one hand on the child.

EQUIPMENT
Different soft materials such as:
Feathers
Terry cloth
Blankets
Satin
Plush toys

© FRED GOLDSTEIN | DREAMSTIME.COM

On the Move
Sequential level 1 activity

In the Know
Sequential level 3 activity

Selecting Appropriate Activities

In our discussion of the Kinetic Scale in Chapter 17, we explained the importance of providing a wide variety of movement experiences not only for the body, but also for the brain. As you select activities, use *variety* as your key criteria. Strive for a balance among the six physicalities over the course of your program, whether it's a single session, a week, or an entire term.

As you thumb through the activities in Chapter 26, you'll notice we've organized them according to the six physicalities in the Kinetic Scale. This should help you plan a well-balanced diet of movement. But a single activity may have multiple developmental benefits, so we've coded each activity with an at-a-glance visual guide to all of the kinetic benefits. The code is based on a three-point scale—high, medium, and low—which you'll see depicted visually through three different sized icons:

low   medium   high

Step 3: Evaluation

How do you know when a child is ready to advance to the next level? When she's becoming confident and capable with an activity, you'll notice one or more of these things:

- She'll do the activity without asking for help.
- She'll do it faster.
- She'll do it with less concentration (automatically).
- She'll want to show you what she can do.
- She'll go back to that same activity repeatedly.
- She'll seek out or invent new challenges on her own.

When you see these signs, it may be time to bump the challenge up one level. If you find a child is not mastering a specific progression and is getting frustrated, do not advance her. Instead, try going back a level to give her extra time to prepare for the bigger challenge, or try a different activity and return to this one later. It's important not to dent her confidence.

So, let's get moving

Chapter Summary

- Smart Steps is a step-by-step program designed to optimize young children's natural need for movement in order to strengthen their physical, cognitive, social, and emotional foundations for early learning and school readiness.

- With Smart Steps, the primary objective is to help children refine and automate their movement foundations in order to unlock their brain power for the thinking, reasoning, and creativity needed for formal learning.

- Respect individuality: make the activity fit the child, not the child fit the activity.

- Repetition is the key to learning for young children.

- Participate and demonstrate so children learn by seeing, hearing, and then trying on their own with your guidance.

- Teach and assess at three levels: On the Move, Watch Me Grow, and In the Know. Use the Movement Can-Do Guide to assess a child's current capabilities and select the Smart Steps activities best suited to help her grow and advance.

- To evaluate when a child is growing capable and confident with an activity, notice whether she can do it without help, is doing it faster or with less concentration, wants to show you what she can do, returns to the activity repeatedly, or is seeking out new challenges on her own.

CHAPTER 26
The Activities: Smart Steps at Play

//

This chapter includes 24 Smart Steps activities. (You will find 12 additional activities in the digital file. See page ix for the URL and password.) The activities are grouped according to their sensory and motor emphasis:

The Senses
Sights, sounds, smells, tastes, touch, massage, eye fitness, object permanence, sorting, sequencing, patterning

1. Fences
2. Oobakeep
3. The Quest Chest
4. Mirror, Mirror

Balance
Rolling, spinning, swinging, rocking, balancing, turning upside down

5. Tip and Dip Dance
6. Over and Under
7. Say Hello, Octopo!
8. Roll-Over Rover

Intuition
Inclines, body awareness, pushing and pulling, lifting and carrying

9. Scarves
10. Fill 'er Up
11. Muddo
12. The Beanbaggles

Power
Crawling, walking, running, jumping, hopping, skipping, climbing, tumbling, stretching, wheel play

13. Hips Tips
14. Runaway Bubbles
15. Narrow and Wide
16. Chicken Switch

Coordination
Crawling, hopping, leaping, climbing, marching, skipping, bicycling, ball play, stepping stones

17. Hands, Meet Feet
18. Farm Gates
19. The Pretzelator
20. Steppin' Magic

Control
Locomotion, stability, manipulative play, targeting, fine motor activities, playground games

21. The Eyes Have It
22. Baby Steering
23. Time-to-Go Games
24. Breaker! Breaker!

Smart Steps at Play #1: Fences

Infant massage is a beautiful way to spend time together while stimulating baby's sense of touch and helping awaken body awareness. Infant massage is often a quiet bonding activity. But it can also be a playful one when there are no fences between you!

GET READY!

Be sure the room is warm. Undress the child and lay him on a blanket on a flat, sturdy surface. Let him know you're with him every minute by staying close and keeping at least one hand on him at all times.

Moving
Fences Up and Down

Use your fingers to draw fences down the child's back or tummy, narrating the story of the fences as you go.

"There are lonnnnnng fences." Slowly run your fingers down the child's back or tummy in a straight line.

"There are wiggly fences." Run your fingers in wiggly lines down the child's back or arm.

"There are prickly fences." Gently tap your fingers over the child's body.

"There are tickly fences." For babies, gently hug the ribs with your fingers but don't tickle. For older children, tickle gently.

"But there will never be any fences between you and me."

Growing
Fences All Over

Now try the same game up and down the child's arms and legs, hands and feet, and the top of his head. This will help him understand the full extent of his body.

Knowing
Funny Fences

Ramp up the giggles and build the child's sensory toolbox by making fences with materials such as feathers, terry cloth, satin, and so on.

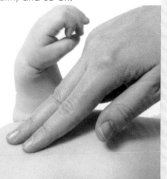

STAGES

Snugglers   Squigglers   Scampers

KINETIC SCALE

Senses Balance Intuition Power Coordination Control

BENEFITS

Sense of touch
Body awareness
Bonding

LANGUAGE FOCUS

The sound of your voice is all the child needs at this stage to stimulate his curiosity about his auditory world.

SAFEGUARDS

Use a sturdy surface. The floor is ideal. For both safety and reassurance, always keep at least one hand on the child.

EQUIPMENT

Different soft materials such as:

Feathers	Satin
Terry cloth	Plush toys
Blankets	

Smart Steps at Play #2: Oobakeep

Oobakeep is the best little hide-and-seeker you'll ever meet. She knows where everything is hiding—especially the things you can't keep track of. Oobakeep knows where you keep your nose and your toes and everything in between!

GET READY!

A twist on baby's favorite peek-aboo, all you need is a blanket and a feather (or anything tickly). A great game to play anytime, anywhere.

Moving
Peekaboo!

Babies love surprises, so start by playing peekaboo. Hide behind the blanket, then reappear. Peekaboo! Classic peekaboo helps develop the concept of object permanence.

Growing
Oobakeep!

Cover the child's knee with the blanket. Ask, "Where did your *knee* go?" Even at the earliest stages, words plant language seeds for the future.

While her knee is hidden, give it a little tickle. "Oobakeep! Oobakeep! Can you find my *knee*?"

Remove the blanket and give the child's knee another tickle. "There's your *knee!*" Combining the tactile sensation of tickling both before and after you remove the blanket will help her sense her own body while you reinforce the idea with words.

Repeat the game with other parts of the body.

Knowing
My First Hide-and-Seek

As the child plays on the floor, hide different objects under the blanket. Be sure the child sees you covering each object.

Ask, "Where did your toy go?" Lift the blanket. "There's your toy!"

Playing hide-and-seek with objects helps baby develop object permanence while moving her body to follow her own curiosity.

STAGES

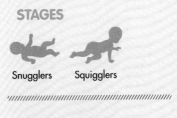

Snugglers   Squigglers

KINETIC SCALE

Senses   Balance   Intuition   Power   Coordination   Control

BENEFITS
Object permanence
Body awareness

LANGUAGE FOCUS
Body parts

SAFEGUARDS
Never cover baby's face with the blanket.

EQUIPMENT
Blanket
Feather (or other tickly texture)

Smart Steps at Play #3: The Quest Chest

Little ones love looking for treasures. And the get-up-and-go it takes is great for physical development, curiosity, and observation skills.

GET READY!

The Quest Chest can be a simple cardboard box or plastic pail, but it's even more fun if the child makes it his own. Get out the arts and crafts supplies and encourage the child to make his own Quest Chest by drawing a picture or writing his name on one side of a cardboard box. Then, after each quest, have him add decorations by gluing on objects he's found.

Creating a ritual for starting this or any game gives the child time to mentally prepare for the activity and builds anticipation for the fun to come. Each time you play Quest Chest, start with "The Quester's Creed."

The Quester's Creed

We're on a quest to fill our chest
With treasures you will never guess!
From north and south and east and west,
We'll find the most AMAZINGEST!

Moving
Treasure Quest

Pick a theme and together go questing! For instance, you might go in search of things that are blue, things that make noise, or things that are soft. Have the child put his treasures in his Quest Chest to build his own sensory collection.

Growing
Treasure Sort

After the quest, spend time with the treasures you've collected. These objects now have special meaning for the child because he found them, so take the opportunity to expand his knowledge and understanding.

First, talk about his quest. Ask, "Where did we find this treasure?" Get the child to tell you his story.

Then, talk about the treasures themselves. How does this fit our theme (association)? What else do they have in common? What makes them different (discrimination)? Sort the treasures by size, shape, or theme (patterning). And be sure to involve as many senses as you can in his evaluation to create a multisensory experience.

Knowing
Use Your Treasures

When a child actively engages with new objects and new ideas, he learns more. And more importantly, he learns to apply what he knows to other situations. That is the beginning of problem solving. Encourage the child to decide what he wants to do with his loot! For instance:

- Make a piece of art using all the treasures you've found.

- Make up a song or story using the names of your treasures.

- Pick one treasure and learn more about it. Take a field trip to discover more. Go to the library and pick out books about it.

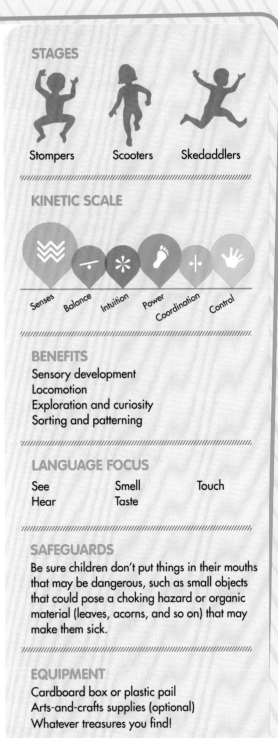

STAGES

Stompers   Scooters   Skedaddlers

KINETIC SCALE

Senses Balance Intuition Power Coordination Control

BENEFITS

Sensory development
Locomotion
Exploration and curiosity
Sorting and patterning

LANGUAGE FOCUS

See   Smell   Touch
Hear   Taste

SAFEGUARDS

Be sure children don't put things in their mouths that may be dangerous, such as small objects that could pose a choking hazard or organic material (leaves, acorns, and so on) that may make them sick.

EQUIPMENT

Cardboard box or plastic pail
Arts-and-crafts supplies (optional)
Whatever treasures you find!

Smart Steps at Play #4: Mirror, Mirror

Kids are natural mimics. They want to do whatever you do. Use that to build children's eye fitness and create opportunities for social growth and development.

GET READY!

Put on some soft, soothing music to set a gentle tone. Start by looking in the mirror with the child and talking about how the mirror always does exactly what we do. "It must be really fun to be a mirror. Will you be my mirror?"

> Mirror, mirror,
> Can you see?
> Mirror, mirror,
> Dance with me.
> Mirror, mirror,
> Let's fly free.
> Mirror, mirror,
> What shall we be?

Moving
Quiet Time Reflections

Sit facing each other. Recite the "Mirror, Mirror" rhyme while moving your hands and arms slowly. Have the child mirror your movements. Moving slowly will help the child follow you and will help her brain absorb the learning more easily. To enhance eye tracking, have her hold her head still so only her eyes are following you.

Next, try the activity sitting side by side facing the mirror. This is a fun way to play with perspective and peripheral vision.

Growing
Reflecting Feet-to-Feet

Repeat the activity by sitting and slowly mirroring foot and leg movements. Once you've had some fun moving your upper and lower bodies, try mirroring whole-body movements.

Knowing
I'm the Mirror!

At the end of the "Mirror, Mirror" rhyme, the verse invites you to switch roles. When the child is ready, encourage her to take the lead so that she decides the terms of the play.

Mirror Memory

For a slightly more advanced version, create a visual movement memory game. Create a sequence with two or three simple movements. For example: *step, clap, step*. Have the child repeat the sequence. As she gets more adept, add another movement to the sequence. For example: *step, clap, step, hop*. Take care not to frustrate the child. Continue until she feels she's fully mastered the challenge.

STAGES

Stompers   Scooters   Skedaddlers

KINETIC SCALE

Senses   Balance   Intuition   Power   Coordination   Control

BENEFITS

Eye-hand coordination
Eye tracking
Sensory development
Social development

LANGUAGE FOCUS

In
Out
Around
Near
Far

SAFEGUARDS

Be sure the movements you choose are
within the child's capabilities.

EQUIPMENT

Soothing music
Mirror

Smart Steps at Play #5: Tip and Dip Dance

When babies can roll over by themselves, they are on the road to independence. They're seeking more physical experiences that will help develop their sense of right side up and upside down. Helping the child experience these sensations gently is as simple as asking him to dance with you.

GET READY!

Put on some music and try this activity's different dance steps to help develop the child's balance.

Before you start, prompt the child by telling him what's going to happen. For example: "We're going to go for a spin this way. Now we're going the other way." Even though the child is too young to understand your words, your voice will reassure him.

Moving

Tippy Time

Hold and support baby around the waist and under the chest (so he is in a facedown flying position). Keep him close to your body at all times for reassurance.

Gently bob, dance, and spin slowly. Tip him gently so his head is above his feet. Then

reverse and tip him slightly so his head is below his feet. Again, do all of this *very slowly and gently* while maintaining full support of the child's body.

Growing
Dippy Time

Repeat the activity, but now hold the baby a little away from your body, fully supporting his chest and neck. This seemingly small change challenges baby to begin using his own core muscles to hold himself up. In addition, this is a gentle way of helping him sense his body independent of you while still feeling you close to him. If baby doesn't like this sensation, stop and bring him back in close to your body.

Knowing
Shall We Dance?

Repeat the dance, turning baby so he's lying on his back. Support him fully behind his neck and lower back. This position challenges the emerging postural head-righting reflex, which may cause some fussing at first. This is quite natural. His instinct will be to try to lift his head toward his chest in this position. He should relax quickly and enjoy the dance. But if it appears to be uncomfortable, change position or stop. Always let the child guide you.

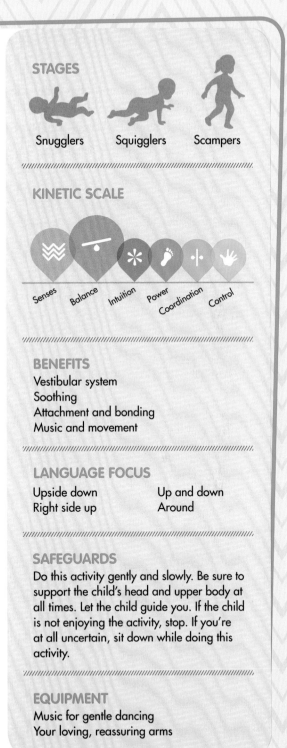

STAGES

Snugglers   Squigglers   Scampers

KINETIC SCALE

Senses   Balance   Intuition   Power   Coordination   Control

BENEFITS

Vestibular system
Soothing
Attachment and bonding
Music and movement

LANGUAGE FOCUS

Upside down   Up and down
Right side up   Around

SAFEGUARDS

Do this activity gently and slowly. Be sure to support the child's head and upper body at all times. Let the child guide you. If the child is not enjoying the activity, stop. If you're at all uncertain, sit down while doing this activity.

EQUIPMENT

Music for gentle dancing
Your loving, reassuring arms

Smart Steps at Play #6: Over and Under

The first way children learn directional concepts such as *over* and *under* is physically. Tangible experiences make such abstract concepts real and meaningful, so the child can one day translate them to formal learning concepts.

GET READY!

Learning *over* and *under* begins with simple play concepts children understand as soon as they begin moving around for themselves. Climbing over a pillow and under a table is a day's adventure for little ones. So clear some floor space or head outside onto the grass, and let's build on those natural play patterns.

Moving
Tunnels and Mountains

Make a tunnel with your legs and encourage the child to crawl through. As she crawls under them, use the word *under* to narrate the play. Make more tunnels with your arms, torso, and in any other way to get the child to tunnel *under* you.

Now introduce the concept of *over*. Challenge the child to climb *over* your legs, arms, tummy, and so on.

Growing
I'm a Tunnel

Encourage the child to make tunnels with her own body. As she does, roll a favorite toy through the tunnel and talk about how the toy goes *under* the tunnel. And of course, have the child make mountains with her body and roll the toy up and *over* the mountain.

Knowing
The Over-Under Journey

Have two children pair up (or you can partner with a child). The object of the game is to cross the room with your partner by going *over* and *under* each other.

Start by deciding where to go. The children may choose a real place, like the other side of the room, or an imaginary place, like the dinosaur forest or the prince's castle! Wherever they decide to go, pick a physical location 10 to 15 feet away as your target for a game of five to six turns.

Next, decide who travels *over* and who travels *under*. Again, let the children decide. Using only their bodies and imaginations, the *over* players must travel each step of the journey by going over their partner. Likewise, the *under* players must go under the other partner.

Here are a few ideas to get you started. By all means, though, let the children make up their own over-under obstacles as much as possible.

- Go over the hill. (One child crouches while the other climbs over her.)

- Go under the bridge. (One child forms a bridge with her body or legs while the other tunnels under her.)
- Go over the tickle tiger. (One child lies down on her back. She tries to tickle the other child as the child crawls over.)
- Go under the gate. (One child lies on the floor and raises one leg in the air up and down like a toll gate. The other child scoots through the gate when it's open.)
- Wiggle over the worm. (One child wiggles like a worm on the floor while the other wiggles over her.)

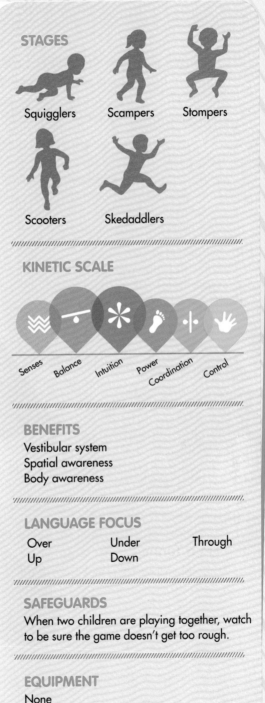

STAGES

Squigglers   Scampers   Stompers

Scooters   Skedaddlers

KINETIC SCALE

Senses   Balance   Intuition   Power   Coordination   Control

BENEFITS
Vestibular system
Spatial awareness
Body awareness

LANGUAGE FOCUS

Over	Under	Through
Up	Down	

SAFEGUARDS
When two children are playing together, watch to be sure the game doesn't get too rough.

EQUIPMENT
None

Smart Steps at Play #7: Say Hello, Octopo!

To master control of their bodies, children must learn balance from all different orientations and positions. Combining body awareness, midline development, and balance, this game challenges children to discover what they can do with different parts of their bodies while keeping their balance.

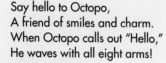

GET READY!

Introduce Octopo: "I wonder what it would be like to be an octopus with eight arms! Just imagine what you could do if you had eight arms to do it with!"

Say hello to Octopo,
A friend of smiles and charm.
When Octopo calls out "Hello,"
He waves with all eight arms!

Moving
Octopo Waves

Have the children get down on all fours and be Octopo. Start the game simply, adding levels of complexity as you go.

Wave your right arm.
Wave your left arm.
Wave your right foot.
Wave your left foot.
Wave your right arm and right foot.
Wave your left arm and left foot.
Wave your right arm and left foot.
Wave your left arm and right foot.
Wave both arms.
Wave both feet.

SARAH ALICE LEE

Growing

Upside-Down Octopo

Have the children stand, reach down and put their hands on the floor, and repeat the game. This creates an upside-down orientation, which makes it more challenging to coordinate arms and legs. It also builds upper body strength.

Knowing

Musical Octopo

Play some lively music while children wave their arms and legs like Octopo to the beat of the music.

When the music stops, call out two parts of the body and have the children balance their bodies on those two body parts.

STAGES

Stompers   Scooters   Skedaddlers

KINETIC SCALE

Senses   Balance   Intuition   Power   Coordination   Control

BENEFITS
Balance
Body awareness
Stamina

LANGUAGE FOCUS
Upside down
Left and right
Body parts

SAFEGUARDS
Use a mat or towel on a hard surface. Be sure each player has enough space.

EQUIPMENT
Music with a good beat

Smart Steps at Play #8: Roll-Over Rover

Roll-over reading helps children develop their language skills and get ready for reading by making storytime an interactive, multisensory experience. And the vestibular stimulation actually helps children focus and concentrate on the story.

GET READY!

Roll-Over Rover can't seem to do anything right side up, unless he's upside down—which makes it hard to remember which end is up! He loves to roll over and over and over because it's fun to see things in new ways!

At storytime today, Rover thought it would be fun to listen to the story upside down. And boy, was he right! Try a little roll-over reading with children, and see what Rover sees.

Note: Do *not* play this game on a bed or any elevated surface.

Moving
Page-by-Page Rollovers

Have the children pick a favorite storybook and lie down on their tummies on the floor to listen to the story.

Each time you turn the page, have the children roll over a half turn (from tummy to back or back to tummy). Before you start, get the children to decide which way (left or right) they're going to roll to prevent traffic jams.

It's difficult for the children to see the pictures while doing roll-over reading. Use that to your advantage. During and after the story, have the children discuss how they envision the characters. For instance, you might prompt them by asking what color the animal character is and what his house looks like. This form of visualization enhances children's ability to imagine and relate what they see in their mind's eye to others, while solidifying the story in their imaginations and memories.

Growing
Key Word Rollovers

Instead of rolling over each time the page is turned, select a key word from the story. (Pick one that appears many times.) Have the children roll over each time they hear that word. This helps children focus especially hard on the story while building auditory discrimination as they listen intently for the key word.

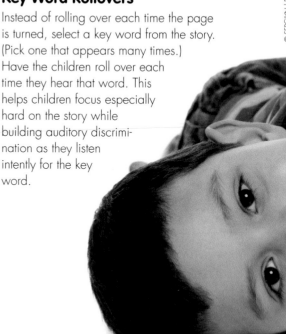

Side Rollovers

To add another level of challenge, when the page is turned, have the children turn a quarter roll so that they stop on their sides. Try to get them to keep their bodies still and straight, so that they have to work at keeping their balance. This may be a bit tricky. It requires more coordination, control, and concentration. The next time the page is turned, children roll a second quarter roll to their other side and stop.

If the children are really enjoying this, add the key word to the activity. When they hear the key word, have them roll all the way over.

Once the children get the idea of the game, have the children decide which movements they would like to use during Roll-Over Rover time.

And when the story is done, everybody rolls all the way across the room!

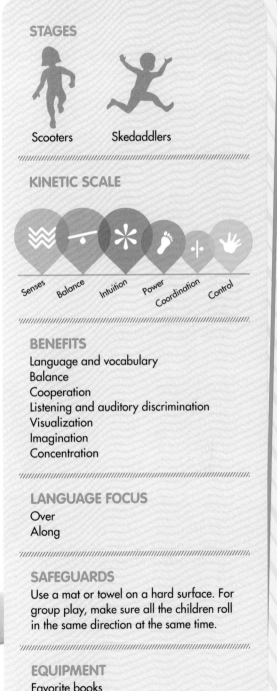

STAGES

Scooters   Skedaddlers

KINETIC SCALE

Senses   Balance   Intuition   Power   Coordination   Control

BENEFITS
Language and vocabulary
Balance
Cooperation
Listening and auditory discrimination
Visualization
Imagination
Concentration

LANGUAGE FOCUS
Over
Along

SAFEGUARDS
Use a mat or towel on a hard surface. For group play, make sure all the children roll in the same direction at the same time.

EQUIPMENT
Favorite books

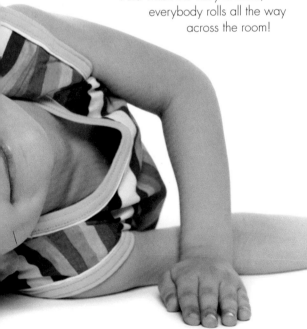

Smart Steps at Play #9: Scarves*

Multisensory experiences foster baby's understanding of herself and her world.

GET READY!

Soft, sheer chiffon scarves create a gentle, colorful playspace for babies. The light and airy touch of scarves provides gentle tickling sensations all over. Scarves are easy for babies to grasp and hold, conforming to little fingers working toward their pincer grip. And when you throw scarves up in the air, they offer a dramatic light show for babies learning to track objects with their eyes.

Moving
Scarves Everywhere

Lay baby on the floor or other safe surface so she can see you kneeling over her. With a chiffon scarf, tickle her face, neck, head, and any part of her skin. As the scarf touches the different body parts, tell her which part you are touching. "I'm tickling your feet."

Growing
Sneaky Scarves

Pass the scarf behind baby's back, under her knees, through and around her ankles, over her head, and so on. Tell her what you're doing and the body part you're touching. Use directional language such as *behind your knee* and *on top of your toes*. Just for the fun of it, try threading the scarf under her shirt directly on her skin, and shimmy it up through the neck or sleeve for a great big smile!

SARAH ALICE LEE

* Thanks to Adele Orangi for contributing this activity.

Knowing
Scarves in the Air

As baby begins moving around, throw the scarf into the air. Encourage her to grasp and then release it. Watch for her anticipation as the scarf comes down, and be ready for giggles to explode when it lands with a tickle. All the while, narrate the playful events. "Oh, it landed on your toes!"

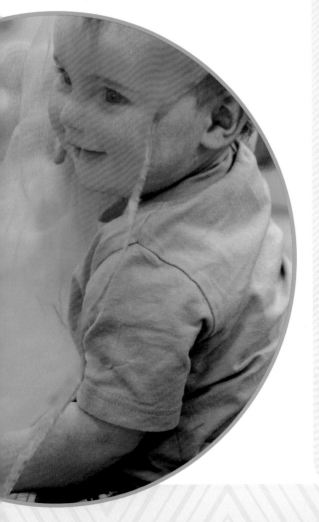

STAGES

Snugglers   Squigglers   Scampers

KINETIC SCALE

Senses   Balance   Intuition   Power   Coordination   Control

BENEFITS

Body awareness
Eye tracking
Sensory development
Soothing

LANGUAGE FOCUS

Body parts   Up   Behind
Over   Down   Top

SAFEGUARDS

Monitor this activity at all times. Avoid wrapping scarves around the head or neck. Keep the scarves away from the airways. Make sure you use scarves made of light, transparent material. Be sure there's enough room for the children to move around during this activity. Do not leave any child unattended with a scarf.

EQUIPMENT

Soft scarf

Smart Steps at Play #10: Fill 'er Up

By understanding how much is too much, too little, or just right (enough), children build spatial awareness and lay foundations for abstract mathematics. A simple way to physicalize these ideas is by pouring. But with pouring comes spilling, so adults don't often let children pour for themselves. Let's give kids practice pouring while minimizing cleanup and building up children's body control in the process.

GET READY!

Play this game indoors or out, with water or sand. The activity is described using water, but we recommend using both materials, so children understand the subtle differences between the two substances. To reduce cleanup, have the children play outdoors or over a sink or tub indoors.

Moving
It's Pouring!

Some children don't have much experience with pouring, so start by handing out two cups and asking them to fill one of the cups with water. Then suggest pouring the water from one cup into the other. This may seem easy, but in fact, the children's proprioceptors are furiously sending messages to the brain to help guide muscle control. As the children pour from cup to cup, talk about how the water is going *out* of one cup and *into* another. Have children use both hands to do the pouring. With a little more experience, try using one hand at a time (both right and left).

Have the children pour with the two cups touching. Once they get the hang of it, have them try separating the cups a bit. Then have them try to raise the pouring cup high and see if they can catch the water with the other cup.

Growing
What's a Little? What's Too Much?

As the children get the hang of pouring, suggest they pour just a *little* into the cup, then *enough* to fill it to the top. Then pour *too much* in so the cup overflows. Have the child use both hands to do the pouring. With a little more experience, try using one hand at a time (both right and left). Again, this seems simple, but it's the way children learn to measure their effort along with the water.

As they play, talk about what a *little* looks like. Talk about what *too much* might be. And help the children recognize when they've got *just enough* in their cups.

Knowing

Don't Sink the Boat!

As the children begin to catch on to the ideas of *too much*, *too little*, and *just enough* and refine their ability to pour carefully, change to a different vessel. This will challenge them to transfer their new abilities and knowledge, showing them that *too much*, *too little*, and *just enough* are ideas that apply to lots of different situations.

Introduce a small toy boat. Demonstrate what happens when a boat takes on too much water. It sinks! Discuss how much water it takes to fill up the cup and compare that to how much water it takes to fill the toy boat.

Now it's the kids' turn. Have them pour water into the boat but try not to sink it. Of course, they're bound to sink the boat. Join the giggles when it happens, retrieve the boat, and try again. Then switch the game and see how fast they can sink the boat!

STAGES

Scampers Stompers Scooters

KINETIC SCALE

Senses Balance Intuition Power Coordination Control

BENEFITS

Muscle strength
Strength management and force
Estimation

LANGUAGE FOCUS

Out
Into
Too much
Too little
Enough

SAFEGUARDS

Supervise children around water at all times. Use unbreakable containers.

EQUIPMENT

Cups   Water
Toy boat   Sand

Smart Steps at Play #11: Muddo

Footprints fascinate little ones. The idea of leaving their imprint on the land not only makes them feel powerful and important, but also helps them learn abstract concepts of time and space. A handprint or footprint is a tangible sign that "I was there" and now "I'm here."

GET READY!

A mysterious, muddy creature called the Muddosaurus lives right in your own play yard. Muddo loves mud. But Muddo is also very shy. In fact, no one has ever actually seen her! So how do we know she's there? Because each time it rains, Muddo comes out to play and leaves her footprints in the mud! I sure would like to meet Muddo someday. Can you help me find her?

Any amount of mud or wet sand will do. If you don't have sand or mud handy, dust the pavement with flour. In the winter, play with Muddo's cousin, Snowasaurus! Also use play dough for a fun finger-imprinting game.

And remember, for generations, soap and water have never failed to conquer any amount of mud a kid can get into!

Moving
Tracing Muddo

If this is the child's first mud experience, start by showing him how to leave a footprint in the mud. Have him clomp around and make lots of prints. Notice how he watches to see the marks he's left behind. For first-timers, this may be enough. But if he wants more, continue.

Growing
Imagining Muddo

Encourage the child to show you what Muddo's footprints look like in the mud. For instance, ask, "I wonder how big Muddo's feet are? I wonder how many toes Muddo has? I wonder how many feet Muddo has? I wonder where Muddo would like to go today? Should we make her a path?" Let the child's imagination be your guide.

Knowing
Meeting Muddo

If you're really adventurous, take the next muddy step. Say, "I wonder what Muddo's hands are like? What would it look like if Muddo put her hands in the mud? Maybe Muddo would come out to play if we drew a picture for her in the mud." And finally, but certainly not for the faint of heart, "I wonder what it feels like to be a Muddosaurus who rolls in the mud!"

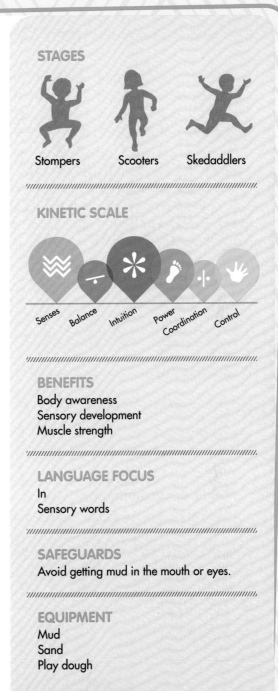

STAGES

Stompers Scooters Skedaddlers

KINETIC SCALE

Senses Balance Intuition Power Coordination Control

BENEFITS
Body awareness
Sensory development
Muscle strength

LANGUAGE FOCUS
In
Sensory words

SAFEGUARDS
Avoid getting mud in the mouth or eyes.

EQUIPMENT
Mud
Sand
Play dough

Smart Steps at Play #12: The Beanbaggles

The size, shape, weight, and texture of beanbags make them ideal trainers for children's intuition. The scrunchiness of a beanbag cooperates with small hands so that the focus of the play isn't compromised, while the weight helps the proprioceptors learn to manage muscle strength and force. And beanbags don't roll away. When you're trying to get little ones to stay on task, a toy that doesn't try to escape helps them stick to the learning.

You can use beanbags in many different ways for many different learning outcomes. Here are three games that foster children's ability to follow instructions, work on short-term memory, and develop the physicalities.

GET READY!

There are some new toys in town, and they're ready to play! They're called the Beanbaggles, and they're out for fun. But there's one little problem. The Beanbaggles don't know any games. Can you teach the Beanbaggles some of your favorite games?

Beanbags are ideal tools for building manipulative skills. They're easy to grasp and don't roll away.

Moving
Meet the Beanbaggles

Handshakes: Beanbags are great for building muscle strength in the hands, so start by simply having the children "shake hands" with the Beanbaggles. Have the children stand in a circle and pass the Beanbaggles to one another. Start by passing to the right. Each child receives with the left hand, changes hands, and passes off with the right hand. Be sure to reverse direction so that both hands get the same experiences.

Over-unders: Alternate one child passing over her head, the next under (between) her legs. Alternating play helps children develop short-term memory, rhythm, timing, and teamwork.

Feet to feet: Have the children remove their socks and shoes, sit on the floor in a circle, and pass the Beanbaggles with their feet. The twisting and wriggling focuses the whole body on accomplishing a simple task.

Growing
Flying Beanbaggles

Throwing: Target games challenge children's intuition, rhythm, timing, and control. Set up a target—a hoop, a bucket, or whatever is handy—and have the children "teach" the Beanbaggles how to fly through the air. Have the children alternate hands, and after each round, have them take one step back from the target to increase the challenge.

Flicking: Have each child place a single Beanbaggle on the top of her foot and try flicking it into the target. This is tricky, so it will probably take some practice. This activity helps develop strength management and one-footed balance. Be sure to alternate feet during play.

Knowing
Nighty-Night, Beanbaggles
When the fun is done, it's time for the Beanbaggles to head back to the toy box for a good night's rest. Turn cleanup time into a fun and challenging game using a simple game of cumulative instructions.

Start with two instructions, then three, four, and so on. Customize the activities to suit the children's abilities and see how many instructions they can follow. For example:

- Put the Beanbaggle on your head and go forward three steps.

- Put the Beanbaggle on your head, go forward three steps, and bend your head forward. (The Beanbaggle will drop to the ground.)

- Put the Beanbaggle on your head, go forward three steps, bend your head forward, and jump over the Beanbaggle.

- Put the Beanbaggle on your head, go forward three steps, bend your head forward, jump over the Beanbaggle, and spin around.

Cumulative instruction games develop short-term memory while providing a variety of physical challenges. When the children have reached their memory limit, give the final instruction to put the Beanbaggle away in the toy box.

STAGES

Scooters   Skedaddlers

KINETIC SCALE

Senses   Balance   Intuition   Power   Coordination   Control

BENEFITS
Rhythm and timing
Strength management
Eye-hand coordination
Precision
Balance
Memory
Teamwork

LANGUAGE FOCUS

Left	Under	Forward
Right	Over	Around
Straight	On	

SAFEGUARDS
Make sure children have adequate space for these activities.

EQUIPMENT
Beanbags

Smart Steps at Play #13: Hip Tips

Rolling over is the first important whole-body movement a child does on his own. It signals that a big new world of independent mobility is not far away.

GET READY!

The trick to rolling over is twisting the hips to create the propulsion needed for the full-body roll. Providing baby with gentle suggestions of those sensations will help prepare him for the day he's ready to go solo.

Moving
Rock-and-Roll

Lie down with baby on your tummy and both of you looking to the ceiling. Support baby and gently rock him in your arms from side to side, singing, "Everybody's rolling, rolling, rolling; everybody's rolling, just like me!" The side-to-side motion gives him a sense of how his body feels when it rolls to the side. (This is a lovely gentle activity when done skin-to-skin as well. See the "Skin-to-Skin" handout in the digital file.)

Growing
Hip Tips

Lay baby on his back on the floor with bare legs and feet if possible. Hold both hips and rock him from side to side so he can feel what it's like to do hip tips—the beginning of independent rolling. As you play, talk about what you're doing and how his little hips roll from side to side. Sing, "Everybody's rolling, rolling, rolling; everybody's rolling, just like me!"

Knowing
Come and Get It!

Lie down on the floor next to baby. As he begins to roll independently, encourage him by holding his favorite toy just out of reach. This will help him reach and extend his body.

STAGES

Snugglers

KINETIC SCALE

Senses   Balance   Intuition   Power   Coordination   Control

BENEFITS

Balance
Muscle strength
Independent movement
Cuddle time

LANGUAGE FOCUS

Over
Back
Front
Side to side

SAFEGUARDS

Do this activity gently and slowly. Support the whole child at all times. Let the child guide you. If the child is not enjoying the activity, stop.

EQUIPMENT

None

Smart Steps at Play #14: Runaway Bubbles

Bubbles are full of sparkling surprises and high-energy hijinks, yet they float slowly and delicately in the air. As such, bubbles make great play partners for young children developing eye fitness, eye-hand coordination, and stamina.

GET READY!

Uh-oh! The bubbles are running away! We've got to catch them all and get them back in their bottle!

For this activity, you'll need a big supply of bubbles. Use store-bought bubbles or mix the following ingredients to make your own. And if you've got one, use a bubble machine for tons and tons of bubble fun.

- 1 cup water
- 2 tablespoons light corn syrup or 2 tablespoons glycerin
- 4 tablespoons dishwashing liquid or baby shampoo

Moving
Pop Go the Bubbles!

Bubbles are on the loose! Encourage the children to catch as many as they can with their hands. After a while, you might wonder aloud, "I wonder if it's possible to catch a bubble with your thumb?" As the children succeed, reinforce their sense of accomplishment: "You can catch a bubble with your thumb! How clever!" Then suggest other ways to catch bubbles: "Hmm. If you can catch those rascally runaway bubbles with your thumb, I wonder what else you can catch bubbles with?" Have the children offer up ideas as well, and let the chase continue.

Growing
Whoosh Go the Bubbles!

This time, instead of popping the bubbles, have the children blow on the bubbles to keep them up in the air. This helps children understand that there's more than one way to effect change in their environment.

Next, suggest they use a piece of paper or cardboard to fan the bubbles back toward their bottle. Fanning the bubbles without popping them requires more controlled movements, so encourage them to fan quickly but gently.

Finally, have children try to catch the bubbles without popping them. They'll have to use very gentle, delicate movements.

Knowing
Clap Go the Bubbles!

Add rhythm to the activity by having children clap and pop the bubbles to this rhyme.

Clap the bubbles here!
Clap the bubbles there!
Clap away your troubles,
Clap the bubbles everywhere!

STAGES

Scampers Stompers Scooters Skedaddlers

KINETIC SCALE

Senses Balance Intuition Power Coordination Control

BENEFITS

Eye tracking
Temporal awareness
Eye-hand coordination

LANGUAGE FOCUS

Up   On
Down   Body parts

SAFEGUARDS

Use nontoxic, tear-free bubble solution for this activity. Be sure the children have enough space to chase the bubbles. This activity is best done outside, but if you play it inside, be sure the floor doesn't get slippery.

EQUIPMENT

Bubbles
Bubble machine (optional)
Pieces of cardboard or paper

Smart Steps at Play #15: Narrow and Wide

When children experience language physically, it increases and internalizes their understanding of the words and underlying concepts.

GET READY!

Narrow and *wide* do everything together, so how can you tell them apart?

Using the body to create the physical sense of *narrow* and *wide* will help children interpret the meaning both to the space around them and the objects in their world.

Moving
Getting Narrow and Getting Wide

Have children sit in a circle and start a discussion about the ideas of *narrow* and *wide*. Give them examples of *narrow* and *wide*, using your own body to describe the ideas. Then have children stretch their legs out in front of them. Talk about how their legs are narrow when they are together. Then have them splay out their legs and talk about how their legs are wide apart.

Have the children stand up and repeat the activity with their legs, standing with the legs together (*narrow*), then spreading them apart (*wide*). Changing orientation like this helps develop a deeper understanding of directional concepts.

Ask children to show you how else they can make their bodies narrow and wide. Start with the arms. What about the fingers? Can they make their mouths narrow? Wide?

Growing
What Else Can Be Narrow? What Else Can Be Wide?

Transferring the concepts of *narrow* and *wide* to other objects is the next step. For this game, start with a long rope and have children watch as you shape it into a V so that one end is narrow and the other end is wide. Talk about *narrow* and *wide* as you lay out the rope and ask the children to show you which is which on the rope.

Have the children step across the narrow end of the rope. Talk about how the distance is *narrow* as they step across. Then have the children jump across the wide end of the rope. Again, use the word *wide* as they jump. This simple physical comparison helps children realize the difference between narrow and wide.

Knowing
Walking Narrow, Walking Wide

To demonstrate the rope's progression from narrow to wide, have the children stand on the rope at its narrowest point and use their feet to walk along the two sides of the rope as it gets wider and wider. Again, use the words *narrow* and *wide* to narrate the play. Then have the children start at the wide end and walk to the narrow end.

When they've got the feel of it, have them walk the rope as different animals. For instance, have them walk like a monkey or do the bunny hop along the rope, and so on.

STAGES

Stompers   Scooters   Skedaddlers

KINETIC SCALE

Senses   Balance   Intuition   Power   Coordination   Control

BENEFITS

Jumping
Balancing
Stability
Body control

LANGUAGE FOCUS

Narrow
Wide
Along
Over
Across

SAFEGUARDS

Be sure the children have adequate space for this activity. Keep the rope on the floor at all times.

EQUIPMENT

Long rope

Smart Steps at Play #16: Chicken Switch

All-out, high-energy play is the easiest, most natural way for children to develop the strength, fitness, and stamina they need while they're moving to learn.

GET READY!

The chickens are all in a flap! They have to find a basket to cradle their eggs before the rooster crows! But with so many chickens and so many eggs and so many baskets . . . well, you can just imagine: the feathers really start to fly!

Count the number of children who will be playing the game. Scatter that number of hoops or paper plates (the baskets) around the floor and give each child a different-colored beanbag (egg) for this game. For the first two sequential levels, there will be the same number of hoops and eggs as there are children. Explain the game as follows.

The chickens each need to find a basket to keep the eggs safe. But here's the thing:

- There can only be one egg in each basket.
- You can't put your egg in the basket closest to you.
- The game starts when the rooster crows.
- The game stops when the rooster crows again. And when the rooster crows again, the chickens have to find a *different* basket for their eggs. Remember, there can only be one egg in each basket.

Moving
Egg in a Basket

Crow like a rooster to start the game. Play slowly so the children understand the concept. Have the children place their egg in their chosen basket and crow again when each child has successfully found an empty basket. If at the end of the round there are two eggs in one basket, encourage (or coach) the children to figure out what they need to do to resolve the problem.

Growing
Chicken à la Hurry Up!

Once the children have the basics down, speed up the pace of the game. Encourage them to scurry and hurry while you shorten the time between rooster crows. This time, don't stop each time the rooster crows. Instead, the chickens now need to hurry and find another basket!

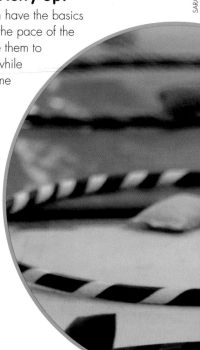

SARAH ALICE LEE

When you spot two eggs in one basket, call it out to the children so they can hurry up and fix it.

Chicken Switch

Get the feathers flying by having the children find a basket while flapping like a chicken. Then have the children hold their eggs between their knees while they're flapping and searching for an empty basket. Expect all-out chicken giggles as they not only stretch their imaginations, but also figure out how to coordinate this unusual movement pattern in henhouse traffic!

Knowing

Fox in the Henhouse

Now that the chickens are ruling the roost, remove one of the "baskets" from the play area for a musical-chairs style game. Begin the game, and when you crow your last crow for that round, one child will have a homeless egg. But she's not out of the game. She just became the fox!

Explain that there's a fox in the henhouse. "Be on the lookout for a sneaky fox who likes to switch eggs!" Start the next round and coach the fox to be sneaky and switch her egg with someone else's. When the round is over, one child will be eggless. Have the eggless child and the "fox" swap eggs and swap roles for the next round.

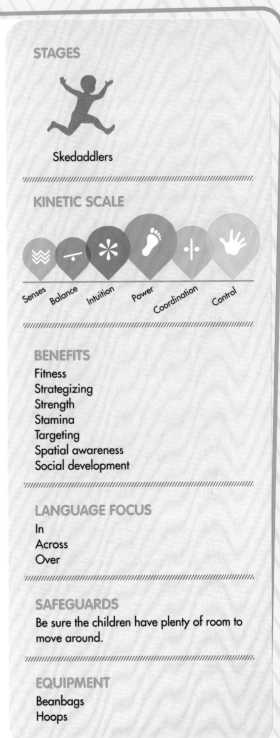

STAGES

Skedaddlers

KINETIC SCALE

Senses Balance Intuition Power Coordination Control

BENEFITS

Fitness
Strategizing
Strength
Stamina
Targeting
Spatial awareness
Social development

LANGUAGE FOCUS

In
Across
Over

SAFEGUARDS

Be sure the children have plenty of room to move around.

EQUIPMENT

Beanbags
Hoops

Smart Steps at Play #17: Hands, Meet Feet

Since babies aren't born with body awareness, it's important that baby gets to know his hands and feet, and that they get to know each other.

GET READY!
Playing with babies' hands and feet can be done anytime—at playtime, diaper changing, or cuddle time.

Moving
Let's Go for a Ride
Lay baby on his back on the floor. Gently move his legs in a bicycle riding motion. "Ride" up the hill slowly, and then down the hill more quickly. This helps his muscles and brain feel what it's like to experience independent movement and change in speed. Do a similar movement with his little hands.

Growing
Hands, Meet Feet
Take the baby's right hand and right foot and gently bring them together. Then stretch the leg out gently. And stretch the arm out gently. Repeat for the left hand and foot. As baby begins to recognize his hands and feet through touch and movement, he is not only learning body awareness but also becoming aware of what it feels like for different parts of his body to move at different times. This will be crucial later on as he begins his journey to independent mobility.

Knowing
Crossovers
Take baby's right arm and gently bring it across his body to touch his left arm. Then bring the left arm over to meet the right arm. Repeat with the legs, doing this several times gently and playfully in a sort of infant dance. In fact, music with a gentle beat is a great accompaniment. For example, "If You're Happy and You Know It" works well. Feeling oppositional movements such as these helps prepare the body and the brain for crawling and walking, which both require complex lateral movement.

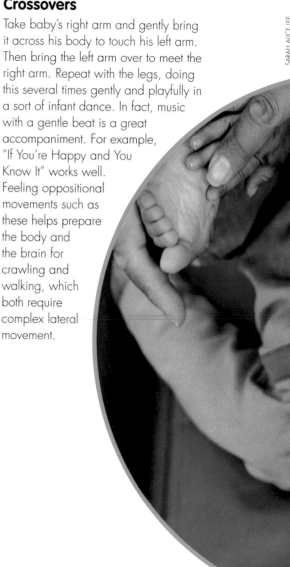

SARAH ALICE LEE

STAGES

Snugglers   Squigglers

KINETIC SCALE

Senses   Balance   Intuition   Power   Coordination   Control

BENEFITS

Body awareness
Muscle strength
Bonding
Security

LANGUAGE FOCUS

Over
Body parts

SAFEGUARDS

Do this activity very gently and slowly and
a little at a time. Let the child's reactions
guide you.

EQUIPMENT

None

Smart Steps at Play #18: Farm Gates

Using different parts of the body in different ways at the same time is great for developing the midlines.

GET READY!

While this activity may look simple, it can be challenging for little ones, so take it slow and build in lots of repetition. Sit on the floor and have the child sit in front of you. Explain that there are two different gates: one for the sheep (your arms) and one for the cows (your legs).

The farmer is very busy today and needs our help minding the gates to let the cows and sheep in and out of the barnyard. Can you help out on the farm today?

To let the animals out, open your arms or legs out to the side. To keep them in the barn, close your arms or legs together in front of you.

For younger children, watch to see what they can do on their own, then gently help them with the more complicated movements by guiding their arms or legs. Even if you have to guide all the movements, the activity will still give children a sense of their midlines.

Moving
Here Come the Sheep!

Start simply. Open the sheep gates (arms) wide and then close them again. Repeat this several times and go as slow as you need to help the child get the idea.

Here Come the Cows!

Now do the same with the legs to let the cows out. Close up the gates again, practicing as much as you need to.

Growing
One-Way Traffic

Next, begin to mix up the steps, varying arm and leg movements one at a time. For instance, it's time to let the sheep out, but we have to keep the cows in.

Do these movements one at a time.

1. Let the sheep out. (Open the arms.)

2. Let the cows in. (Close the legs.)

3. Let the sheep in. (Close the arms.)

4. Let the cows out. (Open the legs.)

Repeat this several times or as often as it's fun for the child.

Knowing
Two-Way Traffic

Now that you're both getting pretty good at gatekeeping, try moving the arms and legs simultaneously.

1. Let the sheep and cows out at the same time. (Open both arms and legs.)

2. Keep the sheep and cows in at the same time. (Close both.)

SARAH ALICE LEE

Then mix it up:

1. Let the sheep out and the cows in simultaneously.
2. Let the sheep in and the cows out simultaneously.

Stragglers

Every once in a while, a calf or a lamb straggles back to the barnyard late. This is a job for an expert gatekeeper! Open one gate at a time, then build up to opening one gate and closing another gate simultaneously. For instance:

1. Open your right arm, then your right leg.
2. Open your left arm while you close your right leg.
3. Close both arms while you open your left leg.

The movement patterns can get tricky as you put various combinations of opening and closing gates together, so do this activity slowly and watch the child's enjoyment level. The cows and sheep will wait for another day if the child is getting tired.

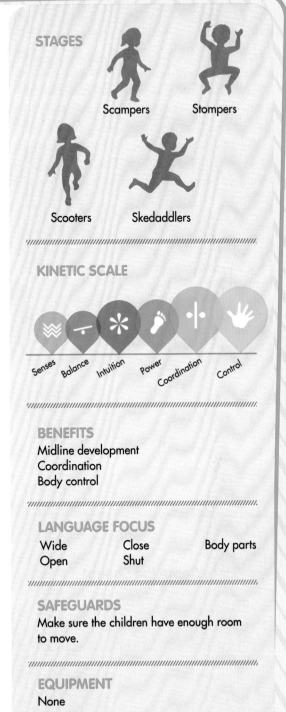

STAGES

Scampers
Stompers
Scooters
Skedaddlers

KINETIC SCALE

Senses   Balance   Intuition   Power   Coordination   Control

BENEFITS
Midline development
Coordination
Body control

LANGUAGE FOCUS

| Wide | Close | Body parts |
| Open | Shut | |

SAFEGUARDS
Make sure the children have enough room to move.

EQUIPMENT
None

Smart Steps at Play #19: The Pretzelator

Midline development, and in particular cross-lateral movements, take many years to automate. Twisting and turning their bodies into pretzels is a great way to encourage kids to cross all three midlines and build coordination.

GET READY!

The pretzels are all mixed up and need our help to unpretzel things!

Midlines are developing for almost all of the early years, so you will likely find children come to this activity at many different levels of ability. Watch closely to be sure children are not frustrated by these pretzely movements, assisting where necessary by helping them cross their midlines.

Moving
Crisscross Grab

Pile toys in the middle of the room and put the basket a short distance away from the pile. Have the children cross their right hands over their left, grab for a toy with both hands, and put it in the basket. Play another round, crossing the left hand over the right.

Growing
Switcheroo

Sit on the floor with the children with your legs out in front of you. Cross the right ankle over the left and have children do the same. When you call out "switch," switch ankles— left over right. After a few rounds, cross the hands in the same manner. And if you get really good at it, cross your right hand over your left foot and keep on switching!

Knowing
The Pretzelator

Using your crisscross grab and your switcheroo ankles, create a pretzel race to the basket! Grab a toy with your crisscross hands, pass it to the next player, and have her make her way to the basket with her ankles crossed!

STAGES

Scooters   Skedaddlers

KINETIC SCALE

Senses   Balance   Intuition   Power   Coordination   Control

BENEFITS

Midline development
Coordination
Body control
Organization

LANGUAGE FOCUS

Cross over
Uncross
Left
Right

SAFEGUARDS

Make sure the children have enough room to move.

EQUIPMENT

None

Smart Steps at Play #20: Steppin' Magic

As children grow and develop, their ability to react to dynamic situations signals maturing body control and brain processing power. That's why it's important to challenge children to think on their feet.

GET READY!

Magic is everywhere, so be careful where you step!

Gather together 12 items big enough for children to step in or on—six of one color (magic steps) and six of another (stepping-stones). Hoops are best for the large movements this game requires, but if you don't have hoops, use another reasonably large item, such as paper plates. Place the hoops or plates in a large circle around the play area.

Explain to the children that six of the items are Magic Steps. When you step in them, something magical happens. And explain that the other six are stepping stones where nothing magical happens.

Moving
One Step at a Time

To start the game, tell the children to step on the stepping stones, and when they step on a magic step, they must spin around. Have the children line up and step onto the path one at a time, stepping and spinning. After each round, change the magic step move

to something different, such as jumping, hopping, clapping, and so on.

Growing
Stepping Up the Magic

Add another activity to do on each magic step. For example, turn around, then touch your toes. As the children get better at the game, add another activity: Turn around, touch your toes, then touch your nose. Next, add another: Turn around, touch your toes, touch your nose, and jump in the air. These cumulative challenges develop short-term memory. Limit the number of magic movements to what the children can comfortably remember.

Knowing
Making the Magic

When the children fully understand the game and have mastered the basics, it's time to turn the game over to them. Discuss what kind of magic could happen on the magic steps. Have the children decide for themselves and play a few rounds under their direction.

Smart Steps at Play #21: The Eyes Have It

Eye tracking begins early and develops throughout the first years of life. Gently encouraging young eyes to focus and move builds the muscles in the eyes that a child will use one day for reading.

GET READY!

All you need for this activity is a simple streamer or soft toy that is attractive to baby's eye and easy for her to grasp.

Moving
Catch the Eye

Lie baby on her back on a safe surface—preferably the floor. Hold a ribbon, scarf, or streamer above her (approximately eight inches from her eyes, as this is the ideal focal length for a very young baby). Slowly sway the streamer from side to side to attract baby's attention. Move it slowly far to the left and far to the right so that it goes out of her range of focus. This encourages baby to move her eyes to follow the streamer. From time to time, move the streamers up and away from baby, then back down to within her focal range. This will help baby's emerging focal abilities.

Knowing
Attention Grab

Encourage baby to reach and grab the streamer by inviting her hands to join in the play. Grabbing the streamer may be a hit-or-miss proposition at this stage, but helping her reach up for it and tickling her fingers with the streamer creates a multisensory experience and gives her the idea that she can reach for things herself.

Later, encourage her hands to follow the streamer while it's moving—a very early form of eye-hand coordination.

Growing
Things Are Looking Up!

Making tummy time a positive experience is great way to help baby advance naturally. When baby is able to roll to her tummy independently, wave the streamer in front of her. This should encourage her to lift her head to watch and track the streamer. Only do this for as long as baby can maintain an upright head position on her own. Don't try to force her to remain in that position longer than is comfortable. Each time she does begin to lift her head, she's building neck and upper body strength, which is a critical ingredient for transitioning from primitive to postural reflexes.

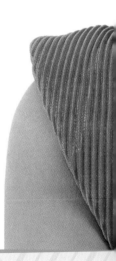

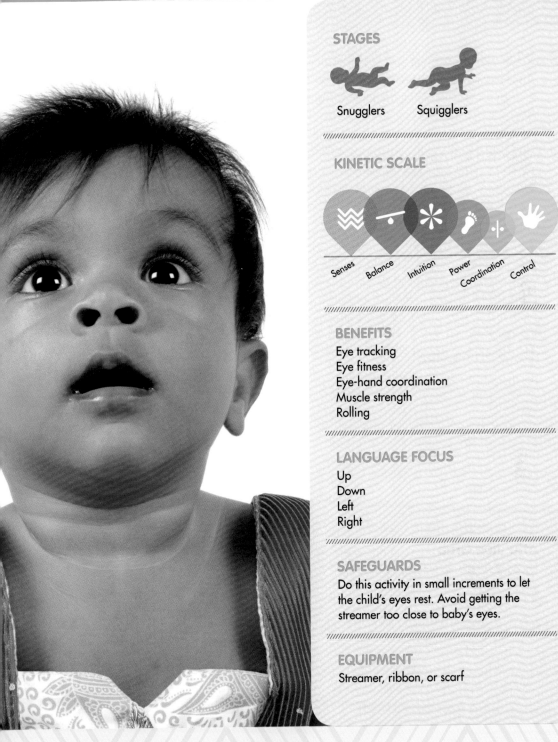

STAGES

Snugglers   Squigglers

KINETIC SCALE

Senses   Balance   Intuition   Power   Coordination   Control

BENEFITS

Eye tracking
Eye fitness
Eye-hand coordination
Muscle strength
Rolling

LANGUAGE FOCUS

Up
Down
Left
Right

SAFEGUARDS

Do this activity in small increments to let the child's eyes rest. Avoid getting the streamer too close to baby's eyes.

EQUIPMENT

Streamer, ribbon, or scarf

Smart Steps at Play #22: Baby Steering

When babies are up and rocking, just before they start crawling, they're not only figuring out how to maintain that position, they're developing balance and releasing the remaining head and arm primitive reflexes so they can get going. But where to go first?

Which way babies steer has less to do with where they want to go and more to do with which parts of their body have more power. For instance, some babies actually start crawling backward rather than forward because their upper body muscles are more fit and ready for crawling than their legs.

GET READY!

Helping new crawlers get where they want to go means getting down on the floor with them. But it doesn't mean doing it for them.

Moving

The Starting Block

To encourage baby to crawl forward, place several of his favorite toys in front of him within his line of sight. If that's not quite enough, get behind him and use your hands as a solid platform or starting block for him to push his feet against. And note: be sure the child is doing the work here, not you.

Growing
Forward, Crawl!

Once baby gets going forward, encourage as much crawling as possible. For instance, babies are often fascinated by lights. Use a flashlight on the floor for baby to track, crawl after, and try to catch.

Knowing
Baby Steering

At first, to change directions, babies will often push themselves into a sitting position, pivot to change direction, then take off again from there. These are early signs of deliberate body control.

To help baby learn to steer while crawling, scatter favorite toys around the room. This will motivate the child to figure out how to get himself from one point in the room to another.

Next, set up a crawling circuit around the room. Set up cardboard boxes to crawl through, pillows to crawl over, furniture to crawl under, and so on. Get down on the floor and encourage baby to move to and through the different areas. Watch how he begins to change direction more easily as his steering improves.

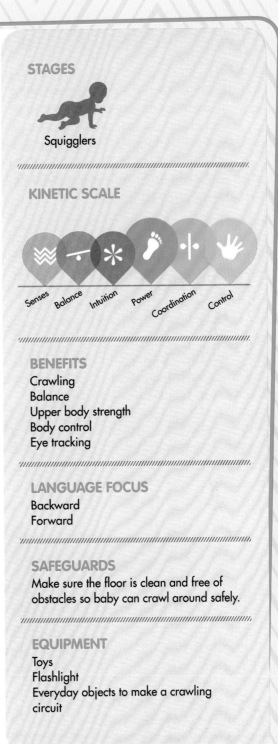

STAGES

Squigglers

KINETIC SCALE

Senses Balance Intuition Power Coordination Control

BENEFITS
Crawling
Balance
Upper body strength
Body control
Eye tracking

LANGUAGE FOCUS
Backward
Forward

SAFEGUARDS
Make sure the floor is clean and free of obstacles so baby can crawl around safely.

EQUIPMENT
Toys
Flashlight
Everyday objects to make a crawling circuit

Smart Steps at Play #23: Time-to-Go Games

Today's kids are shuttling from place to place from the minute they wake up in the morning. From breakfast to school to soccer to bedtime, life is busy, and kids are expected to keep up. In school, too, kids need to make quick switches from activity to activity. But transitions from here to there can be difficult or downright stressful when children don't want or aren't ready to change what they're doing. When that happens, there's only one thing to be done: make it fun!

GET READY!

Animal play makes everything more fun! It engages the imagination and immediately sets the wiggles and giggles in motion. Try these on-the-go games for transitions throughout the day.

Moving
Animal-a-Go-Go!

When it's time to go, wonder aloud what it would be like to get from here to there like children's favorite animals. Ask what their favorite animal looks like. What does it sound like? How does it move?

Growing
Wonderings

Once children decide which animals they want to be, gently offer a few ideas by

wondering out loud: "I wonder how high a tiger can jump? I wonder how a roly-poly bear would climb? I wonder how an octopus would cross the grass?" Wondering aloud prompts children to use their own imagination. For instance, try not to say outright, "Show me how high a tiger can jump." That makes it your idea, not theirs.

Knowing
Animal All Day Long

Once kids get the idea, offer different variations—but always let children choose. For example, if children pick a tiger, suggest making it an all-day game. Call it Tiger Tuesday. Since tigers have stripes, have kids be on the lookout for striped things throughout the day. Practice roaring and running and jumping all day, and don't forget to purr.

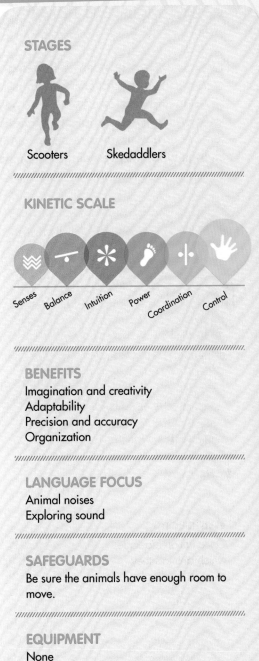

STAGES

Scooters   Skedaddlers

KINETIC SCALE

Senses   Balance   Intuition   Power   Coordination   Control

BENEFITS

Imagination and creativity
Adaptability
Precision and accuracy
Organization

LANGUAGE FOCUS

Animal noises
Exploring sound

SAFEGUARDS

Be sure the animals have enough room to move.

EQUIPMENT

None

Smart Steps at Play #24: Breaker! Breaker!

Role play offers children unique opportunities to experiment with familiar concepts and new ideas. In a group setting, role play builds a sense of shared community. And when we add a new layer—language—children must adapt new ways of participating in the fun!

GET READY!

"Breaker! Breaker! Let's hit the road!"

Get started for long-haul trucking role play by creating your trucks. You can use tricycles or ride-ons for this game, or turn this into an arts-and-crafts project by having the children make their own truck!

To create the truck chassis, use a cardboard box and cut the top and bottom out so only the four sides remain. The kids will need a CB radio, too, so poke a hole into the bottom of paper cup and thread a string through it. Attach it to the cardboard truck or to the handlebar of the child's tricycle.

Moving
What Kind of Truck Driver Are You?

Kids love trucks, so start by asking each child what kind of truck she wants to drive. This is a great opportunity to discuss different kinds of trucks and the jobs they do.

If you're making your own trucks, get to work using paints, markers, crayons, or whatever else you have handy to spruce up your wheels just the way the kids want them.

And every trucker has a nickname or CB "handle," so before you set out on your road trip, have each child select a personal CB handle. Practice calling each other by their CB handles. If you like, have each child draw a picture that represents her handle on the side of her truck.

Growing
Words of the Road!

Establish CB etiquette so the children understand how to communicate when they're on the road. For instance:

- Truckers must call each other only by their CB handles during the game. Creating and remembering special names reinforces memory and language skills.

- Truckers must use their CB radios to communicate with one another. Using a communication tool cements the fantasy for the kids.

- Truckers must ask for permission to speak by starting each communication with "Breaker! Breaker!" Creating language rules helps children understand the concept of socially structured and socially appropriate communication.

- For older children, you can introduce additional CB lingo into the game. Here are a few phrases to get you started. Feel free to make up your own unique lingo, too!

CB LINGO

Put your ears on: Please listen to my call.

Come back: Please respond to my message.

Ten-four: Okay. Message received.

What's your 20? Where are you?

Pedal to the metal: Go faster.

Mayday: Help!

Go-go juice: Fuel.

Honk honk! Blow your horn!

Knowing
Hit the Road

Have the children decide where the truck stop is (the end of the path, the play-ground swings, or wherever they like). Then put the pedal to the metal and head out! Breaker! Breaker!

MOVING SMART

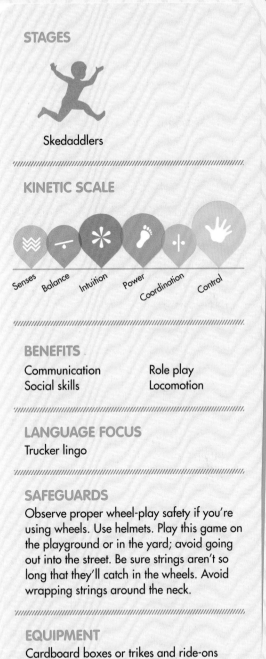

STAGES

Skedaddlers

KINETIC SCALE

Senses   Balance   Intuition   Power   Coordination   Control

BENEFITS

Communication
Social skills

Role play
Locomotion

LANGUAGE FOCUS

Trucker lingo

SAFEGUARDS

Observe proper wheel-play safety if you're using wheels. Use helmets. Play this game on the playground or in the yard; avoid going out into the street. Be sure strings aren't so long that they'll catch in the wheels. Avoid wrapping strings around the neck.

EQUIPMENT

Cardboard boxes or trikes and ride-ons
Paper cups
String
Art supplies (optional)

Notes

Chapter 1

1. Winter, P. *Engaging Families in the Early Childhood Development Story.* Victoria, Australia: Ministerial Council for Education, Early Childhood, 2010.
2. Bulluss, J., and P. Coles. *Smart Start with P.M.P: A Perceptual Motor Program Manual.* Mordialloc, Victoria: Smart Starters, 2007.

Chapter 3

3. Perry, B. "Introduction to the Neurosequential Model of Therapeutics (NMT)." Houston, TX: Child Trauma Academy, 2010. Adapted with permission.
4. Sunderland, M. *The Science of Parenting.* New York: DK Publishing, 2006.
5. Cheatum, B.A., and A.A. Hammond. *Physical Activities for Improving Children's Learning and Behavior.* Champaign, IL: Human Kinetics, 2000.
6. Winter, 2010.
7. Sunderland, 2006.
8. Westwell, M. "Building Capacity for Life in the 21st Century." Presentation to the New South Wales Secondary Principals Council, 2009.
9. Sunderland, 2006.
10. Sunderland, 2006.
11. Winter, 2010.
12. Miller, G. "The Magical Number Seven, Plus or Minus Two: Some Limits on Our Capacity for Processing Information." *Psychological Review* 63, 81–97, 1956.
13. Mindworks Resources. "3 Primary Learning Modalities Every Person Uses." Coppell, TX: 2013.

Chapter 4

14. Cheatum and Hammond, 2000.
15. Hands, B., M. Martin, and P. Lynch. *Fundamental Movement Skills Teacher Resource.* Australia: Western Australia Minister of Education, 2004.

Chapter 5

16. Sunderland, 2006, page 21.

Chapter 7

17. Kopp, C.B. *Baby Steps: A Guide to Your Child's Social, Physical, and Emotional Development in the First Two Years.* New York: Henry Holt & Co., 2003.
18. Hannaford, C. *Smart Moves: Why Learning Is Not All in Your Head.* Arlington, VA: Great Ocean Publishers, 2005.
19. Cheatum and Hammond, 2000, p. 269.
20. Hannaford, 2005.

21. Hannaford, 2005.
22. Cheatum and Hammond, 2000, p. 316.
23. Kuhl, P. "The Linguistic Genius of Babies." TED: Ideas Worth Spreading, October 2010.
24. Guernsey, L. *Into the Minds of Babes: How Screen Time Affects Children from Birth to Age Five.* Philadelphia: Basic Books. 2007.
25. Guernsey, 2007.
26. Day, L., "The Power of Touch." United Kingdom: Baby Sensory, 2008.

Chapter 8

27. Hannaford, 2005.

Chapter 9

28. Cheatum and Hammond, 2000.

Chapter 11

29. Scheve, Tom. "Do Babies Have Kneecaps?" Atlanta, GA: Discovery Communications, HowStuffWorks, Inc., 2013.

Chapter 12

30. Hannaford, 2005.
31. Jensen, E. *Teaching with the Brain in Mind.* Alexandria, VA: Association for Supervision and Curriculum Development, 2005.
32. Goddard Blythe, S. *The Well Balanced Child: Movement and Early Learning.* Gloucestershire, UK: Hawthorn Press, 2004.
33. Hoy, K.E, P.B. Fitzgerald, J.L. Bradshaw, C.A. Armatas, and N. Georgiou-Karistianis. "Investigating the Cortical Origins of Motor Overflow." *Brain Research Reviews*, 46 (2004): 315–27.
34. Chudler, E.H. "One Brain . . . or Two?" *Neuroscience for Kids*, 2011.

Chapter 14

35. Goddard Blythe, S. *What Babies and Children Really Need.* Gloucestershire, UK: Hawthorn Press, 2008.
36. Mehrabian, A. *Silent Messages: Implicit Communication of Emotions and Attitude.* Belmont, CA: Wadsworth, 1980.

Chapter 15

37. Goddard Blythe, 2004.
38. Goddard Blythe, 2004.
39. Goddard Blythe, 2004.

Chapter 24

40. Hannaford, 2005.

Chapter 25

41. Bulluss and Coles, 2007.

Bibliography

"Births—Method of Delivery." *Centers for Disease Control and Prevention*, 2013. www.cdc.gov/nchs/fastats/delivery.htm

Bulluss, J., and P. Coles. *Smart Start with P.M.P: A Perceptual Motor Program Manual*. Mordialloc, Victoria: Smart Starters, 2007.

Cheatum, B.A., and A.A. Hammond. *Physical Activities for Improving Children's Learning and Behavior*. Champaign, IL: Human Kinetics, 2000.

Chudler, E.H., "One Brain . . . or Two?" *Neuroscience for Kids*, 2011. faculty.washington.edu/chudler/split.html

Ciccarelli, Saundra K., and J. Noland White. *Psychology*. Upper Saddle River, NJ: Prentice Hall, 2012, p. 48.

Copple, C., and S. Bredekamp, eds. *Developmentally Appropriate Practice in Early Childhood Programs Serving Children Birth Through Age 8*. Washington, DC: National Association for the Education of Young Children, 2009.

Day, L., *The Power of Touch*. United Kingdom: Baby Sensory, 2008. www.babysensory.com/downloads/TouchEN.pdf

DeBenedet, A.T. and L.J. Cohen. *The Art of Roughhousing*. Philadelphia, PA: Quirk Books, 2010.

Goddard Blythe, S. *The Well Balanced Child: Movement and Early Learning*. Gloucestershire, UK: Hawthorn Press, 2004.

Goddard Blythe, S. *What Babies and Children Really Need*. Gloucestershire, UK: Hawthorn Press, 2008.

Guernsey, L. *Into the Minds of Babes: How Screen Time Affects Children from Birth to Age Five*. Philadelphia: Basic Books, 2007.

Hands, B., M. Martin, and P. Lynch. *Fundamental Movement Skills Teacher Resource*. Australia: Western Australia Minister of Education, 2004.

Hannaford, C. *Smart Moves: Why Learning Is Not All in Your Head*. Arlington, VA: Great Ocean Publishers, 2005.

Hoy, K.E, P.B. Fitzgerald, J.L. Bradshaw, C.A. Armatas, and N. Georgiou-Karistianis. "Investigating the Cortical Origins of Motor Overflow." *Brain Research Reviews*, 46 (2004): 315–27.

Jensen, E. *Teaching with the Brain in Mind*. Alexandria, VA: Association for Supervision and Curriculum Development, 2005.

Kangaroo Care USA, *Skin to Skin Effects in Term Infants and Citations*. Cleveland, OH: Ludington-Hoe and the United States Institute for Kangaroo Care, 2011. www.kangaroocareusa.org/uploads/KC_Effects_on_Infant___Mother_Tables.pdf

Kopp, C.B. *Baby Steps: A Guide to Your Child's Social, Physical, and Emotional Development in the First Two Years*. New York: Henry Holt & Co., 2003.

Kuhl, P. "The Linguistic Genius of Babies." TED: Ideas Worth Spreading, October 2010. www.ted.com/talks/patricia_kuhl_the_linguistic_genius_of_babies.html

Louv, R. *Last Child in the Woods: Saving Our Children from Nature Deficit Disorder*. Chapel Hill, NC: Algonquin Books, 2008.

Mehrabian, A. *Silent Messages: Implicit Communication of Emotions and Attitude*. Belmont, CA: Wadsworth, 1980.

Miller, G. "The Magical Number Seven, Plus or Minus Two: Some Limits on Our Capacity for Processing Information." *Psychological Review* 63, 81–97, 1956. In the online resource *Classics in the History of Psychology* developed by Christopher D. Green, York University, Toronto, Ontario. psychclassics.yorku.ca/Miller/

Mindworks Resources. "3 Primary Learning Modalities Every Person Uses." Coppell, TX: 2013.

Morris, Charles G., and Albert A. Maisto. *Psychology: An Introduction*. Upper Saddle River, NJ: Prentice Hall, 2005, pp. 49–50.

Perry, B. "Integrating Principles of Neurodevelopment into Clinical Practice: Introduction to the Neurosequential Model of Therapeutics (NMT)." Houston, TX: Child Trauma Academy, 2010. www.eusarf2012.org/Portals/13/Documents/nmt_core_slides_2011.pdf

Scheve, Tom. "Do Babies Have Kneecaps?" Atlanta, GA: Discovery Communications, HowStuffWorks, Inc., 2013. science.howstuffworks.com/life/human-biology/babies-kneecaps1.htm

Sunderland, M. *The Science of Parenting*. New York: DK Publishing, 2006.

Westwell, M. "Human Ingenuity: Building Capacity for Life in the 21st Century." Presentation to the New South Wales Secondary Principals Council, 2009. www.aaibs.org/attachments/original/34.pdf

Winter, P. *Engaging Families in the Early Childhood Development Story*. Victoria, Australia: Ministerial Council for Education, Early Childhood Development and Youth Affairs, 2010. www.mceecdya.edu.au/verve/_resources/ECD_Story-Neuroscience_and_early_childhood_dev.pdf

Acknowledgments

To Becky, Milly, and Lucy. My heart in three parts . . . Gill.

To our magic doors of inspiration and purpose, Caitlin and Jacob Brinch.

For your love, encouragement, and unyielding confidence in our cleverness, thank you to Ross Walker.

To Susie Goldsmith, for all of your love, support, and encouragement.

To our field marshal, Diana Jenkin, without whom none of this would be possible.

With gratitude to our friends and passionate advocates of moving children everywhere: Wendy Pirie, Adele Orangi, Ellie Davidson, and Mandy Wilson.

To our friends and colleagues in Australia: Peter Coles, Judie Bulluss, and Robyn Crowe.

With love to our partner Sue Richter for believing in our story, keeping us centered, and making us smarter each day. TBIABS.

With love to Jill and John Payne for your wisdom, strength, and loving guidance.

To our friends in the United States, thank you for helping us on our journey: Matt Mattus, Kevin Mowrer, Steve Drucker, Jan Rimmel, Steve D'Aguanno, Eric Morse, Gentry Akens, David Krumsiek, Kathryn Priestley, Rachel Moran, Susan Polachek, Maureen Johnson, Michele Boyd, Christine Micke, Margaret Kelliher, Dr. Larry Cohen, Matt Brown, and Elaine Leibsohn.

To Meg Bratsch, Margie Lisovskis, Michelle Lee Lagerroos, and the entire Free Spirit Publishing team, thank you for your trust in us, your partnership, talent, and spirit to bring our story to life.

Thank you, Ivan d'Poodle.

And from both hemispheres, a special thank you to Angela Winstone and Laurie Arrow for bringing us together as writers and friends, and for your indefatigable passion to make the world a better place for children.

Thank you, everyone!

Index

About the Authors

Gill Connell is a globally recognized presenter and child development authority, specializing in the foundations of learning through movement and play. She provides developmental expertise to parents, preschools, schools, and companies such as Hasbro, Inc., based on her more than 30 years in preschool and primary education. She is the former national director of Gymbaroo Preschool Activity Centers and the founder of Moving Smart, Ltd. (www.movingsmart.co.nz), which offers resources, tools, trainings, and workshops. She coauthored the book *Moving to Learn: An Essential Guide for All Parents, Carers and Educators.* Gill lives in Christchurch, New Zealand, and travels regularly to the United States.

Cheryl McCarthy is a former vice president of intellectual property development for Hasbro, Inc. She is a 30-year veteran of the world of children's play, specializing in young children's storytelling and entertainment. As executive producer, she managed the creative development of properties such as My Little Pony, Candy Land, Mr. Potato Head, and many other beloved children's icons. She is currently the creative director at Moving Smart, Ltd. Cheryl lives in Attleboro, Massachusetts.

More Early Childhood Educator Resources from Free Spirit Publishing

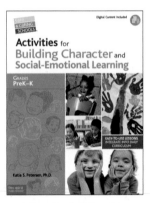
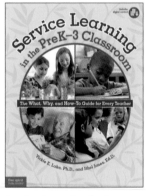